Reading a Japanese Film
Cinema in Context

Keiko I. McDonald

University of Hawai'i Press
Honolulu

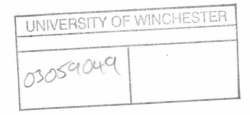

11 10 09 08 07 06   6 5 4 3 2

Library of Congress Cataloging-in-Publication Data

McDonald, Keiko I.
    Reading a Japanese film : cinema in context / Keiko I. McDonald.
        p. cm.
    Includes bibliographical references and index.
    ISBN-13: 978-0-8248-2939-1 (hardcover : alk. paper)
    ISBN-10: 0-8248-2939-5 (hardcover : alk. paper)
    ISBN-13: 978-0-8248-2993-3 (pbk. : alk. paper)
    ISBN-10: 0-8248-2993-X (pbk. : alk. paper)
    1. Motion pictures—Japan. I. Title.
    PN1993.5.J3M365 2006
    791.43'75'0952—dc22
                            2005013946

University of Hawai'i Press books are printed on acid-free
paper and meet the guidelines for permanence and durability
of the Council on Library Resources.

Designed by University of Hawai'i Press Production Staff
Printed by The Maple-Vail Book Manufacturing Group

Contents

Contents

Preface

COURSES ON JAPANESE CINEMA have become one of the most salient features of Japanese studies programs at major academic institutions all across America. Courses with titles such as *Introduction to Japanese Cinema* and *Japanese Literature and Film* are attracting students in ever increasing numbers. Japanese studies majors are joined in these classes by film studies majors, who come from programs that recognize the unique contribution Japan has made to world cinema. The most dramatic increase in demand has come from students whose interest in Japanese culture and society has been linked primarily with electives.

Japanese cinema courses have been a staple of my teaching for many years now. Like so many teachers and scholars, I rejoice to see the audience for my specialty expanding at such a rate, even as I have to lament the relative vacuity of really sound textbooks to serve these eager new students of Japanese cinema in undergraduate classes. Many of my colleagues and students have urged me to respond to this lack, which now I attempt to do.

My title is *Reading a Japanese Film*. This book will draw on my long years of experience teaching in the classroom and lecturing to audiences of Japanese and Asian cinema. The majority are my original essays. Like the other books I have authored, this work is intended to address the basic question with which I have been concerned as a teacher and scholar for more than two decades: How does a person from the Japanese tradition show Western viewers, primarily general audiences, how to see a Japanese film?

Over the last fifteen years scholars and critics of Japanese cinema have produced a number of important books in response to the enthusiastic reception of Japanese cinema on a global scale. They range from historical, generic studies to volumes devoted to single directors: David Bordwell's *Ozu and Poetics of Cinema* (1988), Kyōko Hirano's *Mr. Smith Goes to Tokyo: Japanese Cinema under the American Occupation, 1945–1952* (1992), Donald Richie's comprehensive study *Films of Akira Kurosawa* (expanded ed., 1996), Joanne Bernardi's *Writing in Light* (2001), and Mark Abé Nornes's *Japanese Documentary Film: The Meiji Era through Hiroshima* (2003), to name a few.

Unfortunately, none is designed to serve as a textbook for an introductory Japanese film class, which needs to focus on numbers of filmmakers.

Other useful texts have come and gone, doing their part for the classroom context before going out of print for want of steady sales. It is sad to say that the publisher has no plans to reissue, much less revise and update, David Desser's *Eros Plus Massacre: An Introduction to the Japanese New Wave Cinema* (Bloomington: Indiana University Press, 1988), which was the staple of textbooks for my Japanese film classes for so many years. Then too, some, such as *Reframing Japanese Cinema: Authorship, Genre and History* (1992), edited by David Desser and Arthor Nolletti Jr., need updating.

I know of just one scholarly textbook currently in print that can accommodate the needs of much broader audiences. It is Donald Richie's most recent publication, *A Hundred Years of Japanese Film* (2001), an informative history of the nation's cinema with a selective guide to videos and DVDs.

I have written this book hoping that it would complement Richie's text, which offers invaluable insights into Japanese cinema history but does not focus on individual film analysis. Then too, my book will also complement the forthcoming *Japanese Film: Texts and Context,* edited by Alastair Phillips and Julian Stringer. Their anthology, which provides analyses of major Japanese films from the silent era to the present, will offer a variable set of critical perspectives exhibited an impressive array of some twenty contributors.

Acknowledgments

THIS STUDY was made possible by the generous assistance of so many people. I am deeply indebted to them all. I would like to express my sincerest gratitude to Donald Richie—my mentor of twenty some years and the foremost Western authority on Japanese cinema—who offered me as much professional assistance and warm encouragement as possible.

I offer special thanks to Thomas Rimer, a colleague of mine at the University of Pittsburgh, who read a first draft and provided much constructive criticism. And I am very grateful to Jan-Paul Malocsay, who also read the entire manuscript and made useful comments from the viewpoint of the Western audience. I also owe a great debt of gratitude to David Desser and Linda Ehrlich; each read part of the draft and offered me valuable suggestions.

My special thanks go to Patricia Crosby, executive editor at the University of Hawai'i Press, for her inspirational editorial advice on the manuscript.

Akira Koike and Kyōko Satō from the Kawakita Memorial Film Institute and Kanako Hayashi from the Tokyo FilMex were wonderfully accommodating by making some of the Japanese materials available to me.

I would also like to thank a good number of Japanese production companies for permitting me to reprint stills. I am mostly indebted to Bandai Visual and Office Kitano for its generosity.

Research work for this book, which involved two trips to Japan, was supported by generous research grants from the Japan Iron and Steel Federation/Mitsubishi Endowment, the Toshiba International Foundation, and the University Center for International Studies and the Asian Studies Center of the University of Pittsburgh. To all these organizations, I am truly grateful.

Finally, my special thanks go to the Richard D. and Mary Jane Edwards Endowed Publication Fund.

Introduction

If the American film is strongest in action, and if the European is
strongest in character, then the Japanese film is richest in mood or
atmosphere, in presenting characters in their own surroundings.[1]

DONALD RICHIE offered this engaging observation in his seminal work of
1971, *Japanese Cinema: Film Style and National Character.* Scholars and critics in the West have been teasing out its implications ever since, not least
by laboring to explain how national character can be seen "as the particular through which the humanistic ideals of universal significance are said to
be represented concretely."[2]

National character could be a natural point of entry for any approach to
Japanese culture. Japan has always intrigued the West and rewarded curiosity at every level of interest, from the least to the most committed. Japanese
cinema is uniquely well qualified to bridge the oftentimes puzzling divide
between East and West. The visual allure is there, however strange and at
times mystifying it may seem to outside eyes.

Since this is a book for every kind of viewer, it needs to apprise the
novice, and possibly remind old hands, of a fascinating fact of Japanese cinema: that some knowledge of its history is essential to understanding its
characteristics, achievements, and place in the culture of Japan.[3] Readers
confident of the basics may choose to bypass the following, necessarily brief,
historical overview.

A Brief History of Japanese Cinema

New Art, Old Format: 1897–1920
The first successful Japanese film viewed with the *cinématographe* showed
famous Tokyo sights such as the scenic bridge Nihonbashi in late 1897. The

first-ever commercial film in 1898 reeled off seventy feet of center shots of three geisha dancing. Cinema's gaze remained fixed on the stage for the next ten years. Theatrical traditions in Japan were so strong that the new art could not at first imagine dramatic conventions as its own. This burden of tradition retarded the formation of a specifically cinematic grammar, even as the continuity between old art forms and new did in some respects help film gain its artistic independence.

Three definitive characteristics of Japanese cinema are its use of *onnagata* (female impersonators), *benshi* (commentators), and center-front long shots following strict continuity.[4] Female impersonators continued a unique kabuki tradition from the early Edo period when, in 1629, the Tokugawa shogunate banned women from every kind of theatrical performance. The *benshi* commentators continued an age-old tradition of storytelling manifest in many forms of performance art: bunraku puppet theater, kabuki choral commentary, and specific narrative forms such as *kōdan* historical and *rakugo* comic tales.[5]

The center-front long shot was a natural outcome of cinema's first view of itself as a camera-eye spectator of ongoing stage performance. Most early footage showed what theater audiences saw: entire scenes shot in one long take showing actors full-length. This fixed approach to camera work remained a defining characteristic of Japanese cinema even after the long shot and long take were joined by other more specifically cinematic devices.

The mood Donald Richie sees as definitive refers to effects of atmosphere achieved by aligning characters against a setting viewed in long shot. A telling example in the era of silent film comes in Minoru Murata's *Souls on the Road* (Rojō no reikon, 1921). Two prisoners just released trudge wearily down a country road. The cloudy sky and the desolate fields speak for their sense of being helpless and hopeless in an unkind world.

Cinema's theatrical dependency also led to a clear division of repertoire originating in the *kyūgeki* (old drama) of kabuki and the *shimpa* (New School) reaction to it. *Shimpa* used modern settings for a wide range of plays, comedy and suspense and its mainstay, melodrama, tear-jerkers most often derived from novels of unrequited love in domestic settings. Cinema's genre division fell along similar lines. Films dealing with matters previous to 1868 were *jidaigeki* (period drama), those afterward were *gendaigeki* (contemporary/modern drama). Every student of anything Japanese must know 1868 as the watershed date of the Meiji restoration, which brought Japan into modern world.

Cinema's destiny as mass-market art was decided early on. Nikkatsu

Company's takeover of four competitors in 1912 created a monopoly whose creative drive went in two directions at once. The company's old studio in Kyoto continued to concentrate on its "old drama" specialty, making cinema history with brilliant collaborations such as that between director Shozō Makino (1878–1928) and superstar Matsunosuke Onoe (1892–1923). A new Tokyo studio dedicated to modern variations on *shimpa* melodrama made that *gendaigeki* specialty a market leader. Staple sentimental favorites, such as Tadashi Oguchi's *The Cuckoo* (Hototogisu, 1918), gave a good cry for the money. Separated by war from a loving husband, its heroine of *The Cuckoo* (familiar from a popular novel) suffers melodramatic torment at the hands of her mother-in-law.

Cinema's rapid evolution embraced changes demanded by the *shingeki* (New Theater) movement. A movement for artistic cinema in 1916 called for these technical innovations: subtitles were to replace the *benshi* commentators; Western music would replace the traditional Japanese; acting would be more realistic; and female impersonators would give way to their natural competition. Among the first to film accordingly was Norimasa Kaeriyama (1893–1964), who in 1919 persuaded Nikkatsu to let him direct *The Glory of Life* (Sei no kagayaki). Until then he was known as a film connoisseur and author of the seminal book *The Creation of Photography of the Moving Picture Drama* (Katsudō shanshingeki no seisaku satueihō).[6]

Tradition's stranglehold was not to be broken quite so easily, thanks to well-entrenched special interest groups such as the *benshi* commentators and *onnagata* female impersonators. Still, the pressure for more realistic effects was there, so while Nikkatsu temporized, a bold new competitor moved quickly in the right direction.

Old Conventions Swept Away: The 1920s

The Shōchiku Company was founded in 1920 by a gigantic syndicate with extensive holdings in theaters and acting troupes. The same year, the Shōchiku Kine School of Art was established with Kaoru Osanai (1881–1928), a leader in the *shingeki* movement, as its head.[7] Film directors under his supervision were youths about twenty years old, such as Minoru Murata (1897–1937). Some of them were strongly attracted to those editing techniques such as cross-cutting and parallel montage that D. W. Griffth employed in *Intolerance* (1916). This urge for change from inside was also assisted by those who were trained overseas. Among returning directors and cameramen were Henry Kotani (1887–1972) and Thomas Kurihara (1885–1926). Kotani is considered by many the father of cameramen in Japan. He worked on Shōchiku's pioneering "pure drama" film, *Island Woman* (Shima no onna, 1920). The heroine is a fisherman's daughter whose lover is pursued by another woman. She was played by an actress, a first-time-ever innovation reinforced by Kotani's use of American-style flashbacks and close-ups along with subtitles.

Rival Nikkatsu did respond in kind with films such as *Two Wives* (Tsuma to Tsuma, 1922), directed by Eizō Tanaka (1886–1968). A studio showdown later that year led to a mass walkout of *onnagata*. Nikkatsu temporized again but replaced them all with actresses the following year. Clearly tradition was out and innovation was in, at least in cinema. Even the powerful *benshi* were on shaky ground in 1923 and completely out of the picture by 1928.

The *jidaigeki* period film was also reborn in the 1920s. Star director Makino left Nikkatsu in 1923 to found his own studio in Kyoto. His new style of swashbuckling hero broke with kabuki conventions, moving freely and realistically, apparently under the influence of American films with their emphasis on fast-paced, action-packed suspense. Films in this style earned the name *chambara*, a reference to the entertainment value of its brilliant period swordplay.

The seven years leading up to the coming of sound in 1930 is generally known as the golden age of silent-era *jidaigeki,* which put the more generalized *gendaigeki* somewhat in the shade. Makino made memorable films such as *Chūji Kunisada* (Kunisada Chūji, 1925), derived from the hit stage play of the same title, and *The Sword of Doom* (Daibosatsu Tōge, 1927), based on a popular novel by Kaizan Nakazato (1885–1994). His fame was shared by his son, Masahiro Makino (1908–1993), best known for *Street of Masterless Samurai* (Rōningai, 1928). Nikkatsu's Daisuke Itō (1898–1981) distinguished himself with *Chūji's Travel Diary* (Chūji tabi nikki, 1927), *Servant* (Gerō, 1927), and *Man-Slashing, Horse-Slashing Sword* (Zanjin zamba, 1929). Buntarō Futagawa (1899–1966) directed *Serpent* (Orochi, 1925), a pioneer work of *chambara* realism notable for breaking the superhero mold with a masterless samurai loner protagonist as prone to human frailty as anyone.

The Talkie and the 1930s

Sound tripled the cost of making a film, but that disincentive to taking risks was countered by market pressures favoring experimentation as companies looked to compete with new trademark genres and old ones profitably modified.

Shōchiku led the way with Japan's first successful talkie, *The Neighbor's Wife and Mine* (Madamu to nyōbō, 1931), directed by Heinosuke Gosho

(1902–1981).[8] Like others soon to follow, it gave voice to the company's staple *shomingeki* (drama of everyday lower-middle-class life). Shōchiku director Yasujirō Ozu (1903–1963) resisted the talkie as long as he could, but made important contributions to this genre. The silent film *I Was Born, But . . .* (Umarete wa mita keredo, 1932) deals with a favorite Ozu theme, the unfairness of life. Ozu's touch throughout is lightly humorous and stylistically sophisticated. The repetitions and parallelisms and stationary camera—all hallmarks of his mature mastery—are already in place here.

While Shōchiku went on pleasing ladies drawn to larmoyant sentimentalism, Nikkatsu allowed some directors to explore possibilities of slice-of-life realism. A typical Shōchiku smash hit would be *A Lover's Vow* (Aisen katsura, 1938), directed by Hiromasa Nomura (1905–1979). Tomu Uchida (1898–1970), a veteran of period films, helped Nikkatsu develop more socially oriented films in modern settings, such as his family saga *Theater of Life* (Jinsei gekijō, 1936).

Nikkatsu also continued to profit from its popular *jidaigeki*. Directors such as Sadao Yamanaka (1909–1938) and Hiroshi Inagaki (1905–1980) brought a certain seriousness to period drama, offering insight into the social milieu of the late Tokugawa period. Yamanaka's finest in that vein were *Humanity and Paper Balloons* (Ninjō kamufūsen, 1935) and *The Village Tattooed Man* (Machi no irezumi mono, 1935).

A third major player emerged in 1936, when the Tōhō conglomerate decided to compete across the board with films of every kind. It became a force to be reckoned with, especially in vaudeville-style comedy and musical genres. Tōhō also lavished huge sums on *jidaigeki* historical epics such as *The Ōsaka Summer Campaign* (Ōsaka natsu no jin, 1937), directed by Teinosuke Kinugasa (1896–1982).

Some directors in this decade set out to prove that mass-market appeal could accommodate highbrow scripts as well as best-seller spin-offs. They became known as *junbungaku* proponents of "pure literature." Studio rivalry also played a part.[9] Encouraged by the immense popularity of Uchida's *Theater of Life*, Nikkatsu commissioned other works based on thought-provoking novels. Shōchiku's *junbungaku* stars were the movement pioneer Shirō Toyoda (1906–1977) and Yasujirō Shimazu (1897–1945). They engaged with serious literature in serious ways—this in an age when ambitious fiction could appear first in various serial formats.

A second golden age of Japanese cinema is seen as taking shape in the 1930s, thanks chiefly to the varied, inventive approaches to the *gendaigeki* genre by masters such as Kenji Mizoguchi (1898–1956), Ozu, and Shimazu.

Mizoguchi made classics into classics and sometimes, as with *Osaka Elegy* (Naniwa erejī, 1936) and *Sisters of the Gion* (Gion no kyōdai, 1936), gave original scripts enduring life on screen.

War, Occupation, and Censorship: 1940–1951

War with China in July 1937 gave the film industry a foretaste of World War II hardship. Every aspect of creation, production, and distribution was subject to strict control. Materials were severely rationed. A board of censors scrutinized scripts in minute detail lest they promote frivolous behavior or Western notions of individual freedom. In 1941 the nation's ten film companies were reorganized as two, becoming, in effect, instruments of government policy. Nikkatsu's assets were divided between Shōchiku and Tōhō. In 1942, however, Masao Nagata managed to form the Dai-Nihon Eiga (Daiei).

Even before the rest of the world armed itself with censorship and propaganda, Japanese studios were in tune with the times. Films such as *The Whole Family Works* (Hataraku ikka,1939) by Mikio Naruse (1905–1969) showed life on the home front imbued with the requisite patriotic fervor. The lives of ordinary soldiers at the front were depicted in films such as *Five Scouts* (Gonin no sokōhei, 1938) and *Mud and Soldiers* (Tsuchi to heitai, 1939), both directed by Tomotaka Tasaka (1902–1974) and drawing on popular novels. A year after Pearl Harbor, Tōhō released *The War at Sea from Hawaii to Malaya* (Hawai-Marei oki kaisen, 1942), a potboiler of appropriately heroic proportions, directed by Kajirō Yamamoto (1902–1974).[10]

A generous budget allowed for special effects impressive for the time. Studios also glorified the past in historical "pageants" such as *The Battle of Kawanakajima* (Kawanakajima gassen, 1941) by Teinosuke Kinugasa (1896–1982).[11] To this category Mizoguichi also contributed a period film "without swashbuckling," his two-part version of the Japanese epic *Chūshingura* under the title *The Loyal Forty-Seven Ronin* (Genroku Chūshingura, 1941–1942).

Films of Occupation: 1945–1951

The postwar Occupation brought every kind of change, though film censorship remained an important tool of national policy. Its aim this time was to help recast Japanese society in a distinctly different mold as directed by the Allied Supreme Command. Thirteen themes associated with the "nationalism" of the past were banned. The traditional *jidaigeki* genre suffered most, deprived of its motivating themes of feudal loyalty and heroic self-sacifice.[12]

Even so, the cinema industry set to work, producing 160 films in the second year of the Occupation. At least eight of those were unmistakable instruments of official policy, though some stand out as historically significant. Two dealt with women's new roles in society. *Morning of the Ōsone Family* (Ōsoneke no ashita, 1946) by Keisuke Kinoshita (1912–1999) showed two hard-pressed women in wartime learning to be assertive. Mizoguchi's *Victory of Women* (Josei no shōri, 1946) featured a successful female trial lawyer. He followed that with *The Love of Sumako the Actress* (Joyū Sumako no koi, 1947) and *My Love Burns* (Waga koi wa moenu, 1949) to complete what some consider to be a feminist trilogy.

The young Akira Kurosawa (1910–2000) responded to censorship pressures with *No Regret for Youth* (Waga seishun ni kuinashi, 1946), its plot a paradigm for liberated women seeking self-worth. *The Ball at the Anjō House* (Anjōke no butōkai, 1947) by Kōzaburo Yoshimura (1911–2000) was notable for its boldly modern cinematic style and frank approach to the astonishing spectacle of women taking charge of an aristocratic family's failing fortunes.

No amount of censorship could staunch demand. Long years of war followed by hardships of recovery filled theaters to overflowing—theaters that were in short supply since more than five hundred were bombed. Audiences were looking for entertainment, not indoctrination, so studios rushed to supply every kind of light-hearted musical and comic drama. Shōchiku's first postwar venture was *Breeze* (Soyokaze, 1945), a smash hit musical revue whose "Song of Apples" theme became a pop anthem signifying hope for the future. Tōhō's competing *Song to the Sun* (Utae taiyō, 1945) was directed by Yutaka Abe (1895–1977).

Business was booming but studios suffered their share of strikes, ideological disputes, and money troubles. Tōhō lost staff and gained a competitor when breakaway dissidents formed Shin-tōhō. Daiei, a wartime creation, lost important *jidaigeki* performers to another company, so in 1949 it shifted into melodrama with a highly successful series of *haha-mono* (mother film) tear-jerkers: *Mother and Crimson Plum Blossoms* (Haha kōbai), *Three Mothers* (Haha sannin), and *In Search of Mother* (Haha koi boshi).

A Third Golden Era: 1951–1959

Economic, political, and cultural factors all joined forces to effect a remarkable growth in Japanese cinema in the early 1950s. New construction soon restored the number of theaters to the prewar figure of 2,641. By 1959, that number had nearly tripled to 7,401.

The return to national independence with the San Francisco Peace

Treaty of 1951 (to be effective in 1952) had a direct effect on the development of both artistic and popular cinema. For example, *jidaigeki,* especially the swashbuckling *chambara* variety, returned to captivate an audience hungry for a genre forbidden during the Occupation. This decade showed an impressive array of this genre. *Seven Samurai* (Shichinin no samurai, 1954) by Akira Kurosawa (1910–1998) and the *Musashi Miyamoto* trilogy (Musashi Miyamoto I–III, 1954–1956) by Hiroshi Inagaki's (1905–1980) survive as examples of artistic excellence, and the radio drama turned five-part film *The Red Peacock* (Beni kujaku, 1954–1955) was the pinnacle of popular *jidaigeki.* In *gendaigeki* genre, release from censorship and guidelines of the Supreme Commander of the Allied Powers also offered filmmakers new flexibility in their choice of subject matter. Many directors turned to contemporary themes, some playing to antiwar sentiments, others to the conflict of values in a changing society. The resultant blossoming of creativity in this decade marked what has been termed the Golden Age of postwar Japanese cinema (a third golden era throughout). For example, leftist Tadashi Imai made *The Tower of Lilies* (Himeyuri no tō, 1953), the antiwar film about high-school girls forced to kill themselves during the invasion of Okinawa. The ever-versatile Kinoshita's major works included *Carmen Comes Home* (Karumen kokyō ni kaeru, 1951), a satire on Japan's modernization, and *A Japanese Tragedy* (Nihon no higeki, 1952), a study of conflicting old and new values resulting in a gulf between a poor mother and her children. His fame was most closely linked with a tear-jerker melodrama charged with antiwar sentiment: *Twenty-four Eyes* (Nijū shi no hitomi, 1954).[13]

Outside Japan, Kurosawa's *Rashomon* (1950), the Grand Prize winner at the 1951 Venice Film Festival, awakened the international audience to the rich heritage of Japanese cinema.[14] Mizoguchi vied with him for international recognition as his *The Life of Oharu* (Saikaku ichidai onna, 1952) shared the best director award (the Silver Lion) with John Ford's *The Quiet Man* at the 1952 Venice Film Festival. The following year *Ugetsu* (1953) earned him a Silver Lion.

Other Japanese directors won recognition as well. Teinosuke Kinugasa's *The Gate of Hell* (Jigokukon, 1954) also won the Cannes Film Festival Grand Prize while Kurosawa's *Seven Samurai* (1954) and Mizoguchi's *Sansho the Bailiff* (Sanshō Dayū, 1954) received Silver Lions at the Venice Film Festival. Inagaki also entered the international limelight with his Oscar-winning *Musashi Miyamoto Part I* (1954).

Ozu and Gosho continued to explore the quintessentially familiar theme of the lives of ordinary people. Gosho's *Where Chimneys Are Seen* (Entotsu no mieru basho, 1953) won an award at the 1953 Berlin Film Festival. Despite the highly critical acclaim Ozu's films enjoyed at home, recognition abroad was rather slow to come. When finally *Tokyo Story* (Tōkyō monogatari, 1953) made its way to the 1958 London International Film Festival, it won the Sutherland Award for best picture.

At this new point of departure, the four existing firms (Tōhō, Shintōhō, Daiei, and Shōchiku) were joined by another, the Tōkyō Eiga Company, commonly called Tōei. Tōei made valuable contributions to popular cinema by adapting radio *jidaigeki* for film and putting them in contact with a vast new market of children and teenagers.

Shōchiku began the decade with a familiar emphasis on melodrama and the *shomingeki* drama of lower-middle-class life. The Tōhō captured the white-collar market with a comedy series featuring a company president. The company is also credited with inventing the Japanese monster science fiction film, the prime example being *Godzilla* (Gojira, 1954).

Daiei was notably successful with art films in the 1950s, producing international prize winners such as *Rashomon* and *Ugetsu*. Their popular film success, however, lay in creating a boom in the subgenre named for their series titled *Sex Stories of Teenagers* (Jūdai no seiten, 1953–1954). Nikkatsu was in a difficult position when the company resumed production in 1953. Prosperity came quite by accident in 1956 with the so-called Sun-Tribe (Taiyō-zoku) film. Its subject was a group of youngsters whose response to a materialistic society was the pursuit of sex and violence.[15]

Television and Retrenchment: The 1960s

By 1963 television was reaching 65 percent of the nation's viewing audience. That same year, the film audience shrank to half of its 1955 peak of 1,127 million. Clearly, the film industry had to retrench and reform its products and marketing strategy in line with audience tastes (or popular cinema). Plagued by poor management and a series of strikes, Shin-tōhō went bankrupt in 1961. Tōei hoped to replace its lost *jidaigeki* lead with more timely contemporary Yakuza films (gangsters and professional gamblers genre films). The highlight was *The Story of Japanese Yakuza* (Nihon kyōkaku-den), with eleven films produced from 1964 to 1971.

The Tōhō Company continued to remain strong in its specialties of white-collar comedy and science fiction. In the latter, it continued to populate the screen with Godzilla and his monster look-alikes. Nikkatsu, the most active company next to Tōei, resorted to skillful management of established idols cast in a series of action comedies and the *Migrant Bird* (Watari-dori) series (1959–1962; nine titles).

Daiei profits remained substantial, thanks to a number of action drama series with popular starts. Among them were the *Zatoichi* and *Evil Man* (Akumyō) series, both with actor Shintarō Katsu (1931–1997) and running 1961–1969.

Shōchiku fared poorly in the 1960s owing to a decline in audience interest in domestic drama, melodrama, and comedy. However, in 1969 a Shōchiku comedy comeback began with the first in a series that would continue for the following twenty-seven years: Yōji Yamada's *It's Tough Being a Man* (Otoko wa tsurai yo), commonly known as the *Tora-san* series, the parody of the Yakuza film featuring the vagabond Tora who never quite manages a break free of his home ties.

On the artistic cinema front, a goodly number of new names arrived on the "New Wave," as it was called, because of elements of experiment and controversy reminiscent of French *nouvelle vague*. Notable among them were Nagisa Ōshima (b. 1932), Masahiro Shinoda (b. 1931), and Yoshishige (Kijū) Yoshida (b. 1933), all from Shōchiku. Using bold new techniques, they dealt with themes related to violence and sex to explore new problems confronting postwar Japanese society.[16] Their effort in this line was exemplified by Ōshima's *Cruel Story of Youth* (Seishun zankoku monogatari, 1960).

Nikkatsu's Shōhei Imamura (b. 1926) challenged these New Wave directors. He did so by pursuing the subject of survival instinct in modern Japan with focus on women in the lowest strata of society, as shown in *Pigs and Battleships* (Buta to gunkan, 1961) and *The Insect Woman* (Nippon konchūki, 1963).

In the *jidaigeki* genre, Masaki Kobayashi (1916–1999) made memorable works charged with his antifeudal sentiments, most notably *Harakiri* (Seppuku, 1962) and *Rebellion* (Jōiuchi, 1967).

Production Innovation: The 1970s

In a decade of continuing decline, the cinema industry was forced to make more adjustments that altered the character of some studios considerably. Daiei went bankrupt in 1971. Nikkatsu eventually stopped making regular feature-length films and began with the introduction of a new genre requiring somewhat lower budgets, fewer staff, and reduced production time. This was the so-called *roman poruno* (the American designation would be "soft porn").

Faced with the declining commercial values of stars on a declining cycle, Tōei introduced a successful new series, Kinji Fukasaku's five-part Yakuza film, *Combat without Code* (Jingi naki tatakai, 1973–1974), a twenty-five-year saga of the rise and fall of various Yakuza.[17]

Shōchiku's Yōji Yamada (b. 1931) continued to figure prominently with the vastly popular *Tora-san* series, adding another twenty installments in the 1970s. (The series, a major source of Shōchiku's revenue, ended in 1996 with the lead actor's death.)

Tōhō did not do particularly well in popular genres in the early 1970s. Their comedies became hackneyed, and audiences turned away from their *jidaigeki* offerings. A profitable exception was the *Lone Wolf with a Child* (Kozure Ōkami) series (1972), with six installments. The first three installments were directed by veteran Kenji Misumi (1921–1975). The series featured a banished shogunal decapitator that originated in a comic book. Tōhō's precarious finances were given a shot in the arm by a disaster film, *Japan Sinks* (Nihon chinbotsu, 1973), adapted from Sakyō Komatsu's bestselling book.[18]

In 1976, the Kadokawa Publishing Company entered the cinema industry, with results that would prove to be far reaching. Their Kadokawa Film Company ignored double billing in order to pour their immense capital into single large-scale popular features. Their first production was Kon Ichikawa's murder mystery *The Inugami Family* (Inuegamike no ichizoku, 1976), based on the popular mystery novel by Seishi Yokomizo. It proved to be the highest-grossing film of the last seventy-some years. Kadokawa's publishing connections were the silver lining of their enterprise, with massive advertising organized to promote best-sellers, film versions, and soundtrack recordings simultaneously.

So Much, So New: The 1980s Onward

The year 1980 marked the beginning of the decade of the Japanese bubble economy, which burst in 1991. That spurt of "miracle" growth had an interesting effect on Japanese cinema. A retrenchment on the part of the major studios forced them to cut back on production and concentrate on the far more lucrative business of distribution. Independent filmmakers backed by outside enterprises rushed in to fill the resulting void.

The Kadokawa Publishing Company continued to diversify by marketing books and films together. Its film production division actively engaged in dramatizing popular mystery novels. Fuji Television also produced blockbusters such as Koreyoshi Kurahara's *The Antarctic Story* (Nankyoku monogatari, 1983) and Kon Ichikawa's 1985 remake of *The Harp of Burma* (Biruma no tategoto, 1954). Individual entrepreneurs with no connections to the cinema industry also invested their share of a general surplus of profits for reasons of art, not gain. Generous sponsorship by a former steel mill owner enabled Kōhei Oguri (b. 1945) to make his debut black-and-white film, *Muddy River* (Doro no kawa, 1981), one of the best postwar films about the fate of children.

After the bubble economy burst in May 1991, filmmaking became increasingly difficult. In 1993, Nikkatsu's bankruptcy was followed by Kadokawa's sudden decision to halt all film production for a while. Even so, a number of independent production companies remained successful, among them the Santory-sponsored Argo Project, a consortium of independent filmmakers. Their productions ran the gamut from love story to comedy by a young generation of directors. Apt examples were Takashi Ishii's *Original Sin* (Shindemo ii, 1992), inspired by James M. Cain's classic *The Postman Always Rings Twice* (1946) and a major box office hit, Yaguchi Shonobu's *Waterboys* (2002). Software maker Pony Canyon partnered with the advertising agency Hakuhodo to produce youth-oriented films.[19]

The 1980s turn away from the studio system redirected the nation's cinema by means of two distinct phenomena: the emergence of independent directors, most of them young; and a new line of cinema calculated to appeal to film aficionados, especially young ones with "disposable income."[20] This combination affected literary sources too—light novels and even cartoons, very often scripted with the help of the director himself.

A sampling of those who have gained recognition worldwide might begin with actor-turned-director Jūzō Itami (1933–1998), whose satirical comedies include *The Funeral* (Ososhiki, 1984), *Tampopo* (1985), and the two-part *A Taxing Woman* (Marusa no onna, 1987–1988), who probed the question of "what it means to be Japanese."[21] A second-generation Korean, Yōichi Sai (b. 1949) dealt with themes related to minorities in Japan in *All under the Moon* (Tsuki wa dotchi ni dete iru, 1993) and *The Curse of the Pig* (Buta no mukui, 1999). The multitalented Takeshi Kitano (b. 1947) made a number of violence-oriented films culminating in *Fireworks* (Hanabi), which won the coveted Golden Lion at the 1997 Venice Film Festival.

Some directors who made their mark while still in their twenties and thirties benefited from the PIA Film Festival. Established in 1977 by the Tokyo entertainment weekly magazine *PIA,* the festival served as one of very few avenues open to a new generation of filmmaker hopefuls. A number of PIA winners went on to make a successful transition from small-scale 8 mm/16 mm to commercially viable 35 mm films. Among them were Yoshimitsu Morita (b. 1950), Shinobu Yaguchi (b. 1967), Shinya Tsukamoto (b. 1960), and Kiyoshi Kurosawa (b. 1955). Two names also closely linked with the PIA festival were Naomi Kawase (b. 1969), a female director on the rise, and Masayuki Suō (b. 1956), director of *Shall We Dance?*

(1996). Kawase's semi-documentary *Suzaku* (Moe no Suzaku), the winner of the Caméra d'Or (best first feature film) at the 1997 Cannes Film Festival, brought a personal touch to issues of rural family life deeply rooted in Japanese society.

Among those who had worked in the media were Shunji Iwai (b. 1963) and Hirokazu Koreeda (b. 1962). Iwai's first feature-length film, *Love Letter* (1995), was a romantic drama about a young girl who sends a letter to her deceased lover. Its familiar theme, well served by stylish innovations, got the attention of urbanites who filled a Tokyo theater with standing-room-only crowds for fourteen weeks.[22] Koreeda gained international recognition in 1995 with *Maboroshi* (Maboroshi no hikari), a dramatic account of a widow's obsession with death. A number of festivals singled it out as the first feature-length film of a promising new talent and tendency.

The *anime* animation film was perhaps the most influential genre so far as the international audience was concerned. Katsuhiro Ōtomo's *Akira* (1988), adapted from his own comic book, was a phenomenal success in the United States.

Hayao Miyazaki (b. 1941) and Isao Takahata (b. 1935) collaborated on a number of projects at Studio Ghibli backed by the Tokuma Publishing Company. Their first spectacular breakthrough came in 1988 with Miyazaki's *My Neighbor Totoro* (Tonari no Totoro) and Takahata's *The Grave of Fireflies* (Hotaru no haka). The former, voted best picture of the year by the prestigious film journal *Kinema jumpō,* outranked work with more serious themes. In 1997 Miyazaki wrote, directed, and produced the astonishingly successful *Princess Mononoke* (Mononoke-hime), the highest-grossing film of all time. Hayao Miyazaki's animation *Spirited Away* (Sen to Chihiro no kamikakushi, 2002) made history by earning the all-time highest gross in Japanese cinema. It also won the award for Best Director at the 2002 Berlin Film Festival and more recently won a 2003 Oscar in the Best Animation category.

How does the Japanese cinema industry fare from now? That is beyond the scope of this book and everybody's guess.

A Few Notes on Methodology

This book offers intensive analyses of sixteen individual films altogether. My selection criteria are wide-ranging, in an attempt to address numerous concerns. The films' production dates range from prewar to the present, each representing an important phase of Japan's cinema history. Works by a young generation, such as those of Suō and Morita, neatly balance classics in Japanese cinema. Some films represent specific genres. For example, *The Mistress* is a so-called *bungei-eiga,* a screen adaptation of a Japanese literary work. *The Family Game* is a satirical comedy. *My Neighbor Totoro* is an animated film. The *Musashi Miyamoto* trilogy is a staple of the *jidaigeki,* the samurai film genre. Also included is a work by Kawase, one of the leading female directors today. Readers looking for extensive analyses of classics such as *Rashomon* (1950), *Ugetsu* (1953), and *Tokyo Story* (1953) will find them in my earlier book, *Cinema East: A Critical Study of Major Japanese Films* (1983). They are also widely discussed by other scholars and critics.

Critics agree that Japanese cinema is very rich in masterpieces of silent film. Ideally, at least one chapter here should be devoted to a representative example, even though very few such films are available with English subtitles in the United States. Kinugasa's *A Page of Madness* (Kurutta ippeji, 1926), Ozu's *I Was Born, But . . .* (Umarete wa mita keredo, 1932), and *Story of Floating Weeds* (Ukigusa monogatari, 1934) come to mind. However, these works have been widely discussed by others and I do not think I can really add anything constructive.[23] I would add that *A Page of Madness* is more suited for graduate students of cinema studies, given the director's sophisticated experiments with Expressionism.

Students and teachers will benefit from the fact that except for *Suzaku,* these films are readily available on video and/or DVD with English subtitles.[24] (I am hoping that Kawase's *Suzaku* will soon be made available.)

Since this book seeks to serve a general readership, each chapter opens with a brief introduction whose purpose is to locate the film to be discussed and its director in the larger context of Japanese cinema history. Readers familiar with the larger scheme of things may wish to begin with the body of the text, which is devoted to a detailed reading of the film.

It is important to note that this is not a book on film theory. The readings it offers are not tied to any absolute theoretical stance or ideological commitment. My objectives are those of a classroom teacher and suitably modest. The main text of each chapter will reinforce the student's grasp of two areas of inquiry essential to reading Japanese cinema. The first has to do with cultural specificity: What does the viewer need to know for a meaningful interpretation of a film? That question leads to the next: How does any particular critical method work and what can it tell us about a film?

If pressed to account for my critical method in this book, I would describe it as eclectic, a carefully considered combination of New Criticism, neo-formalism, and a cultural/historical approach. Here let me briefly outline a uniform approach to film. I begin by treating each film as a finished product rather than as a work in progress. I consider each work as a self-contained entity with its own structure.

I also view works from two perspectives: internal and external. The internal perspective studies structure and function: the makeup of parts and how they work together. I will show how structural unity comes by way of complex (and sometimes puzzling) arrangements of basic elements: characters, symbols, events, settings, and the like. And of course since Japanese culture and society are somewhat, if not entirely, alien to their experience, readers will learn to respect the importance of cultural specificity related to these elements. This is a complex business requiring many a shift of critical insight. The film marshals various effects in order to clarify a central problem: the protagonist's manner of relating to his or her world, or to the external world. The protagonist makes choices—issues—in response to the central problem that the given work features front and center. Some choices that are available may seem mutually exclusive; others, uneasily compatible; still others, apparently "free," a matter of roads taken or not taken. In any event, the protagonist's behavior offers us important clues to the worldview at work, whether it is to be taken as tragic or comic, say, or romantic, or ironic.

The other perspective—the external one—refers to the structure the film exhibits in relation to its audience. Seen from this perspective, the work invites us to relate to it in many ways. We are to have feelings about it, to become involved, to make judgments about the good and the bad in characters, actions, and values. As critics, we must decide whether we are being asked to take up an attitude of simple identification with the aspect of the work at hand or perhaps to reject it or maybe to react, to some extent, both ways at once. Can we accept the outcome of the protagonist's action as a logical consequence of his/her or the work's worldview? In short, other issues included here relate to the viewer's point of view, degree of notion of good or bad, and acceptance or refusal of the film's worldview.

Though the focus of the main text of this book tends to be on the internal structure, here and there I do consider how the director's use of certain elements deeply ingrained in the Japanese cultural context—songs for example—is geared to manipulate the viewer's point of view. Needless to say, all the devices of internal and external structure (and deviances from them too) are brought together by the third basic element of cinematic art: technique or stylistics. This is discussed separately, when necessary.

Though the critical format is uniform throughout, the basic constituents of each film—like any cultural icon—will vary from film to film, with analysis varying accordingly. This difference is reflected in subheads I have created for the sake of readability. Each chapter, however, ends with an intensive analysis of the final sequence or scene that clearly demonstrates how the director resolves issues or, as may be the case, leaves them as open.

Notes on Some Practical Matters

Long experience in the classroom has taught me the importance of everyday language and a straightforward, commonsense approach to film analysis. I have written this book in the style I use for teaching—not the style I would use in addressing other specialist scholars. This means that the book is light on critical jargon, even as I look for ways to elicit complex and sophisticated responses from students new to the art of reading Japanese films.

For the sake of readability, Japanese names are printed in the Western manner, that is to say, the first name followed by the given name. Macrons are used for Japanese long vowels. The English release title of a film is followed by the Japanese title in parentheses. For a film never released with English subtitles, I have provided a translation of the title. I have also done away with a glossary of Japanese and film terms in order to avoid redundancy. The first is provided in Richie's *A Hundred Years of Japanese Cinema* and the latter is a staple of many books for introductory film classes.

–1–
Synergy of Theme, Style, and Dialogue
Kenji Mizoguchi's *Sisters of the Gion* (1936)

KENJI MIZOGUCHI achieved sudden, worldwide fame. Few in the West had heard of him in 1952 when he shared the Venice Film Festival Silver Lion with John Ford. Mizoguchi's Best Director film was *The Life of Oharu* (Saikaku ichidai onna); Ford's was *The Quiet Man*. In 1953 Mizoguchi had the Silver Lion to himself. *Ugetsu* (Ugetsu monogatari) edged out the other favorite, William Wyler's *Roman Holiday,* and won the Italian Critics Award as well. Mizoguchi died in 1956, survived by a body of work whose enduring appeal has earned him a place among the masters of world cinema.

A flood of studies testifies to Mizoguchi's worldwide appeal to critics and scholars.[1] Even a quick look at certain aspects of his artistry shows why this is and should be so. Dudley Andrew puts it well, speaking of the thematic constant Mizoguchi made so peculiarly his own from first to last: "In all his periods and within the various genres he practiced, Mizoguchi's most prominent and passionate subject is women. Representative of culture, of the artistic impulse, of the downtrodden, of history, and of revolt, women are at the center of virtually every film he made."[2]

The woman at the center of a Mizoguchi film is a woman in trouble. Her victory, if any, comes by way of defeat in a world where men and money rule. Even in revolt, she is a fighter by way of endurance, since woman's battle cannot be won in any reality a Mizoguchi heroine finds herself in. Japanese audiences are entirely, traditionally familiar with the terms of her conflict between conformity and rebellion, the dutiful obligations of *giri* and the personal inclinations of *ninjō*. Western audiences in need of an introduction to this classical moral dilemma of Japanese culture can go straight to Mizoguchi. He is a brilliant forensic expert on the plight of women caught in the toils of moral dilemma, Japanese-style.

He is also a master dramatist in his chosen area of moral quandary. In *Osaka Elegy* (Naniwa erejī, 1936) his unmarried heroine's futile challenge is to patriarchy and the world of aggressive materialism dominated by Osaka merchants. *The Story of the Last Chrysanthemum* (Zangiku monogatari, 1939) takes us into the world of kabuki, with all its remnants of feudal social structure. A young maidservant loves and lives and dies, entirely devoted to advancing the career of an ingrate actor. The heroines of *The Life of Oharu* and *Ugetsu* are a cut above the majority of their sisters. They take woman's plight to new heights in the Mizoguchi scheme of things, becoming the best, most sublime type of long-suffering womankind: one who can forgive the men who have exploited her, even in the midst of personal misery.

The Crucified Lovers (Chikamatsu monogatari, 1954), like *Utamaro and His Five Women* (Utamaro o meguru gonin no onna, 1946), celebrates the theme of tragic love. This grim tale of adultery's punishment in the merchant-class feudal society of seventeenth-century Japan makes masterful use of its moral tensions. All the forces of social control converge to offer suicide as the only way out for the lady and her servant wrongly accused of adultery. Yet they dare to live, become "lovers," and so are crucified.

Mizoguchi is one of cinema's master stylists. He has a way with the long shot and long take.[3] They frame and define dramatic situations his camera explores with fluid grace. Its movement creates a sense of pleasing control of every effect of famously just-right pictorial composition. A famous example of Mizoguchi's long take virtuosity comes in the boat scene in *The Crucified Lovers*. Osan and Mohei have declared their love and decided to live. They are fixed for several minutes in the camera's steady gaze. It reveals a wealth of subtle detail in this moment of emotional rapture, directing our attention to the slightest visual alteration.

Another example of Mizoguchi's pictorial eloquence comes in the final scene of his last film, *The Street of Shame* (Akasen chitai, 1956). These last two long shots sum up the message of the film: the oldest profession is adapting shamelessly well to the new, postwar Japan. Two prostitutes are shown soliciting side by side at the entrance to their brothel. One is a new recruit dolled up in a kimono. A studied full-length shot draws our attention to her nervous fidgeting. Her companion is clearly at ease in gaudy Western dress. They are all of a piece with the flashy nighttime allure of the setting, genuine playthings of fate, which the film has shown to be anything but kind.

Critics continue to give pride of place to *Ugetsu*, whose first and last views are classics of Mizoguchi's fluid style. The effect is that of a picture scroll unrolling. At the outset, the camera pans across a pastoral valley and passes over a small building before craning down to halt in a long shot of a family in front of their house.

Osaka Elegy (Naniwa erejī, 1936) and *Sisters of the Gion* (Gion no kyōdai, 1936) are considered high points of Mizoguchi's prewar career by viewers at every level of interest.[4] At the time of their release they figured on the list of ten best pictures as noted by the prestigious film journal *Kinema jumpō*. The competition that year included masterworks such as Teinosuke Kinugasa's *Actor's Revenge* (Yukinojō henge, 1936) and Yasujiro Ozu's *Only Son* (Hitori Masuko, 1936). *Sisters of the Gion* took first place; *Osaka Elegy*, third.

Donald Richie and Noël Burch were among the first critics in the West to alert viewers to Mizoguchi's stylistic artistry.[5] My own book *Mizoguchi* (1984) expanded on their views, adding more intensive analysis of the masterful synergy created by Mizoguchi's modes of representation and steadfast thematic concern with the plight of women. Thanks to publishing economics at the time, that book suffered a number of drastic cuts. A number of important scenes in *Sisters of the Gion* got short shrift. Doing right by them now will serve a larger purpose, namely, expanding on an important aspect of cultural specificity overlooked by critics in the West: the linguistic properties of the film.

The *nouvelle vague* director Nagisa Ōshima made the interesting observation that Mizoguchi thinks through his camera. He certainly does so in *Sisters of the Gion*. There we see him letting the camera do the talking in a number of scenes. At the same time Mizoguchi adopts a more direct approach, taking inspired advantage of a fundamental advance, still new at the time: the spoken word on film. In *Sisters of the Gion*, he explored the potential of dialect. He makes subtle dramatic use of the marked contrast between the soft and gentle rhythmic character of Kyoto dialect and the more standard Japanese of fast-talking Tokyoites.

This aspect of his art is all the more interesting for the fact that in 1936 Mizoguchi was gaining notoriety as an unrelenting perfectionist where scripts were concerned. *Osaka Elegy* was his first collaboration with Kyoto native Yoshikata Yoda. They became and remained lifelong friends despite a working relationship requiring heroic forbearance on Yoda's part. It is said that he was desperately ill with tuberculosis when Mizoguchi was demanding rewrite after rewrite for *Osaka Elegy*. Finally, though reluctantly, Mizoguchi agreed to film Yoda's tenth version of the script. Together they worked wonders with the spoken word in *Sisters of the Gion*.

Its linguistic effects are inseparable from the film's aesthetic texture. Kyoto dialect is used in ways that allow for a beautifully nuanced approach to the moral and emotional quandary the sisters find themselves in. The sounds of their voices add much to the words they speak. As we shall see, this dimension of sensitivity is used most effectively in the final scene, where the voices of the sisters illuminate the bitter poignancy of their conflicting views of men and of woman's fate.

The Geographic Setting: The Gion

In *Osaka Elegy,* Mizoguchi dramatized a single heroine's choice of action in adapting to the world of aggressive materialism dominated by Osaka merchants. *Sisters of the Gion* followed with a new approach to a similar conflict through the creation of two character types. The elder sister, Umekichi, is a traditional variety of geisha, one who adheres to *giri,* understood as conformity to the accepted norms of the Gion, especially loyalty to her ex-patron. Her younger sister, Omocha, is a more modern type, more inclined to *ninjō* (indulgence of personal needs and inclinations). She is a graduate of a women's high school (junior high school in contemporary Japan), a rare asset in their profession as she is quick to remind her uneducated elder sister. Omocha grows more acutely asset-aware as the story unfolds. Money becomes her be-all and end-all, the key to survival as she understands it. Despising the pleasure quarter and everything it stands for, Omocha attempts to even the playing field by exploiting the Gion's male patrons all she can.

The heroine in *Osaka Elegy* was forced to change in response to changing circumstances. These sisters of the Gion are inflexible, each in her way, acting on her values to the bitterly futile end. Both are defeated by a system that gives them no real power of choice. The film's thematic progression highlights the various stages of the resulting moral conflict. Each stage gains support from cinematic devices even then becoming hallmarks of Mizoguchi's style. Along with the lateral dolly, his preference for long shot over the close-up is obvious here. So is the tendency to use long take in service of the so-called "one-scene, one-shot method."

Mizoguchi also takes special care to construct spatial dimensions, making effective use of the architecture typical of the Kansai area, as we shall see. All these contribute to his refined synthesis of thematic and aesthetic aims, his perfect marriage of content and form. A good place for analysis to begin could be a simple question: what does setting signify in the overall pattern of thematic progression? The Gion, a licensed pleasure quarter since the seventeenth century, has the force of tradition behind it.[6] It is the paradigm of a male-dominated, money-oriented society. It is restrictive in that the geisha is *giri*-bound. She owes a debt of loyalty to the proprietress who calls for her services at the teahouse. She is also under obligation to her customers there.

More importantly, the Gion is subdivided into a superior A section (*kō* in Japanese) and an inferior B section *(otsu)*.[7] In prewar Japan, the same terms were used for grading a wide range of social phenomena, everything from academic achievement to physical fitness of military recruits.

Umekichi and Omocha live in the B section. Being less privileged, they must be—to put it nicely—more versatile. They are paid less, and respected less, than those in the A section, whose privileged status derives from highly refined accomplishments that give them some power to negotiate with carnal knowledge. The story begins at a low point in the careers of the two sisters. Umekichi has lost her steady patron. Omocha has none. With destitution comes degradation. The two "arts" of pleasing—theatrical performance and sexual compliance—are always in precarious balance with geisha like them. How will the sisters survive? What does survival mean to them? What will it do to them? Those questions have answers as different as these two sisters are.

Marriage of Form and Content: Thematic Progression and Expressive Devices

The opening sequence of *Sisters of the Gion* presents the donnée of the film: a struggle for survival in a world where everything has its price. Stylistically, it is a fine example of Mizoguchi's fluid long take, one much more artistically controlled than those in earlier films. A lateral dolly takes us through what appears to be a merchant's house. The camera moves from the left, past a huge room where an auction is going on. Crossing to another room crowded with creditors, our view glides on to yet another room where items for sale are being sorted. The camera passes a huge pillar and a man holding an objet d'art. This survey has piqued our curiosity. What kind of merchant is being liquidated? This one long traveling shot has exposed us to the extent of his wealth.

As in *Osaka Elegy,* Mizoguchi takes full advantage of the architecture typical of a merchant's house in the Kansai area: narrow in front and deep in back. The scene dissolves to introduce what appears to be an annex at the end of a long corridor.

Mizoguchi is now ready to reveal the merchant's identity: the cotton wholesaler Furusawa. Later we will know him as Umekichi's former patron. Just now we see him with his wife and his steward, Sadakichi. All look sad. They stand in modest quarters stripped bare, in stark contrast to the sumptuous rooms of the house itself. The source of their misery there is conveyed by the distant murmur and bark of the auctioneer's voice. Here, in the opening sequence, movement and stillness are powerfully balanced. The earlier quick lateral dolly corresponded to the brisk auctioneering. Now the stationary camera takes charge. It concentrates our attention on a tense domestic situation. We eavesdrop on a discussion of Furusawa's bankruptcy. Husband and wife must leave their house and return to their hometown. The appearance of supportive common purpose proves deceiving. The camera glides forward to single out the wife, a quick motion, as if anxious to catch her complaint: she who brought her husband an enormous dowry must now return to her family with nothing but the clothes on her back. Furusawa turns to go, clearly upset. His steward cries out, "Master!" His wife, surprised, calls after him too. At the same time the auctioneer's voice grows louder.

Leaving his wife to board with the two sisters, Furusawa extends the theme of instability and conflict, carrying it with him into another area of confrontation between value systems. Here we are introduced to an important controlling image in this film. We see it right after Furusawa storms out from his house. A cut takes us to the small alley where the sisters live. Mizoguchi is scrupulously attentive to this place throughout. A long shot puts Furusawa in this context. He moves toward the camera, then diagonally across the screen from left to right. A reverse-field shot shows him walking straight away from the camera. These shots emphasize the long, narrow dimensions of this sunless, cheerless alley.

Mizoguchi's camera returns to it repeatedly. Later, Omocha will leave the alley in a fashionable dress, by then the mistress of a wealthy merchant. Kimura, a sales clerk enamored of Omocha, will be seen cooling his heels in darkness there while his master goes inside the house to collect a debt from Omocha, only to be ensnared by her charms. It is clear that the alley thematically serves as prelude to each new stage of the sisters' moral conflict.

Mizoguchi uses long shots exclusively for showing people going in and out of this alley. Time and again he alerts us to its stingy, damp, and shadowy measure of human destiny. Women who dream of decent security are doomed to survive on terms as precarious and false as they are niggardly and degrading. Mizoguchi's use of the architectural and geographical confines of the Gion is charged with other symbolic implications as well.

Alleys such as this, which ran behind mansions, served as eating places for feudal retainers. The term zezeura (literally "out back of kitchen") sometimes applied to them lent itself to a pun on zeze (money).[8] The implication for geisha living in the B section of the Gion is obvious: their dependency on money will be more parlous and sordid than that of geisha in the A section.

In the earlier Osaka Elegy, Mizoguchi gave night scenes double duty: to let the audience feel in tune with the heroine Ayako's environment and to establish the "intellectual gaze" as a basic rhetorical stance. Here, he uses the shadowy alley in a similar fashion. He returns to it as a reference point, wanting to make sure that the audience connects with its narrow, dark reality, the only one these women will ever know. He also uses close framing to reinforce the sense of claustrophobia, which stimulates intellectual reflection—a necessary condition for probing Mizoguchi's realistic representation of Gion society.

Significantly, the closed frame becomes a pervasive mechanism for dramatizing the sisters' moral dilemma. We see the first instance immediately after Furusawa walks down the alley. He is seen together with Umekichi and Omocha inside their tiny house. From this point on, Mizoguchi continues to explore the two sisters' different ways of coming to terms with Gion society. As if reluctant to side with one or the other, he keeps the two value systems in tension, sometimes letting them clash, sometimes showing them in parallel. This is seen even in his partial alignment of the two sisters: he intercuts between the two, shooting them now on different locations, now together.

The sisters' first confrontation takes place right after Umekichi sends Furusawa to a public bath. Here Mizoguchi relies heavily on the linguistic property of film—the spoken word—as the sisters air their different views of the situation. Yoda's sensitivity to Kyoto dialect is wonderfully successful here. Umekichi, with her sense of *giri,* is determined to let Furusawa stay at the house until his affairs are settled: "I must observe *giri* as he has taken good care of me as my patron. I may not be able to help him much, but I will be happy to console him by letting him stay with us." Her manner of delivery is very gentle, even demure, yet it conveys moral certitude and strength of character.

Omocha's manner of speaking derives from a rather different aspect of social decorum in Gion society. Mizoguchi himself saw fit to explain it:

> Kyotoites are characteristically keen on courtesy and observing social decorum. . . . The courtesy of a geisha is somewhat different in relation to the proprietress of the tea house and geisha older than herself. That is her private life. Her public life is somewhat different, entailing as it does relations with her clients. Her manner there is much more audacious, at the same time standoffish and flirtatious.[9]

We quickly learn that Omocha is a schemer and a user. Her speech is quite different in public and private. She makes no pretense of observing proprieties in dealings with her sister. She speaks frankly, emotionally, and at length about her resentments. In these situations her speech loses all traces of the gentle, genial Kyoto dialect. She blames Umekichi for letting Furusawa take advantage of her. Same goes, she says, for all the men who take their pleasure in the Gion. "What makes playthings out of us?" she says bitterly. "It's men. Men are our enemies—hateful enemies. They deserve rough treatment. I'll make them pay for this. Sister, you put yourself at their disposal, beguiled by obligation or loyalty. . . ." Omocha's diatribe continues as a change of venue adds an element of irony to a discussion of radically different values whose consistent point of reference on both sides is as profane as money. A cut takes us from their sunless, sordid house to where they go for a walk on the grounds of the Yasaka Shrine nearby. We register a sense of welcome relief after such confinement. Yet the shrine turns out to be a place of conflict, not comfort, for these women. Mizoguchi's camera work provides for a rhythmic give and take of stillness and motion. When the sisters walk, the camera follows; when they stop, it stops with them.

Here too, a radical difference in their manner of speaking helps develop the theme of conflict. Umekichi tells Omocha that society has rules they ought to abide by. Her younger sister counters with a harsh indictment of

Kudō (l., Eitarō Shindō) and Omocha (r., Isuzu Yamada) in *Sisters of the Gion* (1936). Courtesy of the Kawakita Memorial Film Institute.

all such rules: "Then, to be praised by society, you take care of Furusawa. ... Does society treat us like humans? It blames us, as geisha, for causing family problems and moral decay, doesn't it? Why do you have to worry about what people would say?"

The money question adds its cutting edge to their argument when they catch sight of a geisha of Umekichi's generation. Omocha comments that this woman has taken care to save up for her retirement. She adds that her sister's indifference to money is foolish. Umekichi angrily tells Omocha to suit herself.

From this point on, Mizoguchi never loses sight of the conflict that divides the sisters. At the same time he is careful to ration the number of scenes that put the two together. Instead, he puts money in the foreground. There it serves as a consistent point of reference for their conflicting value systems.

When, for example, Mizoguchi cuts to a teahouse, we see Omocha enter alone and sit facing the proprietress, whose ledger lies open between them. The camera steadily rests on them, while compositional flow is provided by other geisha passing by. The proprietress tells Omocha that she is planning to have Umekichi perform in the upcoming geisha dancing festival, one of the major events in the Gion. She does not, however, forget to add that Umekichi must wear a new kimono. Omocha's use of Kyoto dialect creates the expected impression of a dutiful, caring younger sister. She pleads Umekichi's case, adding that she herself, if need be, will raise the money for a kimono. Our curiosity is aroused but held in suspense until the following scene.

A cut to the sisters' house shows Umekichi and Furusawa together. Mizoguchi continues to use the long take here for purposes of contrast. Umekichi's disregard for money is obvious. Again, Mizoguchi puts her sense of *giri* in the foreground. She has bought new kimono material, not for herself, but for the bankrupt Furusawa. She has also bought his favorite sweets. Here too, a sense of spatial flow is created by other people passing through. After Furusawa leaves, a delivery boy brings noodles. Umekichi has to tell him she will pay next time.

The one-scene, one-shot method returns in the following sequence to emphasize the crucial role that money plays in the lives of the sisters and Furusawa. As usual, Mizoguchi begins with a shot of Umekichi coming down the alley. We are alerted to the thematic turning point that follows. She is accompanied by Jurakudō, an antique dealer who used to do business with Furusawa. The camera cuts to the interior as they go in. Its gaze takes note of four people in the room: Omocha, Umekichi, Furusawa, and

Jurakudō. Furusawa asks for a loan but gets much less than he asked for. He calls Jurakudō a tightwad. As they quarrel, the camera takes subtle note of Jurakudō's bulging wallet and Omocha's surprise at the sight of it.

The long take ends with a cut to the exterior. We see Omocha taking an obviously drunk Jurakudō somewhere in a taxi. Mizoguchi offers a close-up, one of very few in the film. Omocha's expression is inscrutable enough to make us wonder what she is up to. A dissolve—Mizoguchi's favorite cinematic punctuation—takes us to a teahouse. We learn that Omocha means to make Jurakudō her sister's new patron. Omocha also has plans for Furusawa. She confronts him in a scene that is a turning point in her conflict with Umekichi.

Again, two shots of the alleyway take us to the house. Mizoguchi cuts to the inside, then fixes the camera's gaze on the inner end of the sitting room. This has the effect of decentering Omocha and Furusawa, confining them to the lower left quarter of the screen.[10] According to Noël Burch, "the principle of camera distance is most stringently observed."[11] Burch is right. But he wrongly ignores the connection between the signifier and the signified here. In fact, he claims that the editing pattern does not reinforce the semantic pattern of the dialogue. Such is not the case. Our first sight of Omocha and Furusawa places them in the upper left side of the screen. That draws our attention to the room they occupy. Stretching our way in front of them is a shabby tatami mat. It dominates the screen. We cannot miss its simple, clear-cut comment of the sisters' poverty.

The camera tracks up a trifle, decentering Omocha and Furusawa in the lower left of the screen. Destitution's visible evidence is joined by Omocha's argument. She speaks frankly to Furusawa, urging him to free her sister by leaving. She gives him money she has wheedled out of Jurakudō—careful to keep half for herself.

Again, Mizoguchi observes their conversation at the low tea table in a steady long shot. Burch faults this choice for leaving too much space open above the speakers' heads.[12] However, there is a very practical reason why Mizoguchi has done this. The rhythmical variations in this long take depend on gestures and changes of position. Omocha and Furusawa reach an agreement and stand up. She helps him don his coat. If the long shot had centered them, their heads would have left the frame at this point. A director such as Ozu would have tracked the camera backward to maintain a centered alignment, which would serve Ozu's preference for individual shots. Two very different cinematic styles are at work here. Mizoguchi's is rooted in emphasis on the sequence of minimum cuts as a basic unit of film. In this he is true to the melodramatic style of his early days at the Nikkatsu studio.

Ozu was trained at Shōchiku, where the *shomingeki* genre of lower-middle-class drama became the studio staple in the early 1930s.

Omocha's success in getting Furusawa to leave marks a turning point in the film. From this point on it follows a steady divergence in the sisters' approaches to life. Umekichi responds to Omocha's scheming by leaving home to join Furusawa, then living with a former employee. Increasing avarice leads Omocha to capitalize on her charms every way possible. Kimura, a young clerk, is in love with her. Disdaining his penniless sincerity, she seduces his boss, Kudō, in order to become his mistress.

As the sisters' estrangement grows, Mizoguchi's camera movements become more calculated. Omocha's seduction of Kudō, an affluent draper, is an interesting example. As usual, a long shot of the alley anticipates a new development in this conflict of values. This time, Kudō and Kimura are seen there. Mizoguchi, true to his method, dramatizes the seduction sequence by keeping cuts and camera movement to a minimum. It is as if he wants to command our attention at this critical moment by focusing on Omocha's decisive control of the situation. A cut tells us that Kimura waits outside while his boss confronts Omocha in the earthen entryway. The wealthy merchant thinks he has come to collect for kimono material this woman persuaded his dimwit assistant Kimura to give her on credit. He finds her seated in the vestibule. Together they occupy the lower left corner of the screen.

Omocha turns Kudō's accusation back on him, claiming that she in fact fell prey to the young man's lascivious scheming. Kimura, she insists, as good as forced her to take the material she admired but couldn't possibly afford. As they talk, the camera takes note of the wordless exchange passing between them. Omocha eyes Kudō's expensive watch and ring. He eyes her appraisingly. The camera's steady gaze sustains the tension we expect to lead somewhere. Yet Mizoguchi chooses not to satisfy our curiosity just yet. In a nicely calculated delaying tactic, he cuts to the outside. Kimura, tired of waiting, paces back and forth.

A cut back inside shows Kudō and Omocha placed as before. She laments her lack of a patron and asks him to help her find one. Her manner of speaking betrays none of the harsh, bitter tone she takes with her sister. Reverting to Kyoto type here, she combines flirtatiousness with plangent persuasiveness. Kudō is not slow to recommend himself as the patron she needs.

All this while the decentered formal pattern combines with nuanced dialogue to prepare us for what transpires. Omocha invites Kudō into the room adjacent to the vestibule. Now Mizoguchi is ready to resolve our mood of suspense. He draws the camera back to the edge of the room to show the two facing each other at the low table. Again, they occupy the left-hand corner of the room, leaving "too much room over their heads."

Here too the placement of the camera reminds us of the poverty that underlies Omocha's action. It makes us see the shabby squalor these women are forced to endure. More importantly, we are again reminded that Omocha is now greeting Kudō not in the vestibule, but in the living room next to it. The low tea table tells us that the house is a typical low-income rental. Situated in a back alley, it has a few poor rooms, all opening into the *doma* (earthen passageway).

Kudō is by now quite willing to listen to Omocha speak of her predicament. She moves around the table to help him with his coat. Naturally, both of them stand. Again, the filmic composition—ample space over their heads—anticipates the movement, leaving Mizoguchi free to control spatial flow without having to move the camera. The point of this choice is clarified by a sequence showing Umekichi with Furusawa in their cheap boarding house. They are seated, facing one another across a low table in a second-floor room. The ceiling is very low, typical of mercantile-class housing in that time and place. Here, centering the two serves to emphasize the contrast between this sorry come-down from the spacious opulence of Furusawa's previous life. The strictly symmetrical alignment also suggests a measure of intimate resignation between the two.

Omocha's determination to beat the system at its own game drives the sisters further apart. Being younger and entirely devious appears to be paying off. Omocha enjoys all the benefits of wealthy patronage. Umekichi appears content with the spiritual gratification that comes of devotion to the luckless Furusawa.

Mizoguchi saves his highly discretionary use of the close-up for the drama surrounding Omocha's downfall. When her dejected suitor Kimura finds out that she has used him to install herself as his boss's mistress, he decides to take revenge. A cut to the familiar dark alleyway prepares us for another turning point in the sisters' moral conflict. A long shot shows us a man walking down it toward the camera. He is Kimura's accomplice, a driver ostensibly sent by Kudō. A sudden sweeping view of the nighttime surroundings has the feel of casual individual witness captured by a handheld camera. A viewer familiar with the area will know that the car is moving away from the Gion district. Sharing Omocha's view of the lovely Kamo River scenery passing by, we share the welcome change from dreary house and alleyway. We might even guess that Omocha is congratulating herself on her success. Although shown in open framing, this atmosphere of night and luxurious mystery is drawing us into an ironic intimate space nothing like what Omocha is expecting.

A series of close-ups inside the car make us witness to what follows. The mystery man riding next to her whips off his sunglasses. It is the furious, vengeful Kimura. The camera gives a close and subtle view of Omocha's change from taunting anger to pleading fear. Mizoguchi keeps us in suspense by putting the outcome on hold, cutting to the outside of the car. A long shot of the car restores our sense of space; the rhythm of spatial flow accelerates fear as the car speeds off into the dark of night.

Omocha (Isuzu Yamada) in *Sisters of the Gion* (1936). Courtesy of the Kawakita Memorial Film Institute.

The Final Sequence

A cut to Umekichi and Furusawa at the boarding house resolves the issue of Omocha's fate and begins a final sequence whose conflict resolution proves less schematic than may at first appear. The narrative gap is filled as word arrives that Omocha is in the hospital badly injured—pushed out of a moving car. Furusawa urges Umekichi to rush to her sister's side.

A cut to the hospital reunites the sisters in a long shot clearly meant to dramatize the elder sister's devotion to the younger. The scene begins with a shot of Umekichi entering the hallway. The moving camera involves us in each stage of her emotional state. It pans in to follow her to the door of an operating room. It stops with her in center frame. Assisted by a nurse, Omocha walks to the right. Umekichi follows to her ward. The camera tags along slowly. Umekichi is out of the frame, but the lateral dolly reminds us that she is moving along behind.

The camera keeps its distance all this while. Here again, Mizoguchi uses the spoken word to convey emotional texture. Even in this moment of crisis, the sisters disagree. Omocha fiercely accuses men: "I won't be defeated by men. Kimura did this cruel thing. I'll make him pay!" Umekichi still insists that Omocha must be sensitive to human feelings. Omocha's reply is rife with bitterness: "They don't treat us as humans. They make fools of us and it's so selfish of them to tell us to act like humans. Who wants to love men?" On that note she disappears behind a lattice screening the door of her room. The camera remains fixed on her point of disappearance. Umekichi must pass in front of it, taking her leave.

The meaning of this long take is syntagmatic: its full meaning is revealed in the subsequent scene. Umekichi returns to the boardinghouse to fetch belongings she will need for her stay with Omocha. She finds Furusawa gone. He has not left so much as a note of thanks, only a message conveyed by the landlady. He has returned to his hometown to become a factory manager there. He advises Umekichi to find a richer patron.

Furusawa's casual callousness seems sadly akin to her sister's slighting reception of her tender concern. Again, the camera bears witness steady to Umekichi's plight. The slightly high angle of its stasis has the effect of diminishing her size. She sits in the middle of the room. The neatness of this composition is clearly ironic, intensifying her isolation. Body language has its say as well. Her drooping shoulder line and the slow-motion raking of the brazier coals speak for her desolate sense of alienation, of devotion repaid with furious ingratitude and outright desertion.

Another significant wordless touch is the double dissolve Mizoguchi uses to end this scene. The first dissolves a shot of her sitting in the room; the second dissolves a similar shot. This device creates awareness of Umekichi's long mourning. It is also an elegiac gesture, one destined to become a distinctive Mizoguchi touch, an expressive indicator of his involvement in the pathos of his chosen subject: woman caught in the toils of misfortune.

The closing scene resolves the sisters' conflict by means of a typically ironic worldview. That view has been suggested all along with the image of the alleyway. Neither sister will escape its cramped and sunless way of life. The geisha's world is so structured that none of her decisions or desires can alter it—or bring subservience a just reward. At the conclusion of *Osaka Elegy,* Mizoguchi let the camera speak for the heroine Ayako's final challenge to society. A final close-up of her defiant expression spoke her piece with wordless eloquence.[13] Camera movement at the end of *Sisters of the Gion* is kept to a minimum while the challenge is made in plain words.

Using the one-scene, one-shot approach, Mizoguchi shows us Omocha in bed with Umekichi sitting alongside. This approach, together with closed framing, fixes our attention on the sisters' predicament. Omocha says: "I'm cold. Cover me with the quilt, sister" *(Nēsan, chotto samuinen. Futon kisetē nā).* This early in the history of talking pictures (and their collaboration) Mizouchi and Yoda crafted this inspired choice of the simplest possible words. They invest the dialogue not just with the local color of Kyoto dialect, but with nuance as well. Omocha's simple words, given that gentle enunciation, are like the expressive monosyllables uttered by Ozu's characters: they say far more than any elaborate technical device. The Japanese audience cannot fail to notice a telling contrast here between the essentially soft texture of Omocha's Kyoto dialect and the harshness of the tone she takes in earlier conversations with her sister.

The point of this subtly stated endpoint will not be lost on an audience of native speakers. Omocha's gentle request conveys a complex mix of emotions. There is the kid sister's tendency to *amae* (childish dependency) along with the sauciness that speaks for the desire for independence.[14] On another level, it speaks for the hard, grown-up fact that the sisters must face the world together since sisterly solidarity is all they have and all they ever will have in the seamy, uncertain corner of the universe they inhabit.

Yet there is more. Umekichi tells Omocha about Furusawa's shabby ingratitude.[15] Even so, she insists that having done what society expects of her is some consolation. Surely now it is her turn to be treated with tender consideration by her sister. But there is to be nothing of the kind. Omocha bursts out in another bitter diatribe. She says, in effect, what can you expect when a geisha is nothing but a plaything for men? ("Omocha" means "toy" in Japanese.) The camera gradually tracks up to her, but stops in a medium shot of her face as she cries out bitterly, "I hate men. Why does the profession of the geisha exist? I wish it ceased to exist!"

Mizoguchi avoids ending this film with a close-up, as he did in *Osaka Elegy*. Yet Omocha's cry is just as provocative and troubling as Ayako's final gaze in close-up. Both devices challenge the entire world—ours included. Dudley Andrew has noted that "Mizoguchi was obsessed with the gait of women, with their swoons, with their averted or penetrating gaze."[16] The same obsessive energy seeks an outlet in Omocha's cry. Even so, we feel something problematic in this ending, a hint of discrepancy between the semantic and cinematic functions. On the surface, Omocha's cry is desperate enough to make us feel spontaneously for both these afflicted women. Yet the camera's position seems to urge consideration of a larger synthesis. We feel compelled seek a larger meaning. Thus our rhetorical stance is neutralized. Our ambivalence suggests that Mizoguchi himself was afraid to take a firmly objective view of the sisters' plight. Otherwise, we think, surely he would have fastened on it more deliberately in the end.

–2–
Dream, Song, and Symbol
Akira Kurosawa's *Drunken Angel* (1948)

AKIRA KUROSAWA (b. 1910) died of a stroke at home in Tokyo on September 7, 1997. He was a grand old man of world cinema—so grand that *The New York Times* gave him one of its longest obituaries in a decade. Kurosawa and Japanese cinema had come a long way together since 1951 when *Rashomon* won the Venice Film Festival grand prize. Its Best Foreign Picture Oscar of 1951 gave American audiences their first real taste of Japanese cinema, a taste whose astonishing growth Kurosawa helped expand and guide for over forty years.

Kurosawa made thirty-two films in his sixty-two year career. Many achieved instant masterwork status by way of awards at home and abroad. Some would be on any world cinema lover's list of must-see classics: *Ikiru* (1952), *Seven Samurai* (Shichinin no samurai, 1953), *Kagemusha* (1980), and *Ran* (1985), to name but a few.[1]

Kurosawa has in fact been the Japanese director most widely discussed in the West. But why? Certainly his thematic orientation has wide appeal. He himself said, "I suppose all of my films have a common theme. If I think about it, though, the only theme I can think of is really a question: Why can't people be happier together?"[2]

An auteurist perspective would point to the fact that most Kurosawa films begin with the premise that the world is fragmented. What follows is an exploration of a central problem shared by individual characters looking for ways to adapt to some variation on social chaos. Kurosawa's worlds tend to be dark, yet not beyond redeeming. The potential for regeneration is always there, but how? *Rashomon* and *Seven Samurai* are definitive in that line. The dilapidated Rashomon gate in twelfth-century Kyoto speaks for a morally and politically chaotic world. Yet Kurosawa insists on a ray of hope, signifying it by means of a gargoyle and signboard still intact in blinding rain. The woodcutter's decision to adopt the abandoned baby at the end of the film is clearly altruistic, clearly a means to save a fallen society. Equally clear there is Kurosawa's conviction that societies in the process of self-destruction are rescued by the compassion of selfless individuals, not institutional responses, as witnessed by the self-serving priest in *Rashomon*.[3]

Kurosawa also makes a case for concerted action, as in *Seven Samurai,* a tale of shabby footloose fighters agreeing to shield a tiny farming village from the evils of civil war in the sixteenth century. What's in it for them beyond shelter and some food? Benevolence, it turns out, a combination of compassion and rectitude transcending the difference in social status. Kurosawa plots are typically deeply committed to some moral ideal.

Time and again he tells a tale on purpose to suggest that positive social outcomes are the property of individuals channeling their altruism into publicly significant action. This universal thematic concern prevails all the way through Kurosawa's last film, *Madadayo* (1993), as I shall discuss in chapter 12. There he appears to meditate on the strength of a bond between a professor and his students, finding in it a source of virtues sadly lacking in today's postmodern world. Needless to say, the *Madadayo* relationship is forged by shared altruistic concern.

Kurosawa had seen his share of decline and fall and hard-won survival and renewal. He studied that process in some powerful postwar films on contemporary issues. A young man confronts the here and now of defeat and recovery in *Drunken Angel* (Yoidore tenshi, 1948). Through him, Kurosawa looked squarely at a difficult world he himself lived in—the society struggling to survive in occupied Japan. Looking back, we can see this film as heralding premises and thematic concerns that will return over and over again in films that belong unmistakably to Akira Kurosawa. His portrayal of an alcoholic doctor who wants to cure both moral and physical diseases was meant to convey a moral message: the importance of altruism.

Kurosawa had this to say: "In this picture I was finally myself. It was my picture. I was doing it and no one else."[4] Donald Richie agrees. He sees *Drunken Angel* as the future master's real "first picture" (Kurosawa had made six others). Richie considers it "the major 'breakthrough' of a major directorial talent who has finally 'realized' himself."[5]

Drunken Angel was a breakthrough in another sense. Kurosawa gave cinema a new face: that of disdainful, charismatic Toshirō Mifune.[6] He became an overnight star at the age of twenty-nine, a case of director and actor, youth and brilliance perfectly matched.

Richie details those aspects of Kurosawa's development in his analysis of *Drunken Angel,* the most comprehensive study to date. Still, Kurosawa's use of music and metaphor in this film can be expanded on. His wide-ranging soundtrack borrows from sources as unlike as Japanese popular song and Viennese waltz. The film's controlling metaphor is the cesspool, along with other, less troubling water images. Kurosawa uses music and metaphor to project a power of insight into the social and cultural milieu of postwar Japan. Their integration into the thematic progression of the film is especially masterful. Their mode of presentation is, as we shall see, as crucial as what they say.

The Central Problem, Thematic Progression, and Water Imagery

As mentioned above, we are apt to see most Kurosawa films beginning with the premise that the world is fragmented. His characters engage us in their ways of exploring alternatives as they strive to survive as individuals by adjusting to various kinds of chaos—moral, political, and social, sometimes all together.

Drunken Angel offers this premise at the outset, in an unmistakable camera cue, a lateral pan to the film's controlling metaphor: the cesspool. Our view sinks to its level, a crater of filthy drainage identified as all that remains of a "bombed-out shelter." The irony is clear: this place of refuge, hit by a bomb, is now a pit fit only to receive the worst in the way of human drainage. Even nature appears to conspire in this degradation. As the doctor explains in the following sequence, the stagnant cesspool water breeds mosquitoes and disease.

The camera studies the surrounding slum. A young man plays a blues tune on his guitar. He does not play it well. This element of discord adds to the gloomy atmosphere as darkness falls. Yawning prostitutes loiter nearby.

This cesspool has been widely discussed. Critics agree on its fitness as a symbol of the social and moral chaos in postwar Japan.[7] I would add a touch of emphasis on an opposing image: the barmaid Gin's dreamy reference to a small clear stream running through a meadow in the country. She mentions it just once, but even this early in his career Kurosawa is asking us to be alive to metaphoric truth, connections real and imagined conspiring to explain the world.

This is his method. The cesspool is a little worldview taking us into the heart of the matter this director makes it his business to explore. The cesspool is a city, a society in danger of falling sick, thanks to being on the receiving end of so much corruption draining out of postwar chaos.

The cesspool shows us characters thinking about its meaning. The hapless barmaid in love with a gangster dreams in opposition to this sinkhole of slum life she lives in. She dreams of that stream in a meadow. The doctor stares into the cesspool. The camera shares his view of its stench, the bubbles of methane gas breaking on the surface of poisoned water. The doctor offers a professional opinion. He compares the bubbling cesspool to an abscess on lungs destroyed by tuberculosis, just one of a plague of postwar diseases he fights a losing battle with. Again, this is Kurosawa's way. The premise is stated in metaphoric terms whose job it is to illuminate a problem central to the film. Here it could be stated baldly as a question: how does the individual come to terms with city life in the chaos of postwar Japan?

It follows that different characters will adapt in different ways. Kurosawa shows them tending to opposite extremes, depending on their view of principles. Some, like Nanae, are flexible enough to pass for unprincipled. Her values are those of the dedicated opportunist. Making the most of her charms, she becomes Matsunaga's mistress. Yet when Okada appears, fresh out of prison, she sees that he is the man of the hour and ditches one man for another.

Thanks to a tidy knot in the plot, Okada's former common-law wife Miho represents a different approach. We meet her in the unglamorous world of Dr. Sanada's office, where she works as a nurse's aide. Under the good doctor's influence, she has come to see Okada as having ruined just half of her life. She now sees herself as being given the chance to build a new and better life, one based on moral integrity. It will not be easy, she knows. Her choice of career is clearly a metaphor that speaks for the kind of dedication this broken society needs to mend it—morally as well as medically.

The medical metaphor is extended to include Dr. Sanada's tuberculosis patient, the unnamed high-school girl whose values stand in clear opposition to those of Nanae and various other morally flawed grown-ups in the film. Suffering has not diminished this girl's sense of self worth. The doctor credits her with facing death more courageously than does the tough guy Matsunaga. Not that she is passively resigned—far from it. Her faith in Dr. Sanada leads her to adopt his view that the most effective weapon against tuberculosis is the will to live.

The barmaid Gin (no metaphoric pun intended) might be called a principled quitter. After Matsunaga dies, she finds the city intolerable. She goes to live with her uncle in the country where she can breathe clean air in sight of that clear little stream in the meadow.

Dr. Sanada himself is too deeply committed to leave the city and all its miseries behind. His dedication goes well beyond the role of medicine in relieving human suffering. He speaks for the director's *idée fixe,* which sees poverty and ignorance as the sources of personal and social fragmentation. Here, as in his other films, Kurosawa is at pains to show how ignorance stems from the individual's lack of self-awareness and the self-worth that comes of moral integrity.

Dr. Sanada is only the first in a long line of heroic, high–minded physicians in Kurosawa's films. The young doctor Fujisaki in *The Quiet Duel* (Shizuka naru kettō, 1949) works with his father to combat syphilis. Red Beard (Aka hige) in the film of that title (1965) is content to run a clinic in the slums when he could be the shogun's private physician. These are just two from a large cast of metaphorical characters Kurosawa developed over the years. And so he begins with Dr. Sanada, whose devotion to curing the physical and moral illnesses of society is clearly a metaphor for benevolence.

That metaphor is central to the drunken angel Matsunaga's conflicted search for a self-image he can understand and accept. Like the musical references on the soundtrack, the metaphors in this film draw us into a world whose sights and sounds resonate with meanings far more complex than the rather melodramatic plot.

As Donald Richie points out, Matsunaga's transformation begins with a medical diagnosis. Like Watanabe in *Ikiru* (1952), Matsunaga is forced to confront himself when he realizes that he is ill. Watanabe begins to live

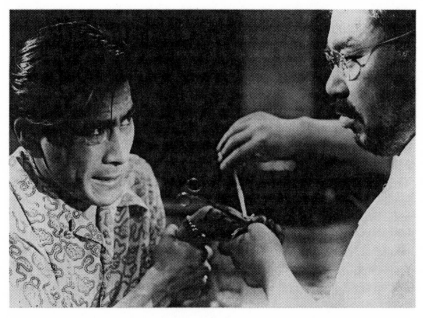

Matsunaga (l., Toshirō Mifune) and Dr. Sanada (r., Takashi Shimura) in *Drunken Angel* (1948). © Tōhō Co. Ltd.

when he is given six months to live. He finds life in devoting himself to working for the good of all.

Thanks to help from Dr. Sanada, Matsunaga's struggle leads him to hope for a cure arising out of a similar change in outlook. Then suddenly his past returns for a fatal showdown when his boss, Okada, is released from prison. From that point on we witness Matsunaga's degradation.

Transition to that final stage returns us to the cesspool image. Matsunaga, sloppy drunk, comes to visit Dr. Sanada. After some argument, he appears to yield to the doctor's advice to get a grip on himself. A cut to the cesspool shows the man we saw at the opening of the film. Here, in a long shot, he plays the same tune, "Blues in the Rain," on his guitar. Someone sidles up to him. The camera tracks forward for a closer view. The stranger sports a crew cut and traditional kimono. He stands over the guitar player. Everything about him speaks of the Yakuza: his stance is that of a gangster; his clothes fit that swaggering way; and he has that hard, aggressive glint in his eyes. He reaches for the guitar. The player gives it up without protest. The Yakuza plays a powerful, sinister tune. The soundtrack amplifies it. Asked what it's about, he says matter-of-factly, "Killing." Later, this same music will return in a dream sequence with richer symbolic meaning. By then we will know that the player is Okada, Matsunaga's crime boss. Just now, we know him as a Yakuza who says he just got out of prison. Looking around, he says that things have changed in the old neighborhood. Everything, that is, but the cesspool. He says it casually, but the message is clear. All is chaos, all is change. Only life at the cesspool level resists all change, taking chaos as it comes.

Again the camera again pans across the filthy cesspool, preparing us for a change of scene. The Yakuza's tune still sounds in the distance as the camera cuts to the doctor's house. Miho trembles as she listens. That tune, she says, was Okada's favorite.

The cesspool returns to lend its ominous message to another sign of lowlife making its way in this difficult world. We see Matsunaga coming out of the doctor's office. The sun is shining now. The soundtrack provides a lively tune played on winds. Matsunaga is wearing a suit. A carnation is pinned to his lapel. This scene offers an upbeat replay of his previous visit to the doctor. That time he came out the door into dismal rainy weather. He had received his diagnosis then. His courage had failed him, and he looked it, too.

Donald Richie has drawn our attention to a sly bit of shadow play now, in this replay on a bright and sunny day. As Matsunaga leaves the doctor's office, a patient given cause to hope, the camera cuts to show his shadow crossing the cesspool. Another shadow follows. The camera pans up to show whom it belongs to: Okada. A glance back at the cesspool shows Matsunaga's carnation floating on the surface, telling us all we need to know about Matsunaga's sudden loss of hope.

His swift decline into physical and moral chaos leads to a dream sequence. In it, two important water images interact with music to convey a sense of futility as Matsunaga fails in his search for a new identity. The scene opens with a shot of him standing by the cesspool. The wind blows over it. A cut to the surface shows what he is looking at: a small doll floating in the filth, a plaything of unkind fate. He already has that sense of his predicament. Later he will know for sure that he has been a lifelong pawn, a Yakuza stooge used while he was useful. Now that he's sick, stricken with TB, his opportunistic boss will sacrifice him in the next raid on a rival gang. More bitter yet, Matsunaga knows that Okada is not playing by Yakuza rules. The traditional boss is supposed to treat his men with the gangland equivalent of benevolence.

A dissolve transforms the cesspool into the sea, that age-old symbol of endless life and bounty, of a world of wishful thinking. The camera settles on a coffin on the shore, centering it on screen. This message from the world of the dead is reinforced by the soundtrack. It replays the tune Okada played on the guitar by the cesspool in his old neighborhood. There he said that the song was about "killing." So whose death does the coffin represent?

Here something very strange takes place, after the manner of a dream. We see two Matsunagas: one in the coffin, one hacking at the coffin with an ax. The one in the coffin climbs out and chases the other down the beach. The one being chased appears to slow down, even as the one in pursuit appears to be picking up speed.

It is easy to see these two enacting a projection of Matsunaga's inner conflict. He wants to break away from his former self, a sick man doomed by disease and his criminal association. That self is symbolized by the shirt and pants he wears in this dream sequence. We saw him wearing them in reality the first time he went to see Dr. Sanada. The other Matsunaga wears the suit appropriate to his confident new identity, the reborn healthy gangster he is so anxious to become. We have seen him that suit before as well, complete with white scarf he sported in the cabaret where he fought with Okada over Nanae.[8]

Drunken Angel is not a reassuring tale of uplift and redemption. The "better" Matsunaga in this dream sequence still wears a gangster's clothes. His vision of social self-worth still suits him up for a life of organized crime. We see clearly, in metaphoric terms in this sequence, that his moral illness will progress unchecked. He will not escape his past. All that remains now is to see how he will die in the wide-awake world of reality.

Not surprisingly, he is killed in a fight with Okada. Yet this fight between the down-and-out henchman and his tough-guy boss is rich in cultural detail. The very fact that this fight takes place shows how gangland values, too, are changing in this postwar society in turmoil. *Jingi,* the code of the Yakuza, entitles the boss to demand absolute loyalty from his *kobun,* or henchman. That loyalty is reciprocal, too. The boss must be a benevolent dictator, a model of rectitude and compassion, where his men are concerned.

Okada himself had been surprised when earlier he showed up at Dr. Sanada's office, expecting to claim his woman. There he found Matsunaga, who intervened on the woman's behalf. Having been in prison, Okada had lost track of the changing times. He quickly learned from his own boss that codes of honor were a thing of the past. What counted now was power— raw power. Henchmen, being weaker, were the means to the given opportunistic end, no more. A boss could use them any way he saw fit and dispose of them, too.

Matsunaga is offered a chance to break with the past and save himself. It comes through the barmaid Gin, who urges him to join her in fleeing the city for the countryside. But he is a man of the city and there he must die, but not before we glimpse something of the angel in the title of the film. Having seen Matsunaga risk his life earlier in a compassionate defense of Miho's newfound moral integrity, we are prepared to see his death in more complex terms than might otherwise be the case. Certainly Kurosawa is at pains to stage the death of this gangster in a way that redeems him as a symbol of human decency all too easily compromised by the breakdown of social and cultural values in the aftermath of war.

This climactic fight scene has been widely praised for its masterful presentation. Many critics have admired the dexterous cut from the strait confines of Nanae's room to the narrow passageway outside and the struggle taking place in a pool of spilt paint. The end of the sequence constructs a metaphor of unexpected subtlety. A long shot shows Matsunaga opening a window to come out on the balcony. As the camera closes in on him, we hear a shot. Next we see Matsunaga lying dead on this commonplace rickety balcony used for drying clothes. He lies bathed in sunlight. We know from the camera's position that the cesspool is down below.

Kurosawa has avoided the obvious here. Matsunaga does not die by the cesspool or in Nanae's room, the room of a woman given heart and soul to opportunistic cunning and greed. We heard him say earlier he could not stand the thought of lying sick in her bed, in such a tiny room, nursed by fellow henchmen. This final shot of him on the sunny, shabby balcony conveys a sense of liberation. The soundtrack replays the music we heard when he stepped out of Dr. Sanada's office, full of hope that he might be cured of his illness after all.

Kurosawa's Use of Music: Tribute to Fumio Hayasaka

Though *Drunken Angel* has the universal appeal of many films, it is also highly encoded with specific cultural information. The soundtrack is especially rich in significant musical references. The score itself was more than usually well arranged and forward looking, even influential. A director as accomplished as Nagisa Ōshima credits *Drunken Angel* with alerting him to the possibilities of music and acoustic special effects.[9] And it's no wonder. In this film, Kurosawa shows the way to an inspired use of sound montage, especially as it concerns borrowing from popular music from the time of the film. Here proper credit must be given to director of music Fumio Hayasaka. He continued on in that capacity for all but one of of Kurosawa's films until his death in 1954 at the age of forty-one. Even so, Hayasaka's legacy includes the scores for *Rashomon, Ikiru,* and *Seven Samurai.*

Tadao Satō writes this in praise of Hayasaka's scoring for the sociocultural milieu depicted in *Drunken Angel:* "Hayasaka's score gets its effects from a well-nigh noisy montage of scraps from popular songs of the day. The result is wonderfully expressive of the heightened sense of nerve and verve characteristic of the desperately stressful social climate in this postwar period."[10] Hayasaka's richly allusive soundtrack shows the way to subtleties easily overlooked in *Drunken Angel.* Satō's astute observation is especially pertinent in scenes depicting cabaret and black market life. What better places to look for a desperately vigorous approach to postwar life?

Needless to say, other directors were also making the most of these energetic lowlife scenes. Hibari Misora's 1948 box office hit *Kanashiki kuchibue* (Sad Whistle) showcased a twelve-year-old's vocal talent in a cabaret scene. Kinji Fukasaku was still using black market symbolism in Yakuza films up into the 1970s.

In *Drunken Angel,* a sound of the blues takes Matsunaga into the cabaret. There he finds a gangster dancing cheek to cheek with the hostess. They dance to the jaunty hit tune "Tonko bushi" (Tonko tune). Its light rhythm contrasts with the hot and heavy feeling generated by these dancers who appear completely oblivious to everyone else in the room. Matsunaga's henchman appears and taps him on the head. Someone outside wants to see him. As Matsunaga steps out the door the music changes to another popular song, Noriko Awaya's "Omoide no burūsu" (Blues of memory).

Dr. Sanada is waiting outside the cabaret, wanting news of Matsunaga's latest X-ray exam. The gangster is in no mood to discuss his dismal state of health. Dr. Sanada is distracted by the music inside. Having no ear for music, he mistakes it for a tango. This small detail adds another piece to our sense of the difference between these two men: the idealistic, unworldly physician and the streetwise gangster. Not only does the doctor wait outside, he can't even catch the drift of the music inside.

Ozu was another director who would get a reputation for using parts of song and even segments of Noh plays.[11] He does this in films such as *Late Spring* (Banshun, 1948), *Tokyo Story* (Tōkyō monogatari 1953), and most notably in *Drifting Weeds* (Ukigusa, 1959). Here in *Drunken Angel,* we see Kurosawa and Hayasaka leading the way.

In this first cabaret scene in the film, the music drifting out the door also binds the doctor and Matsunaga in feelings of loneliness and solitude. Noriko Awaya's song is about sitting alone in a room, assailed by unforgettable memories as a winter storm blows outside.

Later in the film, a popular song in a similar vein offers insight into Dr. Sanada. It is "Anata to futari de kita oka" (The hill I visited with you). He hums it to himself in his seedy office. He is mixing a drink of medical alcohol and water. We see that even this good man must have his poison. But why? The song is about young lovers who climb a hill that commands a fine view of a harbor and ships. Cherry blossom time is coming to an end. Falling petals scatter, some of them coming to rest on this happy pair. The doctor's rueful humming of this tune refines our sense of him. We are not so surprised to learn later on that he is saddened by thoughts of the life he might have led as a family man and respected professional. Others in his class had succeeded where he had failed. He sees it as the price he has paid for having been a playboy in school. And so he hums this melancholy tune, stirring the drink that will only drown him deeper in despair.

The poignant music of the doctor's song contrasts with the hectic gaiety that reigns in the cabaret when Matsunaga returns, introducing Okada to this part of his Yakuza turf. Okada takes a seat and ogles every passing woman. He says they all look beautiful to a guy like him, fresh out of prison. Matsunaga and his mistress Nanae dance to a blues tune, "Yoru no pratto-fōmu" (Platform at night). A band plays the tune without benefit of vocalist, but moviegoers after the war could be counted on to know the words, which tell of two lovers parting in the dead of night. He has boarded the train, leaving her on the platform. As the train pulls away she says goodbye, wondering if they will ever meet again.

As Matsunaga and Nanae dance, a series of quick intercuts studies her awareness of Okada's provocative stare. A viewer aware of the words of the song being played can readily imagine the all-too-human outcome foretold by these glances. This woman dancing with this man will be letting go of him. No, not to stand alone as in the song, but free to dance with the man seated over there, the one who can't take his eyes off her.

Another cabaret scene confirms that outcome. This time, the soundtrack offers a medley of popular songs. Saxophones figure prominently in the opening orchestral work. As Nanae stands between Okada and Matsunaga, a cut to a cabaret hostess looking on asks and answers the obvious question. She wonders aloud how Nanae will choose, adding that Matsunaga is no match for a tough like Okada.

Sure enough, Nanae and Okada dance. They move quickly around the floor as if eager to play out the given scenario, daring events to stand in their way. The music swiftly descends from high-flown operatic emotions to more primal, forceful fare offered by "Janguru Bugi" (Jungle boogie-woogie). This was one of the most popular songs in the repertoire of Shizuko Kasagi, then known as the "Queen of Boogie-Woogie." The singer herself is featured here, a tiny woman made tinier by a high-angled camera view. Yet Kasagi, centered in the frame, fills it with energy, imitating the roar of a tigress as required by the score. Dancers crowd round on every side, moving to the driving boogie-woogie beat. The camera glimpses Matsunaga dancing wildly but alone in the thick of it.

The frenetic scoring here is an obvious evocation of "the unusual vigor and energy" characteristic of postwar Japan. Not every filmgoer at the time would have sampled cabaret life but all could be counted on to know a boogie-woogie song popularized by a performer as famous as Kasagi. In any case, the lyrics of the song make unmistakable reference to the love triangle taking shape on screen. A tigress in the song is referred to as "queen of the jungle" in a scenario complete with erupting volcano. The analogy with Nanae is entirely obvious. She is the heartless predatory female ready to pounce, to seize every advantage in this cutthroat competitive underworld of gangsters and their molls.

The scene ends with a shot of Matsunaga slumping dead drunk in his chair. The boogie-woogie still thunders on the soundtrack, furnishing a shockingly abrupt but effective transition to the diegetic opener to the next scene, a series of sharp slaps administered by the doctor trying to wake his patient. What better way to convey the sharp decline of Matsunaga's health and status in the criminal underworld?

We have seen how the opening theme of the film is the laid-back, rueful "Ame no burūsu" (Rainy blues). The guitarist there looks like a pimp so it is no surprise to learn that Kurosawa originally intended to use the "Mack the Knife" theme from Kurt Weill's *Threepenny Opera*.[12] Finding the publisher's user fee too high, he substituted "Rainy Blues," which served his purpose very well. It was popularized by the "Queen of the Blues," Noriko Awaya. The lyric describes rain falling quietly in a street as evening comes on. A pedestrian feels the rain touching him to the heart. In the film, the tune is given an amateur's bad rendition, complete with discords and awkward phrasing. After all, this blues-loving pimp sits in sight of a cesspool in a blighted, war-torn neighborhood showing few signs of the energy and enterprise required for success in a rapidly changing economy.

What the player does in this scene is prepare us for a change in the storyline. As Steve Prince has observed, the camera's pan across the cesspool connects it with the doctor's office. The doctor complains that the player and the mosquitoes strike up together, one singing, the other whining. A pan back to the cesspool invites us to consider what a plague of mosquitoes

Nanae (l., Michiyo Kogure) and Matsunaga (r., Toshirō Mifune) in *Drunken Angel* (1948). © Tōhō Co. Ltd.

might mean to the health of this unsalubrious neighborhood. That notion is reinforced by Matsunaga coming for another checkup, which, as we have seen, ends in his ill-tempered refusal to follow the regimen required by his disease.

As we have seen, music is used to foreshadow aspects of his personal catastrophe. Bizet did this in *Carmen,* where a "fate" motif looks ahead to the heroine's death at the hands of her abandoned lover Don José. In *Drunken Angel,* we are prepared for the deadly outcome by the blues theme giving way to the song Okada says is about "killing" after he gives it a powerful rendition. As we have seen, that performance took place after his release from prison, on a visit to his old neighborhood, which he finds in ruins and where he plays his song in sight of a cesspool on a guitar commandeered from a pimp. Surely this is symbolism with a vengeance!

But the film has its lighter moments, too. Kurosawa and Hayasaka collaborate on a series of lively ironies playing off contrasts between music and action at hand. For example, Matsunaga's visit to the black market is accompanied by a tune well known throughout Japan: "Aizu Bandaisan" (Mount Banzai in Aizu Province). The audience would have heard it in traditional folk song style complete with the traditional musical instrument, a *samisen.* The song praises the scenic wonders of this sublime "Golden Mountain." Here the tune is scored for strings and winds in a jazzy, upbeat style in telling contrast to the elevated theme of the song. Its streetwise treatment here serves an ironic view of this lowlife, hurly-burly marketplace. And, as if to drive the point home, the camera takes notes of a billboard slogan: "Let's make our town a better place!" Matsunaga himself is in a hearty mood. He slaps a fellow in passing, telling him not to look so sassy. The critic Tadao Satō claims that Kurosawa and Hayasaka found their inspiration for this scene in *Sniper* (1931), by the Russian filmmaker Semen Timoshenko. There a savage irony is served by music in a holiday mood accompanying a group of young soldiers in wartime leaving for the front.[13]

A similar poignant irony is played out in the marketplace, this time in a context more directly related to Matsunaga's declining fortunes. Here the soundtrack offers "a particularly vapid piece of music."[14] It is the "Cuckoo Waltz" by Johann Strauss. Viewers may not have known this less well-known piece of Viennese kitsch, but studious lovers of irony won't miss the reference to a bird whose specialty is taking over other birds' nests. We see that starting to happen in this scene. The unsuspecting Matsunaga exercises his gangster privilege, helping himself to a buttonhole carnation at a florist shop and going on his way. But things have changed. Kurosawa adds this detail to our sense of Matsunaga as a man on the way out. The girl from the shop catches up with him, saying he forgot to pay for his carnation. Matsunaga, incensed, returns to the shop. There he scuffles with the owner, who tells him that this territory belongs to Okada now.

The ironically cheerful waltz plays on as Matsunaga makes his next accustomed stop, the tavern, where he asks the barmaid Gin for sake. The manager calls her into the kitchen to deliver the news: no more drinks on the house for that one. Kind-hearted Gin pays for the drink herself. This is when (as we have seen) she offers Matsunaga a share in her plan to escape the horrors of city life by going to live with her uncle in the country. He cannot imagine going that way. There's no escaping the kind of man he is.

The Final Sequence

The final sequence takes place after Matsunaga's death. It is, in effect, a coda in which music and central metaphor interact to add new meaning to the message Kurosawa has sought to convey. This coda also offers the sense of closure that will become a hallmark of his style in future films.

The sequence begins with Gin and the doctor standing in sight of the cesspool. A cold wind sweeps over the water and ruffles around them. The day, like the place, is made for mourning. The irony is that neither of these mourners knows what we know: that Matsunaga underwent significant transformation before his death. The fact that these two faithful friends still mourn the badly flawed man that he was his whole life is one of the film's most poignant ironies. Still, this scene brings two compassionate people together. Dr. Sanada has his altruistic mission; Gin, her steadfast decency. She is the one who paid for Matsunaga's funeral, something none of his underworld associates would do. At least these two friends know that Matsunaga was capable of compassion too.

This coda also connects the central problem of the film with important moral questions, namely, can the better world we envision really come to pass? Can this chaotic, postwar society really remake itself according to such high standards? Even this early in his career, Kurosawa is a moralist eager to persuade us that society can be improved by individuals motivated by compassion. Obviously, his view of morality is deeply rooted in Buddhism. But Kurosawa's morality insists on a measure of social and political activism. This is the difference between the doctor and the barmaid in this film. Dr. Sanada's vision of a better future requires significant public action. Gin's vision depends on the "little acts of kindness and of love" (to borrow Shakespeare's phrase) of compassionate individuals acting in private.

Here too, we see another defining characteristic of Kurosawa's lifelong work: the utopian vision of what nowadays might be called top-down benevolence. This is his Confucian dimension, his trust in hierarchical arrangements based on the ideal of rulers who rule by virtue of benevolence. Here again, Dr. Sanada serves as the paragon, or the best available in the desolate neighborhood of the film.

Enter the anonymous young girl whose tuberculosis the doctor had treated earlier. She returns now, all smiles, to tell him that she is cured and has graduated from school. Not one to leave a point un-underscored, Kurosawa directs his camera to pan upward to take appropriate note of the sky. It fills the screen with unironic clarity.

A pan back down to the cesspool shows water untroubled by the wind now, a surface open to glancing sun. Satō has this to say about this moment: "The filthy cesspool behind the black market shines with a touch of alluring beauty even though it is filled with the debris of a corrupt society. It serves as a wonderful symbol of the spiritual state of the Japanese in the aftermath of the war."[15] And of course it also lends a glow of hope for the future of this girl who already reciprocates the doctor's helpful trust in her. Here too, Kurosawa's message is resolutely upbeat. One of these days, this stinking cesspool will vanish—in its place perhaps a bold new building will

Matsunaga (l., Toshirō Mifune) and Gin (r., Noriko Sengoku) in *Drunken Angel* (1948). © Tōhō Co. Ltd.

reach for the sky. Who knows? Maybe this same girl will live and thrive right here, in a better world reclaimed from such a dreary wasteland. What better metaphor for the remaking of Japan and Japanese society than the imagined virtuous willpower of this girl?

A cut looks down a passageway through the busy black market. Dr. Sanada, arm in arm with the girl, walks toward the camera. He sings "The Hill I Visited with You," the song we heard him croon earlier as he mixed his lonely drink. Back then, the song spoke for a world of merely wishful thinking, of marriage and family life, of simple human happiness as a lonely failure might imagine it. Now of course his song brings this other, more genuine message home. He is not alone now. He will be the trusted mentor and friend to his patient. She will be his family now.

The camera pans to the sky once more. It looms above the busy crowd. Strings on the soundtrack return to music used twice before. First it expressed Matsunaga's hope of being healed after all. Then it mourned his pitiful end, lying dead on that balcony somewhere near this parting scene. Now that music returns in a livelier tempo as befits Kurosawa's vision of Japan as a country in ruins destined to rebuild itself.

–3–
A Meiji Novel for the Screen
Shirō Toyoda's *The Mistress* (1954)

SHIRŌ TOYODA (1905–1977) was all of twenty-three when he directed his first film, *Painted Lips* (Ayarareru kuchibiru), in 1929. He was in good youthful company at the Shōchiku Kamata Studio, working alongside fellow future masters Yasujirō Ozu (1903–1963) and Heinouke Gosho (1902–1981). Toyoda made sixty films in his forty-seven year career, a body of work that gave him a master's ongoing renown in Japan.

In the West, however, he got nothing like the recognition accorded Ozu and Gosho. This is partly a matter of marketing, since few of his films were distributed abroad. It also has to do with the genre Toyoda made his own with such notable success among the Japanese: the *bungei-eiga* film (adaptation of serious literary works). Distributors were no doubt sometimes right to think that audiences might not connect with scripts based on unfamiliar books.

The years 1935–1937 are generally recognized as marking an upsurge of interest in the so-called *junbungaku* (pure literature) movement in Japanese cinema. "Pure" in this case means serious in the sense of high artistic purpose. Certainly studio productions schedules for those years indicate a vigorous market response to the public's interest in serious literature adapted for the screen.[1]

One of the first was Yasujirō Shimazu's *Okoto and Sasuke* (Okoto to Sasuke, 1935), adapted from Jun'ichirō Tanizaki's novel *A Portrait of Shunkin* (Shunkinshō, 1933). Many such works soon followed, among them Tomu Uchida's *The Theater of Life* (Jinsei gekijō, 1936) and Toyoda's *Young People* (Wakai hito, 1937), based on contemporary novels by Shirō Ozaki and Yojirō Ishikawa, respectively. Set in a mission school, *Young People* concerned the exuberant passion of youth and the sufferings of an intelligentsia faced with a dilemma posed by exalted notions of freedom at odds with the rigid social discipline. The following year Toyoda did two more adaptations. The plot of the screenplay for *A Cry Baby Apprentice* (Nakimushi kozō) followed Fumiko Hayashi's short story rather closely: a fatherless boy's mother passes him from one aunt to another. While Hayashi's story is a sensitive psychological portrait of an unwanted child, Toyoda's film is more interesting for its portrayal of women coping in different ways with their roles as the weaker sex. The other film, *The Nightingale* (Uguisu), drew on the story of the same title published that year by Einosuke Itō. In it, the various episodes focused on the comings and goings of people whose victories and defeats created a microcosm of the world at large.

Many critics credit Toyoda's careful control of narrative and creation of pictorial style with giving real substance and vitality to the *junbungaku* movement. Ever since then he came to be known as director par excellence of *bungei-eiga*.

Toyoda's postwar *bungei-eiga* show his mastery extending to an impressive array of modern novelists. *Wild Geese* (Gan, 1953) adapted an Ōgai Mori novel published between 1911 and 1913.[2] (The film was released in the United States as "The Mistress.") *A Certain Woman* (Aru onna, 1955) adapted the 1919 novel by Takeo Arishama. The leading writers of the 1930s still interested him after the war. In 1956, he made a film of Jun'ichirō Tanizaki's 1936 novel *The Cat, Shozo, and Two Women* (Neko to Shozō to futari no onna). In 1960 he did the same for the "naturalist" Kafū Nagai's 1937 *A Strange Story from East of the Sumida River* (Bokutō kidan). *Snow Country* (Yukiguni, 1957) adapted the Nobel laureate Yasunari Kawabata's novel written between 1934 and 1947.[3]

Snow Country and *The Mistress* are probably best known in the West, thanks to video distribution. They share a kind of heroine that fascinated him and was poignantly different from her counterpart in the original: a woman whose courageous approach to a difficult life derives from a rebellious gift for challenge and confrontation. At the end of *Snow Country,* the catastrophe that involves Yōko's disfigurement in a fire serves to submit Komako to life as a geisha in a society whose focus on money and male ascendancy lays such intolerable burdens on women. Yet Komako faces her maternal responsibilities with a heightened awareness of the plight of her sex. Similarly, instead of silently suffering from the male-dominated and money-oriented society, Otama in *The Mistress* strives for a sense of freedom, as we shall see.

The heroine of *The Mistress* made a good first impression in very good company. Toyoda's film was number eight on the *Kinema junpō* list of best films of 1953. It was a year for masterworks. The top three films were Imai's *Muddy Waters* (Nigorie), Ozu's *Tokyo Story* (Tōkyō monogatari), and Mizoguchi's *Ugetsu.*

Toyoda's genius for literature being what it is, no appreciation of *The*

Mistress would be complete without consideration of his approach to the book he brought to the screen. As we shall see, Toyoda's approach to adaptation is freely interpretive. His heroine, like the novelist's, confronts Meiji society, but goes beyond resistance to outright rebellion. This radical shift in values raises a number of thought-provoking questions. Why does Toyoda change Otama's character? What weight should we give the issue of "contemporaneity" he excelled at addressing? How does this shift in thematic thrust change his narrative? What cinematic qualities did he find in the novel, and what use did he make of them? What did he gain from the familiar basic principles of deletion, alteration, and addition?[4]

Historical Setting and Central Problem

The narrator in *The Wild Geese* gives the date of his story at the outset. The year is 1880, twelve years after the Meiji Restoration. The new government has a policy of strengthening the nation through Western technology. Foreign cultural influences, especially from Europe, are beginning to transform Japanese society. A new class of intellectual is looking for ways to move with this mainstream modernization. The literary scene is awash in translations. The Japanese are reading the likes of Shakespeare and Goethe, Ibsen and Wilde. Politicians are looking for ways to emulate the German legal system.

Ōgai's novel depicts a country in the throes of transformation. The mixture of old and new is exhilarating and disorienting, too. As the story begins, Old Edo still casts a long shadow over this brave new world of imported novelties. University students, policemen, and geisha have a somewhat different look, but underneath they are still profoundly, traditionally Japanese.

The newly adopted capitalist ethos has given the city some unmistakable monuments to conspicuous success. The narrator mentions the Iwasaki mansion on the southern side of Muenzaka. Alert readers will immediately know it belongs to Yatarō Iwasaki, the founder of Mitsubishi Company, one of the new ruling corporate conglomerates, or *zaibatsu*. Bicycles were a socially challenging novelty in the West in 1880, so one can readily imagine the sensation they created in a Japan seeking Western technology. This explains why the narrator takes special note of a bicycle track as "one of the most unusual transformations in this world."[5]

Toyoda lets the camera do the talking, taking full advantage of film's intrinsic gift for telling descriptive detail. Deep space and panning supply narrative verve and economy throughout. This is evident from the first. Opening credits flash on a background series of scenic watercolor views of

Reading a Japanese Film

places typical of Old Edo. Shinobazu Pond in Ueno Park is there, complete with a shoreline pavilion.

The first few sequences sketch in evocative glimpses of manners and customs in process of change. A back alley row of tenements speaks for the life of poverty led by those least affected by change. A cut to a restaurant shows us a *sukiyaki* party for students from Tokyo University. Western beef was a highly exotic novelity. Naturally young men destined to join the governing elite of the new Meiji society would key on this exciting new experience. The novel and the film share the central problem posed for a woman such as Otama in this new sociohistorical milieu: how will she, whose only assets are youth and beauty, confront a self-consciously "new" society still bound by traditional customs and values oppressive to women?

Toyoda's male prototype in the piece is the novel's: the loan shark and pawnbroker Suezō. His like has always epitomized male egoism in control of so many women's lives in a male-dominated, money-driven society. Add to that his value as symbol of the new aggressive materialism imported from the West and Suezō becomes a force to be reckoned with. A woman such as Otama serves the ancient double standard made worse by the new capitalist mentality. A mistress is yet another status symbol money can buy.[6]

The central problem revolves around the familiar dichotomous choices: conformity versus rebellion. The former engages with values of *giri* (social obligation), the latter with those of *ninjō* (personal inclination). The novel and the film both dramatize various stages of Otama's conflict as she reacts to the facts of her life. Yet each takes a different approach to dramatizing the conflict, as we shall see.

The Thematic Progression and Narration of the Novel

The first half of Ōgai's novel details Otama's submission to the traditional pattern of life and its values of conformity, dependence, and suppression of ego. Then, midway through, she shifts ground, doing all she can to achieve an attenuated sense of freedom and independence. Significantly, Ōgai accentuates each stage of Otama's conflict with visual images that manage to be deftly placed without drawing too much attention to themselves.

Money sets the story in motion. Otama's father cannot provide for his family. She barely made it through elementary school and has no professional skills. She must do what dutiful daughters have done time out of mind in Japan: sacrifice herself to help her family. The policeman she marries turns out to be a bigamist with wife and children in the country. Even in the new Meiji society Otama is damaged goods, a woman robbed of her virginity,

52

the indispensable marketable asset required for a decent marriage. Again, she does the dutiful thing. A go-between arranges the only match available now. Otama will become the mistress, on a generous allowance, of the prosperous "merchant" widower Suezō. He is in fact nothing of the kind. He is a loan shark and pawnbroker, both highly despised in Meiji society. His money is tainted. He has a wife and children. Unbeknownst to her, Suezō has cheated Otama of any hope of respectability.

Even before she has any inkling of the truth, she feels degraded and oppressed. Images of confinement underscore the theme of a life of captive frustration. Suezō is master, she, the slave, afraid to leave the house lest he come and find her gone. She looks out at life through a window lattice, rarely speaking with anyone. She finds herself shunned. A fishmonger's wife considers herself entitled to snub Otama's maid. Ōgai describes Otama's silent resignation this way:

> In her feeling the sense of injustice done by the world in general and men in particular was almost absent. If she had such a sense, it was that of the unfairness of her own destiny. She had done nothing wrong, yet she was to be persecuted by the world. This pained her. . . . When she had learned that the policeman had deceived her and deserted her, she had used the same words for the first time in her life: "It's not fair! How cruel!" . . .
>
> Gradually her thoughts settled. Resignation was the mental attitude she had most experienced, and in this reaction her mind adjusted itself like a well-oiled machine.[7]

Otama's turning point comes when she discovers the truth about Suezō. Yet what can she do, a poor woman forced to sacrifice herself not once, but twice, to filial piety? Her first impulse is to take what comfort she can by confronting patriarchy head-on. She goes to her father's house, fully intending to let him know of her misfortune. Yet she cannot break free to that extent. She decides not to burden the old man. That is her first taste of victory: she leaves him almost light of heart, thanks to a newfound feeling of inner independence. Ōgai conveys the essence of this moment with an image that might be missed in the West, though the Japanese audience can be counted on to appreciate its value: the folded parasol. "Already above Ueno Hill, the sun blazed with its heat and dyed the Benten Shrine on the pond's inner island a deeper red. In spite of the glare Otama walked on without opening the small parasol that she carried."[8] Otama, being a sheltered, traditional woman and a kept woman as well, is asserting her right to fend for herself, beginning with a thing as a simple as sunlight.

Ōgai's narrator reinforces the point elsewhere: "Her aim in life had been her father's happiness, so she had become a mistress, almost forcibly persuading the old man to accept. . . . Whatever pain the decision might cost her, she was determined to keep her sadness to herself. And when she had made this decision, the girl, who had always depended on others, had felt for the first time her own independence."[9] Her sense of liberation is that limited at first, yet it foments rebellion equally discreet at the outset. Otama's screened-in view of life passing by in the street furnishes an object of uncommon interest. She becomes obsessively curious about Okada, a young medical student who passes her house around the same time every day. Day after day she watches and waits. Finally, she works up the courage to be out in front of the house just as he passes by. They do not speak a word. They only bow.

Otama's love for this young man remains the stuff of dreams in a context of psychological drama more concerned with social issues than with a heroine's chances for personal fulfillment. Ōgai marks a crucial turning point in Otama's development with an image that cannot fail to generate critical discussion on many levels: a snake makes its way through the bars of a cage and attacks a pair of linnets.[10] The symbolism is almost too obvious to need explaining to readers nowadays. The snake is an archetype of man's libido. Here it is suggestive of Suezō, who exploits Otama's femininity. What counts is its dramatic intensity as an expression of Otama's sense of her situation. The birds confined but content in their cage might serve well enough as a projection of any such woman's dream: marriage and a peaceful life. One bird, obviously symbolic of Otama, dies, unable to fight the victimizer, and so does Otama's dream. At another level, the two birds —one dead and the other still alone—may eternalize Otama's *giri* and *ninjō*. Okada, who has killed the snake, serves as a catalyst in her conflict as he comes into her life.

Thus, seeing that image come to pass had a paradoxical liberating effect on Otama. She feels no compunction about dreaming of Okada, even in Suezō's presence. Free of guilt in fantasy, she can dare to hope for the guilty reality. She plans with all appropriate care. When her master is out of town she will invite Okada in to dine, and then . . . . But fate plays an ironic trick. That day, for the first time ever, Okada passes her house accompanied by someone else. It turns out to be the narrator who later will become her friend. She does not know that yet and neither do we. What is obvious is that the would-be rebellious mistress has missed her chance.

The novel suggests that concubinage is the nonchoice of choice for a woman in Otama's position in Meiji society. Ōgai makes his point by way of a symbol for the vicious circle his heroine cannot escape, for all her willingness to rebel. Okada and his friend have thrown a stone at a wild goose in the pond and killed it. They meet Otama on their way home to feast on their kill. Here too the symbolism is not hard to read. The wild goose was free to fly to a faraway place to make its summer nest. Otama, a bird in a gilded cage, will never break free. Even in the self-consciously new Meiji society, women are still valued at the feudal rate, as chattel, captives of male convenience. Here of course the symbolism is doubly ironic since the man of Otama's dreams has helped his friend kill the goose whose freedom she dreams of sharing by freely choosing to love him! Her loss is real in point of fact as well, since Okada is leaving for medical study in Germany.[11]

The novel's complex psychological topography is laid out by the narrator, who befriends Okada at the outset.[12] His knowledge of Otama's state of mind is obviously secondhand, though he appears perfectly confident in his detailed assessments all the way along. He even breaks in on his own telling, behaving like the omniscient narrator in a book. Time and again we find ourselves wondering how he knows what he claims to know. Ōgai, of course, has indulged the novelist's privilege of withholding information. He waits till the end to complete the puzzle: "I learned half the story during my close association with Okada, and I learned the other half from Otama, with whom I accidentally became acquainted after Okada had left the country."[13]

Film versus Novel

Toyoda's film script puts the camera in charge of telling the story. The narrator is replaced with cinema's gift for free and fluid attention to visual detail. The viewer becomes witness and interpreter as Otama's circumstances, moods, and choices unfold a drama rich in outward manifestations of a life of inward desperation.

The novel's thematic thrust is unchanged: this is a classic Japanese story of conflict between *giri* and *ninjō*. Toyoda does tilt the balance in the direction of *ninjō*. Otama's rebellious spirit plots more forcefully in the film. She is no silent sufferer resigned to her fate. She dares to yearn for a better life, and to do her best to bring it about. She has a certain willful flair for challenge and confrontation. This shift in emphasis makes sense, given that the novel's Meiji heroine "lived" (so to speak) before war, defeat, and occupation had conspired to give Japan a new constitution guaranteeing women equal rights. Viewers in 1954 would have a natural and immediate interest in a more self-directed Otama, even one whose story still ends on the same old, same old note of tragic dependency, Meiji-style.[14]

Toyoda also enriches the causal line that binds Otama to Suezō. This gives more narrative legibility and plausibility to each stage of her struggle for freedom. This is most obvious in the climactic open confrontation between the two. Toyoda does the same for Otama's relationship with Okada, working with the principle of addition and expansion. The novel's young man glimpsed in passing becomes a knowable character whose potential as a lover is credible, if never realized. The resulting film is a 104-minute melodrama rich in scenes of highly charged emotion.

One might say that a director's commitment to the communicativeness and contemporaneity of his medium gave Toyoda even more creative freedom to modify and transform Ōgai's original. That being the case, the dynamic interaction between the two yielded a film more like a fine "interpretation" than a faithful adaptation. This difference itself deserves study.

Toyoda begins his script with an event not described until halfway through the novel. Shifted forward, it still serves the donnée provided by Ōgai: Otama's decision to follow *giri* by sacrificing herself to rescue her father. Toyoda makes the most of her first meeting with Suezō. She and her father and a go-between are waiting to meet her future master in the same restaurant where Okada and his medical school friends are having their *suki-yaki* party. What film script writer/director could resist concocting an entrée so rich in dramatic potential?

The sound of student merriment contrasts with a palpable tension surrounding Otama and her father. She opens a window and looks out. The camera follows her line of sight to Okada near a small pond in the garden. He has stepped outside for a breath of fresh air after being hounded by the loan shark, who crashed the student party. It is of course Suezō mixing business with the pleasure of a more intimate transaction in another part of the restaurant.

These facts are by way of narrative glimpses thus far. They do not yet add up; they do not yet need to. A beautiful young woman is looking out a window at a handsome young man. She looks out and he looks up. Admiration and interest flow both ways. Brief close-ups tell us that. Otama slides the window shut. The die is cast. The love-interest pattern of gazing/seeing/spying so important in the novel has taken on its foreshadowing cinematic form. Already Toyoda is freely reinventing Otama's story. The relation between film script and novel might be described as creatively elastic.

Otama's next encounter with Okada shows how this is so. It follows the plot of the novel, but gives full weight to the gazing motif by making it move both ways. Here the camera's wordless witness does the work of Ōgai's narrator. Otama is seen returning home from the bathhouse. Okada has stopped to look at the birds in the cage outside her door. Okada bows as she passes on in the door. Inside, she goes to the lattice window and looks out at Okada. He looks that way and sees her. The camera closes in on her. An over-large close-up of her face shows more than the woman Okada sees; it conveys the impression she is making on him. She smiles. The camera backs away in the next three shots, taking note of the lattice that blocks his view.

The camera turns to follow Otama's gaze at Okada continuing his stroll. Toyoda elaborates a cinema-novelist's sense of this moment. Otama goes to the mirror. The next shot of her reflection shows that she has added a ribbon to her hair. This touch of hopeful maiden ornament speaks for her wishful thinking: Okada would make such a handsome suitor.

After such introduction, what feminine derring-do? Here too, Toyoda adds to the incident taken from the novel. In the film, the snake incident is expanded. After Okada kills the snake that has killed one of the birds, Otama brings out a basin so that he can wash his hands.

Their brief exchange as he washes makes two important connections. The first one they share. Each acknowledges having seen the other at the restaurant. Otama hazards the comment that she remembers that encounter very well. Okada is less forthcoming, mentioning only that their student party was spoiled by a gate-crashing loan shark. The second connection is one we share with Otama alone. Okada has no idea that Suezō is her master. That aspect of the knot will tighten later on. Just now, the connection made by Okada's casual remark is for her alone. It confirms her suspicion that Suezō is not the respectable merchant he pretends to be. We are prepared to understand why Otama's attitude to Suezō hardens into rebellion.

Okada leaves just ahead of a downpour. Here, Toyoda invents a sequence ready-made for a heroine far more daring than her novel counterpart. Seeing rain begin to fall and thinking how Okada has no umbrella, Otama goes out in search of him. She finds him taking shelter under a tree and lends him an umbrella.

Toyoda enriches the theme of her daring rebelliousness with narrative complications not found in the novel. His Otama is no mere window-view victim of infatuation. She trails her beloved all the way to Tokyo University.

Her success is cruelly ironic. She sees Okada carry an expensive medical book into a pawnshop. She steals a look inside and to her horror sees that the pawnbroker is Suezō. He is a loan shark and this as well. She has every good reason to feel cheated and disgraced. Worse yet, this proof is doubly poisonous. The man she loves is bound by debt to the man she hates. Suezō is master over more unhappiness than he knows. As it turns out, the amount Suezō offers him is just too insultingly low. He sells his book to a secondhand shop nearby. Otama has followed him there, too. After he leaves, she slips in and buys the book. She plans to return it when he comes with her umbrella. That will be doubly sweet revenge—loving justice done with money supplied by the cheat Suezō himself.

Even Ōgai's heroine is moved by revulsion to inward rebellion against the *giri* that rules her life. Toyoda's heroine, having given in to *ninjō* more ambitiously, suffers more accordingly, as the camera is at pains to show. It ducks around Suezō's embrace to steal a look at Otama's face. She has turned away from him to hide an expression of overwhelming disgust.

The film from midpoint on charts Otama's increasing indulgence of *ninjō* in her abortive attempt to gain her freedom. Here too, Toyoda freely

Okada (l., Hiroshi Akutagawa) and Otama (r., Hideko Takamine) in *The Mistress* (1953). © Daiei-Kadokawa Co., Ltd.

invents supportive incidents. Otama takes sewing lessons from a neighbor, hoping to acquire some means of livelihood. She even dares to confront Suezō with the truth about his profession. But of course it is love, not tainted respectability that drives her *ninjō* quest for a better way of life.

Things come to a head when Okada arrives with her umbrella. Otama keeps him waiting outside while she makes herself presentable. Suezō arrives just then. Okada now knows what Otama is and who her keeper is. Suezō passes on into the house. The look in his eyes shows clearly that he sees Otama's interest in this young man. Okada's book is there to confirm his dark suspicion. Jealous and vengeful, he confiscates it. This confrontation only serves to harden Otama's determination to assert herself. Like her novel counterpart, she plans to invite Okada for a meal. Ōgai does not elaborate on her motives. Toyoda is satisfied to let the camera take note of a subtle detail that shows she is thinking of this meal as a tryst: the delicate flower arrangement near the food laid out. Otama has never done the like for Suezō.

Ōgai also does not tell his reader much about Okada's sense of his final encounter with Otama. He merely passes on, an unwitting major figment of an unhappy woman's imagination. Her lovesick hopes are dashed by the narrator, who, ironically, will befriend her, and seek to understand her, later on. Toyoda finds a different way for that ironic twist of fiction to play out on screen. He brings the novelist's muted pantomime to life with a fully developed encounter that leaves no doubt about the emotions and intentions of all involved. The camera's expressive power is seconded by every melodramatic device from plangent strings on the soundtrack to the movement and placement of actors in postures that speak of separation unhappily conclusive.

The scene begins with Otama just inside her door. Hearing Okada's cheerful whistle, she steps outside and walks uphill toward him. Using deep space, Toyoda lets an extreme long shot show Okada walking down with Otama in the foreground. The music of their first encounter creates an effect of fatalistic circularity. A series of close-ups brings them together. The camera's leisurely pace allows a detailed reading of every nuance of motion and expression. Okada's embarrassed surprise suggests a need to hide his true feelings for Otama. A cut to her smiling face yields to another close-up view of Okada, reinforcing our sense that he feels nonplussed.

A following close-up shows that Otama's smile has faded. A line of sight shot shows why. Okada's friend Kimura has caught up with him. Seeing her approaching, Kimura nudges him. We don't know much about Kimura's awareness of Okada's interest, but we see what Otama sees—the last thing a woman wants to see in a situation of this kind. Kimura offers to leave the two of them alone. Okada says "Don't go." Otama leaves the frame. Can this be the melodramatic end? Not quite.

As the two men continue on downhill the camera finds Otama hiding near her door. She makes one more daring move as they pass. Gone is the woman who yearned in hiding behind a window lattice. She steps out toward Okada. Another series of close-up cross-cuts conveys a sense of silent dialogue. Here it speaks clearly of inevitable, final separation. Okada's expression is solemn. She smiles one last time, but sadly. Okada bows and tips his hat to her. Her smile fades into a mix of resignation and despair. Deep space is used effectively to show Otama in the foreground, watching the two men vanishing in the distance.

Toyoda prolongs this scene in a way that seems redundant. Okada and Kimura talk of the impossibility of crossing class barriers. Even in the "new" Meiji Japan these young men take that for granted. As they continue on their walk, Okada says that Otama has her own world to live in. Kimura adds that Okada has his own.

Toyoda's Effective Use of Stylistic Devices

The Mistress contains a number of scenes noted for stylistic embellishment. By relying heavily on the camera's expressive power, Toyoda or his cameraman, Mitsuo Miura, lets us see Otama's inner conflict as she reacts to her oppressive life. A few examples will suffice to illustrate this point.

Halfway through the film Otama is seen leaving the house Suezō has provided for her father. Unlike her novel counterpart, she has told her father all, only to be told that he knew about Suezō all along. Their parting begins with a medium shot bearing witness to the strength of character adversity has given her. "I'll not be fooled!" she cries. "I'm not a child!" The next shot puts her remarks in context. Using deep space, Toyoda tells us at a glance what Otama's father had to gain from helping deceive his daughter. It is a lovely summer's day. They are standing near a bridge in the foreground. Two workmen approach along a pleasant alleyway. A woman is sprinkling water to settle the dust. This is a quiet, pleasant, middle-class neighborhood, a far cry from the sunless slum where they used to live. The alleyway there was a gravel path that skirted an open sewer. Women cooked outside. Thanks to his daughter, the old man escaped that squalor.

The following shot shifts our attention to another distant prospect, the quiet neighborhood where Otama lives. Deep space shows a woman at the top of a slope and Otama at the bottom. A sudden, refreshingly stylistic overhead shot of two open parasols in close-up delivers a startling message. The parasols are identical—the same that Suezō gave Otama and his wife, Otsune. The women of course have no idea. It is we who see the two parasols moving gracefully toward a socially awkward rendezvous. Two medium shots confirm our fears. They meet. A line-of-sight shot speaks for Otsune's head-to-toe survey of her husband's concubine. The alert viewer sees that Otsune has more to anger her than youth and beauty shaded by a parasol identical to hers. We have seen this kimono material handed over to Suezō in his shop by a woman who has fallen on hard times. The wife was insulted first by her husband's offer of goods tainted by another woman's misfortune; the insult is doubled when she sees that same material worn by her husband's mistress.

A close-up of Otsune shows the angry, middle-aged woman Otama finds facing her in the street. She does not need the parasol to tell her that this is Suezō's wife. She can only think to hurry on into her house. Now Otsune knows where she lives. The scene ends with a long take. Strings play as the camera follows Otama passing into her living room. It stops on her as she sits frozen, hiding in a corner. Then it moves to the lattice win-

Otama (Hideko Takamine) in *The Mistress* (1953). © Daiei-Kadokawa Co., Ltd.

dow, looking out at the furious Otsune peering in. The music rises to a crisis crescendo.

From this point on, Otama is haunted by that image of the furious wife. Their second confrontation is equally captivating stylistically. The two women come face to face in the alleyway in pouring rain. A cross-cut moves from Otama's fear to Otsune's spite. Otama runs horrified into her house, pursued by a close-up of Otsune's demonic expression.

The sense of tension eases somewhat as the camera cuts to the puzzled maid. Otama retreats to a corner of the living room furnished with bamboo curtains, telling the maid to fetch the sewing instructor from next door. A cut to the alleyway shows the maid and neighbor woman together. They come into the house to report that no one is out there. No one has been out there. Otama is hallucinating. Several shots pick up clues to her state of mind. The spattering rain reflecting on the bamboo curtains creates an ominous shadow-play. Outside the lattice window, the curtain of rain itself seems menacing. Otama sits motionless in a medium shot, literally and visually cornered.

The sewing instructor sits down next to her. The camera frames their dialogue. Otama exclaims that her life has become unbearable. The sewing instructor tries to reason with her, explaining how difficult it is for a single woman to make a living. She mentions Oshige, a widow with several small children. We know whom she means. Toyoda has supplied this instance. Unable to pay back a loan from Suezō, Oshige left the kimono material at his shop. Otsune was there to receive it—and to recognize it on Otama. The sewing instructor reports a familiar outcome: Oshige has become a streetwalker. The scene ends with two close-ups of the agonizing Otama still prey to near-hysteria. The rain still flickers its menacing light. The music reaches another height of tension as Otama cries out: "Do I have to go on living this way? Is this the only life for me?" The camera suggests the answer.

Another rainy scene speaks for Otama's hope of a better outcome. Here too, shot design is skillfully used to highlight conflicting values. One example is a long shot of Okada taking shelter under a tall tree. Otama comes into the frame to lend him an umbrella. Here the shot is used to draw a curtain of rain around the two figures, bringing them close in a touching vignette. This is the rain she walks through, following Okada back to the university. Like Otama, we experience this stroll as a welcome release from her usual confinement. Strings play softly as she keeps a discreet distance from herself and the man she loves. Here, in place of rigid lattice, we have a close-up view of water lily blooms, petals stroked by drops of rain. Farther on, the camera pauses to reflect on a pool near a row of stone lanterns. The water mirrors the storied rise of a magnificent pagoda. The beneficent spell cast by these lyrical images is rudely broken when she reaches her destination—when Okada enters the pawnshop, unwittingly exposing her to yet another intolerable fact of her captive life.

The Final Sequence

The outcome of the novel is quite clear. Otama is not and cannot be free. She will be a man's mistress, not mistress of her own destiny. Toyoda gives his film an ending just as melodramatic—maybe more so, in fact. But he freely elaborates a closing sequence better suited to an audience facing the challenging new freedoms of postwar Japan. That audience could be counted on to appreciate a timelier twist of fate: that a heroine who dared to take the initiative could end, not just unhappily, but inconclusively. One might say that this is melodrama for the thinking wet hanky.

Toyoda's interest in Otama's daring desperation does lend itself to exaggeration as he builds to a climax. The final sequence begins with the tryst she planned and Suezō foiled by arriving unexpectedly. Okada has come and gone, having met Suezō on her doorstep and having seen how things stand. Shame and chagrin carry Otama over the edge. Suezō sees her transformed from suspected malcontent to outright rebel. He came in on a feast laid out. She pointedly puts it away. He confiscates Okada's book and informs her that her young friend is leaving for Germany. Students all "fly away," he adds. The camera cuts to a close-up of her stricken expression.

Otama runs from the house. A cut to the street shows her running away from the camera in deep space. A procession of pilgrims approaches. They meet halfway. The ceremonial drum beats a steady tattoo as if keeping time with her sense of urgency. The pilgrims are draped in the white of death and mourning. The inference is clear—doubly clear to viewers acquainted with Shinoda's later use of the same effect in *Double Suicide* (Shinjū ten no Amijima, 1969). There Jihei, who has been contemplating on suicide with his love, Koharu, crosses a bridge where he meets a procession like this one halfway across.

The following brief scene confirms Suezō's claim. Otama passes the restaurant where she and Okada first glimpsed one another. This happenstance is cruelly rich in ironies. That glimpse was followed by the negotiated sacrifice of her happiness. The go-between had been at pains to point out that anything better—like marriage to a man she loves—was out of the question for damaged goods such as her. Now, outside the restaurant, Otama meets Kimura. Ironically, another student party is going on inside. This one bids a boisterous farewell to Okada. Worse yet, in this brief moment, Otama learns the worst bad news. Kimura tells her that she was an object of more than passing interest to his friend, that Okada often spoke of her.

Otama had snatched up Okada's book as she left the house. She hands it to Kimura. Kimura's revelation leads to a series of scenes Toyoda uses to suggest the foolhardy desperation of a woman caught in the toils of fore-doomed desire. A cut to the fishmonger shows her using Suezō's money to buy an expensive gift for Okada. There's more to this than getting back at her master and society. The woman who waits on her is the one who snubbed her earlier. Now Otama lays the considerable sum of money down and says, "Deliver it to me—the concubine! You know where I live." A close-up speaks for her mood of furious audacity.

From that to another blow-up with Suezō is a natural step. She goes back home and tells him that she can't go on living as his concubine. He reminds her that marriage to Okada is out of the question. She breaks down. An over-large close-up of her tearful face emphasizes her desperation as she cries: "I know who I am, but that doesn't mean I can't have a dream!" The fishmonger arrives. Suezō, in a rage, orders her out. Otama grabs the fish. Suezō grabs her. She breaks free, shouting, "I won't live in bondage any-more!" The scene ends with a medium shot of Suezō's determined face, as he is left alone. He says, "I won't let you go free. I won't!"

Much is condensed into two final scenes. Here Toyoda's working prin-ciple revolves around motion: Otama hurrying to a last glimpse of Okada, then wandering around the pond; Okada's carriage speeding away; and a wild goose swimming then flying away.

In terms of narrative, the first scene brings closure to the Otama-Okada causal line by finalizing the impossibility of their union. The act of spying and gazing returns, echoing earlier instances of Otama's stealthy look at Okada. A rickshaw is seen from her line of sight. A series of cross-cuts con-nects her with the rickshaw. Like her, we glimpse the passengers, Okada and his German mentor. A close-up of Otama's face suggests sadness and resignation. Another cut to the rickshaw gives foreground magnitude to its spinning wheels. That measure of Otama's sense of loss yields to a shot of students going their separate ways after waving goodbye.

The following shot studies Otama's solitary lovelorn figure. She tight-ens her shawl and moves across the bridge away from the camera. Its distant gaze diminishes her. She becomes a tiny figure blending into the gloaming.

A similar long shot opens the final scene. Otama wanders along the shore of Shinobazu Pond, one of the scenic views shown as the opening credits flashed on the screen. A close-up singles out a lone wild goose swimming. Another takes note of Otama looking pensively its way. A cut to the goose shows it taking off. Otama in close-up watches it go. Two more shots follow the goose to a vanishing point in an immensity of sky. What better symbol of tender farewell denied her? What better bird to express her yearning to be free, to fly far away herself?

The film ends with a close-up of Otama's face. The yearning romantic theme returns. She is still gazing into the sky. Her blank expression gives no hint of the future she has in mind. After such drama, is there no closure? No comforting or confrontational certainty of outcome? Toyoda, apparently, will have it so.

–4–
Period Film Par Excellence
Hiroshi Inagaki's *Samurai* Trilogy
(1954–1956)

HIROSHI INAGAKI (1905–1980) learned his craft at a time when studio production schedules stressed filming on the double-quick by specialists in this or that genre. That in part explains Inagaki's amazing career total of a hundred films in forty-two years. The first twenty-nine of them were *jidaigeki* (period films or samurai action pictures) made between 1928 and 1943.

The script for his first, *All's Right With the World* (Tenka taihei-ki, 1928), was written by a fellow *jidaigeki* specialist, Mansaku Itami (1900–1946). Its hero was played by the enormously popular superstar Chiezō Kataoka (1903–1983). Inagaki made the genre his own right from the start, giving his period films a distinctively modern character. His approach to samurai derring-do was lighthearted, lively, and agreeably akin to the films exploring contemporary manners and mores other directors were making—not for him the darkly nihilistic undertone of so many solemnly self-important samurai films. The mood of an Inagaki film was notably optimistic.

Three characteristic Inagaki films came out in 1931: *Fishmonger Tasuke* (Isshin Tasuke), *A Mother's Image* (Mabuta no haha), and *The Sword and the Sumo Ring* (Ippon gatana dohyōiri). Those were all silent pictures. Another distinctly Inagaki film was the talkie *Yatarō* (Seki no Yattape, 1935). It was a collaboration with the period film expert Sadao Yamanaka (1909–1938).[1]

Finally, in 1943, Inagaki switched genres for his thirtieth film, *The Rickshaw Man* (Muhō Matsu no isshō). This *gendaigeki* (modern drama) was set in the Meiji period. It looks to a feudal past whose moral tone has much in common with the samurai film. The lowly rickshaw man is in love with his master's widow, but in the end doesn't declare himself. Class is a barrier that cannot be crossed. Loyalty to his betters, in this case alive and dead, means the rickshaw man must choose *giri* (social obligation) over *ninjō* (personal inclination).

Inagaki made other *gendaigeki* after the war but won the Venice Film Festival Golden Lion for his 1958 color remake of *The Rickshaw Man*. His leading man was Toshirō Mifune, already famous East and West. Inagaki's gift for history in living memory is manifest in *The Storm* (Arashi, 1956). This adaptation of the novel by the Meiji writer Tōson Shimazaki (1872–1943) covers the twenty-year struggle of a widowed professor raising four children on his own.

Still, Inagaki will be remembered as a versatile master of the period film genre. He also distinguished himself as a maker of the classic remake, a justly famous specialty of Japanese cinema from the earliest days to the present.

The record is held by the epic *Chūshingura,* thanks to Japanese cinema known round the world as *The Forty-Seven Loyal Ronin.* Eighty-four versions have been made since the first featured the legendary Kabuki actor Nizaemon Kataoka in *Chūshingura Act Five* (Chūshingura godanme, 1907). As the title indicates, this complex morality play lends itself to piecemeal adaptation. The plot is rich in subplots, all in service of the tragic obligation of loyal retainers to avenge the death of their lord, even as doing so condemns them to ritual suicide. In whole or in part, *Chūshingura* offers no end of opportunities for dramatic highlights and star-studded casting.

In 1962, Inagaki joined the *Chūshingura* elite with a lavish two-part version in Cinemascope, *Flowers* (Hana no maki) and *Snow* (Yuki no maki). Both display his gift for the human touch in the most forbidding contexts.[2] Here that means probing more deeply into the *ninjō* personal inclinations of characters doomed to fulfill the oppressive *giri* obligations of a feudal society.

Another enduring classic of high-minded heroics is the story of Musashi Miyamoto, a social outcast country rube who evolves into a Buddhist paragon of severely principled philosopher-fighter. He is too much alone in the limelight to generate remakes on a par with *Chūshingura,* but a dozen versions, some of them classics still available, speak for his enduring fascination.

Cinema's first Musashi was the enormously popular *jidaigeki* star Matsunosuke Onoe in *Miyamoto Musashi* (Musashi Miyamoto, 1914).[3] Chiezō Kataoka, mentioned above, played the hero in Kintarō Inoue's *Miyamoto Musashi* (Musashi Miyamoto, 1929). That hit was followed not by a competing remake, but by a best-selling novel with the same title by Eiji Yoshikawa (1892–1962). Yoshikawa's work was published first as a newspaper serial between 1935 and 1939.[4]

The cinema industry moved quickly, releasing two *Musashi* films, one in 1936 by Eisuke Takizawa (1902–1980), the other in 1937 by Jun Ozaki (date of birth unknown). Eight more have been made since. Yasuo Kohata's version for Tōei Company in 1950 is notable for portraying Musashi as an amoral opportunist.[5] Tōei returned to a more traditional view of the hero in Tomu Uchida's five-part version of 1961–1965.[6] The *Musashi* best known worldwide is Hiroshi Inagaki's Eastman Color trilogy made for the Tōhō Company in 1954–1956. Toshirō Mifune, a regular in Kurosawa films by then, was cast as the hero. Part 1 won the 1955 Oscar for Best Foreign Picture.

Inagaki also projected a serial remake featuring his hero's nemesis Kojirō Sasaki, but no spin-off could compete with his trilogy. Even today it is recognized as the *Musashi* classic. Though it is widely available on video as *Samurai Parts 1–3* with English subtitles, critics in the West have tended to neglect Inagaki's masterpiece—all the more reason for Western viewers to see Musashi through Eastern eyes, especially since the style and content of heroism are apt to need "translating" East to West, just as they are West to East.

Musashi Miyamoto is a hero of epic proportions, a marvel of a man who actually lived in Japan from 1594 until his death in 1645. History accords him legendary status. He was a master swordsman and the inventor of the style known as *nitōryū,* literally "two swords as one." Between the ages of thirteen and twenty-eight he fought and won sixty-six duels. He was also an accomplished artist and calligrapher and author of a treatise on the strategy of warfare, *Gorin no sho* (The book of five rings, 1645).[7]

All three parts of the trilogy contrive to answer this question: How can Musashi achieve a holistic vision of life? This hero's rise from humble beginnings fits the narrative pattern of a search for identity, a self-image acceptable to him. Each film's adventures unfold a stage of Musashi's martial, spiritual, and aesthetic growth, leveling up to the ultimate achievement of his heroic journey's end in Part 3.

Each part stands on its own as it records the progress of crucial phases of Musashi's education. Then too, as we shall see, each part develops the director's use of different structural principles. Most significant are various dichotomies, oppositions of insider/outsider, civilization/wilderness, and mentor/pupil. The first two are derived from cultural anthropology, as Will Wright has shown in his brilliant study *Six Guns and Society.*[8] The last dichotomy is the staple of many samurai films that deal with the so-called *mushashugyō* (errantry). Inagaki's mode of representation is equally telling.

He buttresses dramatic highlights with impressive stylistic devices ranging from experimental uses of color to fluid camera movement.

Samurai Part 1 (Musashi Miyamoto)

Central Problem and Thematic Progression

This part offers two choices of action available to the hero's quest for identity: opportunism versus integrity. The opportunist is content with an animal-like existence. His progress is regress, defined by images of stagnation, decline, confinement, and chaos. Integrity is the hard-won choice, requiring stern commitment to the tenets of *bushidō,* the samurai code of conduct. This choice is associated with images of flow, ascent, openness, and cleanliness.

At the outset of the film, the protagonist is called Takezō, a name suitable for the farmer he is. Musashi is a more distinguished name fit for a samurai. Here, the viewer unfamiliar with the Japanese writing system needs to know that there are two ways of reading the Kanji characters assigned to the hero's name: Takezō and Musashi. We meet this Takezō in the context of his social group, a tight-knit farming community. He is instantly identifiable as the rogue, the unsettled, alienated bad boy dreamer. Something clearly has gone wrong in his family life, some lack of parental guidance and affection. As a result, we see him viewed as something of an outcast, a mischievous misfit dreaming of escape up the social ladder.

The opening subtitle sequence clues us in to the historical context of the tale about to unfold. The credits are imposed on scenes of soldiers on their way to the Battle of Sekigawara in 1600, a decisive event in the civil war then dividing the country. The social turmoil of wartime offered malcontents such as Takezō a chance we see him seizing as he leaves the village with his sidekick, Matahachi. Their choice sets the theme of the film: the questing malcontent. Specific to Part 1 is Takezō's pursuit of higher social status, with crude opportunism as his guide.

The subsequent battle sequence shows him failing miserably. He cast his lot with the losing side, the Toyotomi clan defeated in the Battle of Sekigawara. Still, he has not learned. He follows where opportunism seems to lead, taking shelter in a makeshift community whose values are represented by a mother and daughter, Okō and Akemi. Like Takezō, these women are wartime opportunists. They are battlefield scavengers, selling whatever they can loot from the samurai dead.

This sequence is thematically important because this rustic fellow

Takezō is shown to have a remarkable gift: amazing strength and coordination, which are put to the test when bandits attack the women who have taken him in. His manner of fighting is entirely unsophisticated, but he acquits himself brilliantly in show of ungentlemanly derring-do, routing this pack of murderous ruffians with a makeshift wooden sword.

Still, this film is no mindless celebration of brute force. The plot unfolds a series of events whose purpose is to show how Takezō comes to learn what he needs to know to become the Samurai of his dreams. But first he has to learn that learning itself is key. That is why his learning curve is low and slow at the outset, marked by a series of defeats and humiliations.

Takezō's sidekick, Matahachi, serves to show what happens when a village dreamer is made of weaker stuff. He is not just an inferior fighter, but morally inferior, easily led into commonplace compromise. The two women rescued from bandits by Takezō's first show of solo fighting skill know a good thing when they see it. They are, after all, wartime profiteers. Yet Takezō is not about to become a bodyguard for such as them. He is even loutishly dismissive of Okō's advances and leaves in a huff. Matahachi settles for the way of least resistance, seduced by Okō.

The film turns around when the monk Takuan captures Takezō and ties him in a tree. The tree he dangles from is huge, serenely unshaken by his kicking, cursing, clownish fury. The contrast is all the more telling since this tree stands in the temple courtyard. Takezō's fate is in the hands of the wise priest Takuan. He could be killed like a dangerous animal. Or, if he would stop shouting and listen, he could become a fighter worthy of his gifts. And so Takuan becomes his mentor and guide to the inner quest of Part 1. In it, the hero learns to confront himself, know himself, and become the right kind of samurai: the virtuous, selfless, enlightened warrior.

But Takezō is no easy conquest, not even for his own good. He is taken to Lord Ikeda's castle and locked in a room alone with many books. They are of course the right books, classic texts offering instruction in personal integration. A cut to the future shows us Takezō transformed. The wild-eyed fighting country bumpkin is no more. Three years of studious confinement have refined him all out of recognition. We see Lord Ikeda attest to the change in a ceremonial affirmation of his samurai name, Musashi Miyamoto. The village that spurned him is honored in the name.

Even conflict now becomes him. He is torn between peaceful settlement and solitary roaming. He can become one of Lord Ikeda's court retainers and lead that life. Or he can become a *rōnin*, a virtuous, selfless, high-minded fighter roaming the world on a lonely quest for greater self-knowledge. Musashi chooses the latter even though it also means painful separation from his love, Otsū, who has waited for him for all those years.

Shift in Imagery Patterns

The film's thematic progression is simple, but deftly structured around a distinct, easily identifiable image pattern. That pattern favors movement from one extreme to another as Takezō/Musashi's heroic journey proceeds from descent to ascent, obscurity to clarity, stagnation to flow, and scarcity to plenty. These and other contrasts contribute to a paradigm exploring the poles of human behavior, from the unthinking violence of Takezō's wildman rebelliousness to the highly civilized fighting skills of the philosophically accomplished samurai. Inagaki does all this by making inspired use of the most unassuming cinematic devices, as the following examples show.

Takezō (l., Toshirō Mifune) and Takuan (r., Kuroemon Onoe) in *Samurai I.* © Tōhō Co. Ltd.

Takezō's first stage of unconning opportunism shows him in a state of nature—the nature of untamed wilderness. The villagers think of him as a wild man. Certainly he is rough and uncouth, strikingly at home in the tree he climbs to catch sight of the distant army. But he is anything but free. He is confused, chaotic, getting nowhere in life. No wonder he dreams of finding glory in battle. Inagaki shows us that reality in a series of long shots of a pitched battle between warriors on foot and horseback. We see how nasty the carnage is, how awkward and confused, not to mention out of tune with the natural serenity of a landscape wrecked by this reckless strife. It all reflects badly on the would-be hero's formless state of being. And where is he all this while? Digging a ditch—a defense as the army he has joined is defeated in a bloody rout.

The camera reinforces our sense of Takezō's confinement when we see him take shelter with Okō and Akemi, the women who loot the battlefield dead. Closed framing dominates this scene. Takezō is shown aligned under the low ceiling against a pillar. This entire sequence studies the wilderness embodied by this man. We have seen him try to control a horse by unconning brute force. Everything about him suggests a rough, unsavory character. He looks like a tramp. His manners—especially the way he wolfs down food—are appalling.

His capture marks a decisive point in Takezō's learning process, his need to escape this chaotic existence. He needs a mentor, a figure Inagaki uses to introduce the mentor/pupil dichotomy, a configuration of civilization/wilderness opposition. As might be expected, this polar paradigm will become a recurrent narrative device used to advance the story throughout the trilogy.

Inagaki's working principle for highlighting this decisive moment is an expressive use of verbal and visual cadences. Zen Buddhism stresses the importance of a teaching device known as a *kōan* (intellectual riddle) for those who seek enlightenment. Most *kōan* take the form of an intellectual riddle discussed by mentor and pupil. The wise priest Takuan, knowing his pupil's limitations, speaks to Takezō in the most elemental terms. He points out that his strength is brutish and untamed, the strength of an animal. Takezō cries out that he does not want to die like an animal, tied to a tree. Thus begins his long and difficult learning process. He begins to understand what it means to be alive. He begins to be vaguely aware that true swordsmanship combines strength and wisdom.

Here the camera also lets us see a transition of imagery from confinement to openness, from descent to ascent. At the most visual level, open framing is used. The camera moves vertically upward to show Takezō swinging from a rope high in a tree whose profile points, pointedly in fact, at a night sky complete with full moon. One does not have to be a Buddhist to read this image, though the moon for Buddhists signifies enlightenment. We are scarcely surprised when Takezō, after a show of clownish resistance, says to Takuan, "I begin to understand what you are saying!" Still, Takuan leaves him hanging. His parting suggestion is that Takezō take this opportunity to meditate on the meaning of life.

The rainstorm sequence reinforces our sense of Takezō's rebirth. Still, we wonder what makes it possible for him to experience this waking self-awareness. The story itself offers clues as it unfolds. We see hints of a better man inside this village ruffian. He does have a friend or two, most notably his sidekick, Matahachi. And he does take the momentous risk of returning to their village to tell his friend's mother that her son will not be coming home. Unlike his friend, he does not settle for the disgraceful compromise it is to share the battlefield pickings of Okō and Akemi. He is even proof against temptations of the flesh. When Okō throws herself at him, he storms out of the house and stalks into a pond, clearly having in mind to wash away some horrible contagion.

Image after image reinforces Inagaki's view of this fellow as the right heroic stuff but raw and unstable, in dire need of some civilizing influence. He is neither here nor there with respect to human and animal life. The horse we see drinking from the lake is in its element. Why should it yield to this fellow, whose grasp of horsemanship is all about brute force? He is equally at a loss when it comes to finding food in the woods. And yet what draws him out of the darkness into the light of the lonely house he comes across? Otsū's flute is the music that charms this savage beast.

We see that Takezō is headed in some right direction, but Inagaki is in no hurry to take him there. Time and time again he plots a variation on captivity and escape. Each time, of course, we learn more about Takezō's potential. When he and Otsū escape from the village a long shot shows them crossing a stream. The quest image there is obvious. More surprising is the first brief glimpse of a theme enlarged on throughout the trilogy. Otsū's hands are raw and bleeding, cut by the ropes she struggled to untie. Takezō notices as they go to cross the stream. He does his best to bandage them, saying how sorry he is. He is capable of compassion. As we shall see, Takezō's transformation comes about through cultivation of the more complex awareness Buddhists characterize as benevolence, a combination of rectitude and compassion. It is also one of the major tenets of *bushidō*.

When Takezō is recaptured and imprisoned in a room high in Lord Ikeda's castle, one noncommittal shot outlines the donjon against the sky as seen from his line of sight. That and his gaze out and up at it clearly speak for his yearning for personal integration. After such yearning, what disciplined aspiration? The leap ahead three years for the coda of Part 1 tells us by showing Takezō become Musashi Miyamoto. He receives his samurai name, makes his knight-errant choice, and proves by every move he makes that he is a hero worth hearing more about.

The coda also offers closure in the form of completed narrative. We see that Matahachi and Okō now pass for respectable man and wife, living with Akemi in Kyoto. We see Okō and Akemi on their way to an Okuni kabuki performance, a form of theater named for its originator, the early seventeenth century priestess-prostitute Okuni. This forerunner of classical kabuki would have been the choice of common folk. Here it is used to con-

Otsū (l., Kaoru Yachigusa) and Takezō (r., Toshirō Mifune) in *Samurai I*. © Tōhō Co. Ltd.

trast their expediency with his friend's more difficult, but in the end success-ful, rise to a much higher level of understanding. A cut to Lord Ikeda's court shows Musashi in the audience for a Noh performance. Noh drama was developed under the patronage of various medieval shoguns. It would be the choice of the ruling samurai class and cultivated souls such as Musashi.

The Final Sequence

The coda condenses a great deal of information, some of it possibly escap-ing the attention of viewers unfamiliar with Japanese history and culture. For example, anyone can see that Musashi considers himself not yet worthy of a place among Lord Ikeda's honored retainers. But why must he become a roving *rōnin,* a masterless samurai, to continue his education? Because the decisive Battle of Sekigawara introduced at the beginning of Part 1 brought peace, and with it, no opportunity to learn from battlefield discipline.

The last point made is a tender one. Musashi leaves the castle and goes to bid farewell to faithful Otsū. She begs to go with him. He resists, then relents. She runs to get her things. A long shot shows Musashi standing on a bridge. This view of him contrasts with that early scene of him enmired in a battlefield trench. What better indication of his rise from degradation to this new hard-earned challenge? The camera cuts to the stream below. It runs clean and clear, waving green pennants of water plants. This image dissolves into one suggesting more emphatic motion. This cinematic punc-tuation signifies time lapse—time out for a troubling, difficult decision. Clearly it has to do with conflict between love and duty, Otsū and still more solitary learning. We know the answer soon enough in these last few minutes of Part 1.

What must be noted here is what the Japanese viewer sees at a glance: all manner of cultural cues to Musashi's stream of consciousness. At an ele-mentary level, the free-flowing fullness of the stream represents the personal enrichment of his educational process. The water and wavering plants them-selves speak for his awareness of *mujō,* the fleetingness of all earthly things.

This traditional aesthetic idea is deeply rooted in Buddhism: "The flow of water is never the same."[9] This famous opening passage in Chōmei Kamo's *Hōjōki* (An account of my hut, 1212), one of the classics represen-tative of literature on *mujō,* exemplifies this concept. The waving water plants are traditionally emblematic of it. In these last moments too, the camera glances at the name inscribed on the bridge: "Bridge of a Flower-ing Field." Flowers are also emblematic of our human awareness of the fleetingness of life.

Fully aware that the life of a samurai is emblematic of *mujō,* Musashi makes his decision: he will follow the path of personal integration. And so he crosses the bridge. When Otsū arrives, she finds his message carved on the railing: *"Yuruse tamae"* (I humbly ask your forgiveness). The honorific diction speaks for Musashi's acquisition of linguistic skills appropriate for a samurai. The film ends with a long shot of him vanishing in the distance. Inagaki makes use of a subtle textural detail to hint at Musashi's state of being. His greenish outfit does not blend well with the scenery around— traditionally an extension of a human life. This subtle discord suggests that he has still a long way to go to achieve inner harmony. How does he do it? We learn in Parts 2 and 3.

Samurai Part 2 (Duel at Ichijōji Temple)

Musashi's Fights and His Mentor Figures

In the first part, we have seen Masashi win out in a conflict of values, choosing personal integration over opportunism. He has chosen the right path, but has some way to go, so he makes another difficult choice: sacrificing the ease and security of life in the castle to the perils and hardships of a solitary *rōnin.*

In Part 2 we see Musashi follow through on his choices, going from adventure to adventure in his quest to become a true samurai, one skilled in martial arts and endowed with a high degree of mental strength as well. As might be expected, the narrative is organized around two important structural principles: one is a series of battles Musashi engages in; the other involves his encounters with teacher/mentor archetypes. From each event he derives a valuable lesson and cultivates his skills. In this process, he improves his grasp of some major tenets of *bushidō,* the discipline that brings him closer, step by step, to becoming the ideal samurai swordsman.

These events are rendered chronologically. Some stand out as fine examples of Inagaki's stylistic forte as he deftly varies color, shot size, composition, and filmic texture. Let us see how the synergy of form and content is achieved in a few major episodes.

The film begins with Musashi's duel with Baiken. It is an unequal contest, since his opponent is not a swordsman but a specialist in combat with the left-hand sickle and right-hand ball and chain. The novelist Eiji Yoshikawa describes Baiken's technical advantage this way: "Baiken went on and on, telling Musashi . . . about how the chain was like a snake, about how it was possible by cleverly alternating the movements of the chain and the sickle to create optical illusions and cause the enemy's defense to work to his own detriment."[10] The camera follows the fight, beginning with a series of long shots. As the duelists shift positions, sizing one another up, their relationship to their surroundings indicates that they are equally matched. As the fight intensifies, a succession of medium shots contrasts each man's weaknesses and strengths. Shots take on an anxious brevity as the hiss of whirling chain merges with the wind to create a confusing sound. The sky turns red, a fitting sign of crisis used throughout the film. Musashi is clearly in trouble. He is tense with eagerness to win. He has yet to develop the fluid ease of a polished fighter, the samurai's oneness with nature.

A sudden cut to the two bystanders—the child Jōtarō and a priest—brings the battle to an end. This flash of discretion obscures all but a rapid shot of Musashi brandishing two swords and another quick shot of Baiken falling. What does this mean? Put to this test, Musashi has learned that a man with two hands can fight with two swords. The short sword in his left hand surprised his enemy and won the day. This is a significant moment in Musashi's learning process. He has discovered the fencing style he would be famous for, *nitōryū* (two-swords-as-one style). The scene ends with Musashi talking with the priest. This mentor figure points out that Musashi's physical strength is his weakness. Musashi learns that he needs to control his primitive instincts, the ones that put brute force ahead of qualities of soul.

This episode ends in another configuration of the mentor/pupil arche-

Musashi (l., Toshirō Mifune) and Baiken (r., Eijirō Tōno) in *Samurai II*. © Tōhō Co. Ltd.

type. Musashi takes the orphan Jōtarō under his wing while he himself is still a student. A viewer might wonder why Inagaki suddenly introduces a shot of crows flying in the evening sky. The Japanese audience will readily recall the children's song "Nanatsu no ko" (Seven baby crows). The song speaks of a crow's strong love for her young ones. Musashi and Jōtarō are orphans denied that affection. Now they bond as teacher and pupil.

Musashi's second fight is with students of the distinguished Yoshioka School. One by one they accept Musashi's challenge, and one by one they fall. The camera takes notes of bruised and bleeding students lying all around, wounded by Musashi's wooden sword. He is a far better swordsman now. It is he who ends the bloodshed. He has that generous self-control, refusing to fight any more adversaries not skilled enough to match swords with him. Instead, he issues a challenge to the master of the school.

Musashi's combat takes place in the dojo of the school. Closed framing says a lot about Musashi's deft use of limited space. The sense of confinement and stuffiness created by this technique also indicates the traditional, hidebound nature of training at the school. Ironically, fighting technique at the school is largely a sham, thanks to the warped sense of honor inculcated in its pupils. Musashi is bound by genuine honor. This samurai concept encompasses many virtues, notably bravery allied to sincerity and, most importantly, to self-knowledge. Yoshioka students put the school's reputation first and plot accordingly. Their idea of honor includes acting together to ambush and kill Musashi to prevent him from fighting the head of the school. Needless to say, their failure forwards the plot by delaying the inevitable showdown between the master and Musashi.

Meanwhile, Musashi's encounter with a sword polisher and the aesthete Hōami marks another significant stage in his growth. Both are commoners, men far beneath him socially, yet Musashi approaches them with humility and respect. The sword polisher teaches him that the sword is the mirror of the samurai's soul. Hōami shows him how to cultivate the aesthetic side of his high calling. Thus we see Musashi painting. Hōami also teaches him that learning to relax is an important aspect of samurai life.

The mentor-pupil relationship is further enriched by Musashi's acquaintance with Yoshino, a renowned courtesan. The scene following his duel with Denshichirō consists of a few shots, one of them a long take. Musashi and Yoshino are seated in her room, next to a charcoal brazier. In an earlier scene she showed no surprise at the spots of blood on his clothes. Asked how she has gained such composure, she replies, "You lack compassion!" Musashi still has a way to go before he channels this important virtue into his relationship with others, even with his opponents.

Musashi's battle with the Yoshioka students leads to his climactic duel with their master, Seijurō. The title of Part 2, *Duel at Ichijōji Temple* (Ichijōji no Kettō), refers to this episode. The earlier duel with the master's younger brother, Denshichirō, provides a smooth transition to that final set piece. Denshichirō has just returned from his time as a wandering samurai. Vainglorious and overconfident, he challenges Musashi. The depiction of this fight is brief, but visually adroit. An opening shot frames Denshichirō in the foreground. Snow is falling. The main hall corridor of a temple opens in the background. The alert Japanese viewer will recognize the place as a famous Buddhist temple in Kyoto, the Sanjūsangendō (Hall of thirty-three spaces). This hall is famous for having the longest frontage of all such places in Kyoto, nearly two hundred feet long.

Musashi (l., Toshirō Mifune) and Yoshino (r., Michiyo Kogure) in *Samurai II.* © Tōhō Co. Ltd.

Brief as this scene is, we see how the setting plays an important part in Musashi's fighting strategy. He realizes what it takes to overcome the formal style of the Yoshioka School. We see him decide not to be drawn into a combat ritual favorable to that style. He takes charge of the situation. First he makes his opponent wait at the far end of the enormous space between them. Musashi pauses, a menacing apparition. Then he runs to face Denshichirō. The time it takes to cover the long distance between them puts his opponent at a psychological disadvantage. The scene ends with a medium shot of the two facing each other. The camera's long silent gaze takes in the stillness of temple and grounds, the soundless chill of falling snow. The very stillness of the fighters creates dramatic tension and adds aesthetic richness to the scene. Even so, it does not tell us much about Musashi's state of mind. For that, we must turn to the novelist Yoshikawa: "The will to win had been forgotten: he saw the whiteness of the snow falling between himself and his opponent, and the spirit of the snow is as light as his own. The space now seemed an extension of his body."[11]

We see nothing of the fight itself. A cut returns us to Yoshino's quarters in the Gion where Musashi has been staying. The courtesan's child attendant is playing in the snow, singing a folk song. The falling snow and her bright red kimono are the only visual links to the previous scene where white and red would have such a different meaning. Musashi enters. As Yoshino and the girl brush the snow off him inside, the child sees a spot of blood. Yoshino, composed as always, says, "That's not blood. That's the petal of a peony." That and a glimpse of Seijūrō vowing vengeance over his brother's body laid out for burial are all we know of the fight. Inagaki spares us the gory details of fight scenes in general, like other directors of *jidaigeki* in the 1950s. Graphic portrayal of violence came in the 1960s, led by Kurosawa's *Yojimbo* (Yōjinbō, 1961).

The Climactic Battle and the Anticlimactic Ending

Musashi's genius for strategy comes to the fore again in the climactic battle that pits him against overwhelming odds. Akemi has warned him of an ambush by dozens of Yoshioka students planning to kill him before he can fight their master. The odds are overwhelming, but Musashi feels honorbound to appear for his duel at the appointed time. A long shot of Yoshioka students taking cover in a field is bathed in the uncertain gray light of dawn. The texture and tone of this scene conveys a mood of dire foreboding, and rightly so, given the sharp outlines of so many weapons massing against a solitary swordsman.

A cut to Musashi shows him leaving the road to approach the temple by a less obvious route. A series of tracking pans frames his progress through field and forest. He moves quickly, confidently, a man at home with nature and at ease with his own strength and agility. This man is so different from the rustic Takezō we saw rushing headlong through a similar landscape, a panting strongman lashed by the underbrush he crashed through in mindless panicked flight.

Here a series of dramatic shots records the progress of the fight. Most are long shots emphasizing Musashi's control of the situation, the presence of mind he shows by turning the very ground underfoot to his advantage. He leads his pursuers into rice paddies where they flounder while he takes the farmer's narrow walkways in stride. Here the erstwhile wild Takezō's experience of country life becomes an asset for the mindful, agile samurai Musashi.

This battle clearly speaks for Inagaki's interest in the nature/nurture (or wilderness/civilization) dichotomy. Musashi is self-taught, a fighter who learned by fighting fights that really count. The Yoshioka students are citified schoolroom warriors. They fight by the book and have never fought for real. Worse yet, they have learned nothing from the previous sorry outcomes of challenging Musashi. Even now, they think that cowardice en masse can kill this champion.

Still, this is no easy win for Musashi. The fight on screen lasts minutes, but the attentive viewer will know that Musashi fought for his life some hours. Dawn gives way to sunrise and the sun is high overhead before Musashi escapes his pursuers. He has killed a number of his opponents one by one in a running fight, yet he is in a truly heroic fix. The enemy seems numberless. Every avenue of escape seems blocked by more. And since these bad-guy samurai have no sense of fair play, archers are called in to finish the swordsman off.

A cut to bystanders watching from a distance confirms our anxiety. One of them is Kojirō Sasaki, Musashi's deadly opponent in Part 3. He wishes Musashi well, in fact, wanting an even more famous fighter to kill at some future date. But now he thinks that Musashi has made a fatal mistake, pressing ahead to fight against such overwhelming odds. His only hope now, Sasaki thinks, is to break and run. And how can he do that, with archers taking aim?

A cut to Musashi shows a swordsman whose self-possession wins the day. Musashi finally puts distance and cover between himself and pursuers on so many sides. A cut to his panting exhaustion as he drinks from a pool sets the stage for the long-delayed duel that has energized the plot of Part 2 from the outset. Even as Musashi catches his breath, Seijurō steps into the forest clearing.

Again, the camera cuts away from the duel itself, relying on standard cinematic conventions to indicate its progress and outcome. A cut to the sky shows birds in flight as if to escape the murderous atmosphere. Rapid cross-cuts show the action mostly in medium shots. Musashi is in full control. Seijurō, whose master's title was inherited, not won, is no match for him. A medium shot shows a cowardly face, then the sprawling fall of a battle lost. Musashi's back is to the camera. A reverse field shot shows his approach, sword raised for the killing blow.

A cinematic pause arrests that motion in a visual commotion that takes us into Musashi's stream of consciousness. The sky flushes red, then the screen is awash in what could be blood and water flowing together. The soundtrack music swells as voice-overs speak from cameo portraits of those who have helped Musashi achieve the greater self-awareness of the ideal samurai. The itinerant priest, a witness to Musashi's fight with Baiken, speaks. So do the priest Takuan and the courtesan Yoshino. They all advise and accuse. "*Bushidō* is always chivalrous." "You are too strong. Control the

Musashi (l., Toshirō Mifune) and Seijurō Yoshioka (r., Teruhiko Hirata) in *Samurai II*. © Tōhō Co. Ltd.

brutal force in you." "You lack compassion." They speak through the shimmering swirl of the color veil, which lifts away to signal Musashi's enlightened view of this moment when vengeance is just a quick and easy thrust away. *Bushidō* forbids it. The sword should have no taste for blood. Here, it must be sheathed for reasons of benevolence—the samurai virtue that tempers rectitude with compassion. He turns and walks away, leaving Seijurō to live with his shame.

The coda is brief and in a way anticlimactic, dealing with the element of romance. Here, for the first time, Musashi adjusts his core values to accommodate the idea of settling down with Otsū in a small hut on a riverbank somewhere in the back of beyond. Being here with her, he says, "is like a dream." Here, finally, Musashi is overcome with passion. He embraces her in sight of water swelling and dashing over rocks, fit image for his state of being. Yet Otsū turns away. He is understandably at a loss. We know what he does not: that Otsū had the misfortune to see Akemi in his arms. Otsū was too far away to hear his politely firm refusal of a woman he had no interest in—one whose evil nature she has seen. And so Musashi leaves Otsū weeping by the river. The last time we see him, he is on the road alone again. This time his sense of personal inadequacy leads him to renounce all ties to women. A cut to Kojirō ends the film. Watching from a distance, he bids him a malign farewell: "Musashi, the greater you become, so much the better for me."

Samurai Part 3 (Duel at Ganryū Island)

Musashi-Kojirō Opposition

Musashi's pursuit of personal integration continues in Part 3. As the title suggests, the plot proceeds by way of a duel subject to a series of postponements. We see the Kojirō/Musashi opposition grow and intensify through a series of narrative cross-cuts. The water imagery used so effectively in the previous parts returns, this time to enrich our sense of the character opposition the plot elucidates.

Until the climactic duel, the narrative advances two lines of causality related to the swordsmen through parallel and contrast. One makes use of the wilderness/civilization, outsider/insider dichotomies to structure scenes, which explain the difference between these men. The other line of causality brings closure to the romantic subplot as two such different women vie for Musashi's love.

Part 3 also covers more ground as a natural consequence of Musashi's continued *mushashugyō* for samurai perfection. He goes from the ancient capital Nara to the shogun's headquarters city of Edo. He spends time in a remote country village near Mount Fuji and travels all the way to Kyūshū to fight with Kojirō.

Musashi's self-made *nitōryū* (two-handed fighting style) has served him well. Even as he flees notoriety, his fame spreads far and wide. That is a given at the outset of Part 3. The emphasis here is on the educational value of his approach to feats of arms. His quest is for balance, for a masterful swordsman's even-handed prowess of body and mind together. Musashi's ideal samurai cultivates harmonious humility, whereas Kojirō's is fixated on self-centered superiority.

The film opens with Kojirō posturing proud ambition against a backdrop of a sheeting waterfall. A misty rainbow arcs low behind him. His arrogant boasting is made apparent by his slicing a passing swallow out of the air. "Not everyone can do that," he says coolly, as Akemi, who we know by now, has yearning for Musashi, recoils in horror.

A cut to a field near a temple in Nara shows Musashi and Jōtarō, his boy companion, in a crowd of common folk watching a rather crude display of combat. Everything about Musashi's appearance and bearing speaks for his quest of virtue. This is a fighter whose inner strength is humble and self-effacing, based on the austere self-discipline practiced by Zen priests.

Agon, one of the temple priests, has been taking on all comers. The ground is littered with the moaning conquests of this loudmouth boor. There is no one left to challenge him. Musashi has already turned to leave, dismayed by this lowlife display, when Jōtarō, his boy companion, indulges a bit of boyish bravado. He challenges Agon, who promptly drags him into the ring. Musashi comes to the rescue, not with force of arms, but with respectful apology. Rebuffed by Agon, he apologizes again, with even greater grace. But Agon forces the issue, thrusting his lance at Musashi, who has no choice but mount a holdfast defense in a contest of strength for possession of the weapon. After a struggle—Agon is built like a bull—Musashi wins, though the priest in charge of the proceedings declares Agon the winner and champion. Musashi humbly accepts this judgment.

The priest himself we recognize as the one who witnessed Musashi's duel with Baiken in Part 2—the same who reproached him for being too strong to be truly wise. A cut now shows Musashi as the honored guest of this wise man. He praises Musashi's maturity: "The ruthless Agon is what you used to be. You have learned a lot." He insists on giving Musashi a letter of introduction to Lord Yagyū, the shogun's fencing instructor in Edo. The priest explains that this important man is yearning to meet Musashi.

Musashi and Jōtarō do make their way to Edo, where we see them staying not as guests of Lord Yagyū, but in a run-down inn teeming with lowlife ruffians. Musashi has adopted an even more rigorous regimen of self-discipline in his quest for ideal swordsmanship. He has discarded the letter of introduction that would open doors to worldly success. As Takezō, he had ignorance to thank for making him an outsider. As Musashi, he makes himself an outsider in order to pursue greater self-knowledge. Still, he is clearly undecided what to do next. Day after day he sits carving a piece of wood into a statue of Kannon, goddess of mercy or Bodhisattva of mercy. Jōtarō comments that the face he has carved is a likeness of Otsū. Musashi is visibly moved. A flashback to the coda of Part 2 relives that shameful moment when Otsū struggled to escape his passionate embrace. We see that his present indecision has something to do with a torment of guilt and desire together. The statue of Kannon in Otsū's image shows that his love has moved to a higher plane, where it serves as a source of moral strength.

Musashi's roaming life begins anew, this time with two companions, Jōtarō and the comic lowlife Kuma. Kuma joined them at the inn when Musashi defused a potentially dangerous brawl by calmly continuing to eat and just as calmly using his chopsticks to pluck flies off his food and clothes and even out of the air. The astonished and terrified rabble dispersed. Ignagaki, too, has made his point by way of a telling likeness between this bril-

Musashi (l., Toshirō Mifune) and Jōtarō (r., Kenjin Iida) in *Samurai III*. © Tōhō Co. Ltd.

liantly humble example of samurai virtue—self-control—and Kojirō's arrogant murder of a swallow in mid flight.

The director illustrates Musashi's acquisition of many virtues that help him bring him closer to his ideal swordsman. We see him do right by four students killed in a duel with Kojirō. He delivers the corpses to the head of their school, who refuses to accept them. Musashi answers that wrong by doing what is right, performing the burial rites owed them by their master. In this scene we see that his studies have included mastery of some priestly functions. He has gone that far in cultivating the all-important *bushidō* value of benevolence.

Kojirō appears at the burial ground to challenge him to a duel. Musashi may be an unprivileged, masterless samurai, but his grasp of the proprieties is nonetheless exact. He begs leave to fight Kojirō later, in another place, in good conscience. Unlike the arrogant, irreligious Kojirō, Musashi is bound by scruples of piety and honor. A fight on holy ground would be sacreligious, and in this case reduce their duel in the public's mind to a grudge match, making Musashi the champion of a master who refused to do the right thing.

The duel is postponed (as required more than once by the plot). Musashi's quest takes him to the remote small village of Hōtengahara. There he appears to take root once and for all. He helps the villagers fend off the bandits who all but destroyed their way of life before he came. His life is harmonious on many levels. Ironically, he finds himself loving the farmer's hard life, the very life he hated and fled before. Now, having come full circle, he is at peace, aware of being one with nature, with forces larger than himself. He works half-naked and in rags like the other peasants. A simple brownish cotton kimono, which blends with the soil he tills, is all he needs now. Musashi's heroic strength and skill now serve him in the role of benevolent mentor in this village. He is its champion and leader in moments of crisis, but shows no sign of social superiority. He has risen above the need to enlarge himself that way. By and by, even his secret anguish appears to be easing, thanks to Otsū, who comes in search of him.

This short sequence finally closes the prolonged causal line related to rivalry between Akemi and Otsū. Akemi, too, arrives on the scene. Again Musashi's devotion to Otsū stands in the way. This time, Akemi's spite costs many lives, her own included. Thanks to her, the bandits take the village by surprise. Masushi rallies a rustic defense and acquits himself heroically in a fiery nighttime fray rich in conventions derived from samurai films and melodrama. Akemi is killed by the villain she has stabbed to save Otsū, whom earlier she tried to kill herself. She dies in Musashi's arms, at last, wishing him and Otsū happiness. That possibility is postponed by a formal letter of challenge from Kojirō. Musashi, Jōtarō, and Otsū must leave the village so he can prepare himself.

Kojirō's history all this while has been covered in periodic cuts to scenes that compare and contrast the progress of two such different samurai. When the film opens, Kojirō is still a masterless samurai. Though technically an outsider, his fencing style is "in." He holds a formal certificate from a noted fencing school. His self-assured arrogance stands in the way at first, yet he achieves a kind of odious progress in cynical self-promotion, learning from his mistakes and achieving great success.

Various narrative events are carefully crafted to highlight strengths and weaknesses diametrically opposed to Musashi's. For example, our opening view of Kojirō's boastful posturing shows his complete indifference to nature. He kills the fleet and graceful swallow with the sword that is the image of a samurai's highly polished virtue—the virtue of benevolence especially. (His fencing style is known as the *tsubame-gaeshi,* or "swallow twirl," style.) He turns his back on the enchanting waterfall and rainbow that lend such loveliness to this unsettling scene. At the end of the film he will face a blinding rising sun in the most decisive moment of his life, the one he boasts

Akemi (l., Mariko Okada) and Musashi (r., Toshirō Mifune) in *Samurai III.*
© Tōhō Co. Ltd.

of here as destined to ensure his fame. Inagaki uses any number of such contrasting parallels to give his film the moral resonance that lies behind its tale of adventure and romance.

Kojirō's progress in the art of dissembling is beautifully laid out in the scene where he applies for the position of Lord Hosokawa's fencing instructor, a magnificent opportunity Musashi has declined. His opponent in the demonstration match is Lord Hosokawa's principal lancer, armed with the padded weapon used on such occasions. Kojirō proudly asks that the sharp point be exposed, since it will be quite harmless to him. And so it is, in fact. Kojirō, armed with the wooden sword of practice bouts, easily defeats the man. He also cripples him for life. That failure of compassion was also a failure of self-control. Kojirō could see that it cost him the job. As he says himself, "No lord will hire an instructor who cripples his vassal." Even so, Kojirō attempts some damage control. He visits the injured lancer, who is completely taken in by his elaborately insincere apology. This charade also does him good with those whose good opinion really matters. And so Kojirō succeeds in passing himself off as an exemplary samurai. He becomes a retainer, one increasingly associated with every cultured and sophisticated aspect of the privileged life. His elaborate silken wardrobe is as ostentatiously self-centered as Musashi's simple cottons express his selfless high-mindedness.

Inagaki calls on nature time and again to make his point about these men. Musashi is repeatedly associated with water flowing free or stretching away to unbounded horizons. Kojirō is more often posed like the artificial man he is, in contexts where water is confined by human artifice. He bids farewell to doting Omitsu in the narrow confines of a courtyard garden, a replica of nature. The setting itself suggests that this love affair is doomed to fail. When Musashi and Otsū are reunited once and for all, the camera frames them strolling along a beach in sight of ocean without end. As Kojirō goes to leave for the duel, he unties a falcon tethered to a perch. He does not offer it the freedom of the wild. Instead, he says to the bird, "Go back to the castle."

The Final Sequence
The climatic duel, which the film has kept postponing, takes place on the island of Funajima off the coast of northern Kyushu. It was later renamed Ganryū Island, the defeated swordsman's official name being Ganryū Sasaki Kojirō. The tension built up by repeated delays gives this climactic sequence its full measure of suspense. The wilderness/civilization dichotomy works

strongly here too, as does the director's stylistic penchant for rich aesthetic effects.

The sequence leading up to the duel makes the expected cross-cuts between locations, contrasting styles of combat readiness. Kojirō, as befits his status, sits in a prominent position surrounded by well-wishers, who include Lord Hosokawa himself. He is dressed even more resplendently now, his gaudy attire accentuated by a red vest. Nothing about his manner or appearance connects him with his oceanside surroundings. Even the nosegay he holds and affects to smell from time to time is as artificial as he is himself. And since Kojirō has never learned what humility means, his parting words to his page are "Watch me carefully. You'll see the best of my Ganryū style!" Ironically, those are the last words he will ever speak.

Musashi's approach to this dread event is all of a piece with his spiritual growth. Every detail of his boat ride speaks for the humility, sincerity, and serenity he has come to know through so much study and self-discipline. He and the boatman are alone, moving slowly across this stretch of vast and endless sea. It is an affecting sight, so human and so natural, a fitting image of this warrior's highly civilized *bushidō* tenets in harmony with nature. Musashi is clad in a simple, dark blue outfit, the gift of a humble innkeeper. Musashi starts carving an oar into a wooden sword. As an accomplished strategist now, he knows that he must be equipped with a very long weapon to match Kojirō's famous "cloth rod." Inagaki introduces a touching element of human frailty here as evidence of Musashi's genuine humility. He asks the boatman to do him a favor: to ferry his body, if need be, the long way back to Shimonoseki, to Otsū.

The duel is the most breathtaking battle scene in the trilogy. We know here at the outset that Musashi is arriving late on purpose. As we saw in his duel with Denshichirō in Part 2, he knows the value of keeping an opponent waiting, the psychological advantage it gives.

Inagaki's masterful dramatization of this duel is built on contrasts adroitly balanced: motions fast and slow, fighters seen from near and far in horizontal and vertical alignments. An opening long shot frames the two men between huge pine trees against a backdrop of ocean vastness. The symbolism here is instantly intelligible to Japanese viewers. The evergreen pine is a symbol of longevity. The samurai is traditionally associated with the cherry tree, whose blossoms are emblematic of fleeting beauty. A samurai's wish is to die dramatically at the height of his powers, not to linger on into feeble old age. These pines make us more keenly aware of the brevity of the samurai's life, especially here, where one must die.

As the battle begins, the camera work emphasizes Musashi's fluid one-ness with nature. He has taken his stand, as it were, on land and sea, for the most part moving back and forth in the shallows, sure-footed, in touch with the ebb and flow of the sea, at one with the pulsating rhythm of nature's immensity. At one point, a dissected image of his legs appears as a powerful reinforcement of this affinity. Kojirō, not surprisingly, keeps to the beach, earth-bound on shifting sand. Both fencers move back and forth in relation to the shoreline. Time and again a long shot view frames a moment of sudden perilous motion or a calculating freeze, both emphatic testimony to the fact that each of these fighters is a match for the other. The tension mounts accordingly.

Then suddenly a medium shot catches Musashi frozen, wooden sword held high, the sky flickering red behind him. The sun has risen from the sea. On one level we have time to sense that the fight in real time has been long and hard. On another level we are aware of Musashi's harmonious relation with nature. The next shot of Kojirō blinking affirms the latter. He clearly has not reckoned on the rising sun. Now it is clear why Musashi took up his position in the sea, putting his back to the rising sun, using the forces of

Musashi (l., Toshirō Mifune) and Kojirō (r., Kōji Tsuruta) in *Samurai III*. © Tōhō Co. Ltd.

nature to his advantage. The alert viewer will not miss the link between the rising sun and Musashi's red headband. Red has been the signal color of moral and emotional crisis for him throughout. Here it is clearly emblematic of life force. Kojirō's headband is white, the color symbolic of death in Japan.

Kojirō attacks. The camera follows this sudden flurry of motion. In the next shot Musashi leaps backward. This shot captures motion so swift and abrupt that it catches us off guard. What exactly happened? A medium shot of Musashi shows him holding two swords. One is wooden, extra long, carved from an oar. The other is shorter, a steel of the usual length. True to his own invented *nitoryū* style, he has used two swords as one. Yet blood begins to drip from a short, deep cut in his forehead: a palpable hit. Is it a close call? And what about Kojirō? A shift to close-up catches the sardonic expression of one whose faith in his own superiority is absolute, a smirk no sooner seen than gone. His eyes flutter. He falls. His distinguished formal style is no match for Musashi's self-taught discipline. The novelist Yoshikawa describes the outcome this way: "What was it that enabled Musashi to defeat Kojiro? Skill? The help of the God? It was neither of these. Kojiro had put his confidence in the sword of strength and skill. Musashi tested the sword of the spirit. That was the only difference between them."[12]

As Musashi's *nitōryū* style suggests, "harmony" is the key to his personal integration. We have seen how Part 3 charts his progress in cultivating this virtue at every level. Musashi's skillful coordination of wooden and metal swords is a clear indication of the way he has harmonized the positive attributes of civilization and nature, combining the two into one. Then too, the ocean image subsumes all the water images that have run through the trilogy. The sea of fertility becomes an archetypical representation of the consummation of Musashi's quest.

The last few shots seem anticlimactic. Musashi sits facing the prow as the boatman stands behind him, rowing back to the mainland. The boatman is overjoyed. He says, over and over again, "I am so glad. I am so glad." A medium close-up of Musashi shows him in tears, something we have not seen before. But why? Samurai stoicism forbids such tears. No doubt it has something to do with Musashi's compassion for his greatest opponent.

Yet there is more to it. One of the most distinctively Japanese aesthetic ideals has to do with fleetingness—the Western sense of "the passingness of things." Kojirō was said to be in his early twenties, in the flower of his youth. The camera took note of his youthful forelock. Clearly, Musashi weeps for him as the epitome of all that is beautiful, yet perishable in this world. This focus on the fleeting nature of life, tinged with appropriate rue, is known in Japanese as *aware*.

Inagaki's trilogy itself is an acknowledged classic among *jidaigeki* films, a five-and-a-half-hour samurai saga with enduring universal appeal. It offers every pleasure the genre is famous for—battles and duels, plots and counterplots, loyalty and betrayal. Even its touch of romance adds to the plot and narrative suspense. It could have been blood-and-thunder as usual, but Hiroshi Inagaki gives his version of Musashi's story the benefit of artful cinematography and moral earnestness unmatched now for half a century.

–5–
Simple Means for Complex Ends
Yasujirō Ozu's *Floating Weeds* (1959)

THE YEAR 2003 marked the centennial of the birth of Yasujirō Ozu (1903–1963), the master dubbed "the most Japanese of all the directors" by Donald Richie. Cinema lovers around the globe celebrated, re-viewing Ozu films with the tender regard and renewed fascination he elicits like few others. Ozu's own experience of worldwide renown was late in life and brief, beginning at age fifty, when *Tokyo Story* (Tōkyō monogatari, 1953) put him in the international limelight. It later won the First Sutherland Cup for the best film screened at the British Film Institute in 1958.[1]

Ozu (1903–1963) made his directorial debut with the period film *(jidaigeki) Sword of Penitence* (Zange no yaiba, 1927). He was drafted into the army infantry before it was quite finished. He went on to make films for thirty-four years, but he never made another *jidaigeki*. This one early brush with the genre is worth mentioning because it was a low-budget, run-of-the-mill project thrown his way by the studio, Shōchiku's Kamata, whose staple was films in the contemporary setting *(gendaigeki)*.

Thus from his second film on, Ozu's films were consonant with the company production policy aiming at a more cheerful vein of comedy involving common people. His earliest films ranged from "nonsense" comedies, such as *Wife Lost* (Nyōbō funshutu, 1928), to films about college students, such as *Days of Youth* (Wakaki hi, 1929) and *I Graduated, But . . .* (Daigaku wa deta keredo, 1929).

Even so, in the earlier 1930s, Ozu's films achieved a consistency and sophistication suited to the *shomingeki* genre—films about the lives of everyday people, lower-middle-class types especially. Of course, this genre, along with the more inclusive *kateigeki* (home drama), was destined to become a staple of the Shōchiku studio. From the late 1930s on, Ozu promoted his characters to middle-class status, as in *Late Spring* (Banshun, 1949). Some he raised to upper middle class, as in *Brothers and Sisters of the Toda Family* (Todake no kyōdai, 1941).

No matter what their social status, Ozu's characters served the theme he returned to consistently throughout his career, making it seem peculiarly his own: the life of an ordinary family whose relationships are affected by everyday events. This thematic staple is most evident in his postwar films. *Late Spring* tells of a widower's attempt to find a husband for a daughter past her prime. *Early Summer* (Bakushū, 1951) shows an extended family scattered by a daughter's marriage and grandparents forced to move.

Tokyo Story, which everyone agrees is "quintessential Ozu," brings a special poignancy to his theme of family dissolution.[2] The old couple's trip to Tokyo reveals a world of starkly contrasting values bred of radical social change. Their own grown-up, citified children prove insensitive and uncaring, whereas their widowed daughter-in-law shows them nothing but kindness and gentle understanding. The old lady's death in the city, away from home, is the very epitome of the failing family bond.

In *Ohayo* (1957), Ozu studies conflict between parents in their prime and children whose sense of entitlement is strikingly up-to-date. The children stage a silent, sullen protest to back up their demand for that most telling consumer item of the 1950s: the television set their parents initially refuse to buy.[3]

Ozu's approach to any story line is famously understated. Donald Richie has this to say about his obvious preference for "story-like" scripts over plot-oriented scripts: "Any Ozu, however, is in a way a pretext. It is not the story that Ozu wants to show so much as the way his characters react to what happens in the story, and what patterns these relations create."[4] Nothing he does is elaborate or overplayed. Most of what we see on screen is an extension of our own lives, though his mode of presentation has always been a matter of great concern for critics both amateur and professional. His tempo is leisurely, even slow. His views for the most part are quite literally fixed; a camera on the move would defeat his sense of stylistic economy.[5] An Ozu character typically faces the camera, talking to it directly. His shots are entirely conventional: long, medium, and close-up. Since personal relations are his forte, the medium shot is the basic unit of his style. Close-ups are used sparingly. Most often they highlight emotional crises, but even then they are never overlarge. Sequences, too, exhibit a standard method. They tend to open with a rather formal patterning—cutting, for example, from empty exterior to empty hallway to empty room, which a character enters, or which is discovered to contain someone. In the West, Ozu scholars, most notably Donald Richie and David Bordwell, have long discussed this aspect of his art.[6] Ozu's mode of representation is also well documented by his fellow countrymen, Tadao Satō and Kijū Yoshida especially.[7]

Ozu's art is so artless, its power is something of a mystery. How can Ozu move us so deeply using such simple means? I am tempted to add that wonderful old English phrase and say that in Ozu's hands we are "hearts moved to pity" by a story of everyday human destiny. I have chosen *Floating Weeds* (Ukigusa, 1959), a remake of the prewar *The Story of Drifting Weeds* (Ukigusa monogatari, 1934), to illustrate this because it has been treated rather dismissively by scholars and critics. Then too, this film was one of the few films Ozu made outside his own company, Shōchiku. Its rival, Daiei, commissioned it, and the result was a wonderful collaboration between him and Kazuo Miyagawa (1908–1999), a director of photography whose name and fame are most closely associated with *Rashomon* (1950) and *Ugetsu* (1953).[8] Another collaboration came from two veteran star actors, working with Ozu for the first time: the renowned kabuki actor Ganjirō Nakamura (1902–1983) and Machiko Kyō (b. 1924), perhaps best known for her roles in Kurosawa's *Rashomon* and *Ugetsu*. These newcomers joined forces with Haruko Sugiyama (1909–1997) and Ryū Chishū (1906–1993), both Ozu regulars, enriching the film immeasurably.

Let us see the way Ozu's genius simplicity evokes complex responses in the viewer.

Simplicity in Narrative and Use of Literary Images

The story is a simple three-part tale of an aging actor's relations with his family and mistress. Part 1 brings him home to a remote coastal town after twelve years away on tour. Part 2 works with motifs of reunion and confrontation. His attachments complicate as his common-law wife and his mistress clash, and a son discovers that this grand old man of the theater is not his uncle but his father. Part 3 is brief. It brings the story full circle as the actor leaves home again.

The screenplay by Ozu and his longtime collaborator Kōgo Noda (1883–1968) is in their usual vein. It evokes a world of complex meanings through simple dialogue. Commonplaces of greeting or comments on the weather take us inside the speakers. Everyday gestures, too, convey shades of meaning not expressed in words. Even the circumstantial givens of life are apt to be charged with emotive overtones or contemplative moods as Ozu invites us to contemplate an empty alleyway, for example, or a room lit by a solitary lantern.

Ozu's penchant for inviting contemplation lies behind his choice of metaphor for the title of his film. That choice itself speaks for the help non-Japanese viewers need to connect with Ozu's genius simplicity. It is too bad that the best available word in English—"weed"—works against the poetic tone and meaning of the title metaphor. Yet the viewer attuned to Ozu needs to know more—aspects of *ukigusa* (floating weeds) more culturally specific to Japan. On the most obvious surface level, the Japanese viewer will instantly see *ukigusa* as a reference to the traveling actor's vagabond way of life. Learning that, the Western viewer culturally attuned to a film tradition much closer to home might think of the cowpoke equivalent: "drifting along with the tumbling tumbleweed."

Yet it does seem possible to say that the floating weeds of *ukigusa* are more culturally enriched than the tumbleweed. Why? *Ukigusa* is in fact a major metaphor in Japanese classical literature. There it is used to convey the traditional Buddhist view of the world as fleeting and impermanent. *Mujō* is the word used for this condition. A classical instance of the floating weed metaphor is found in these lines by the renowned ninth-century poet and beauty Komachi Ono (Ono no Komachi):

So lonely am I	*Wabinureba*
My body is a floating weed	*Mi o ukigusa no*
Severed at the roots.	*Ne o taete*
Were there water to entice me,	*Sasou mizu araba*
I would follow it, I think.	*Inamu to zo omou*[9]

Here, the notion of impermanence relates to a lover. The poem makes fanciful use of Buddhist logic to explain the ephemeral nature of love. The actual outcome is left tantalizingly in doubt. Has her lover deserted her? Has she given him the brush-off? Komachi was a notorious flirt, famous for mocking her many suitors. Whichever the case, she is clearly waiting for a new love to appear.

Ozu's creation of the traveling actor Komajūrō explores another avenue of *mujō*: the restlessness of life spent on the road, with all its days and nights of uncertainty and change and contact with other people almost by definition casual and fleeting. The famous haiku poet Bashō Matsuo opens his book *Oku no hosomichi* (The narrow road of Oku, 1689) with an extended metaphor admired in Japan as a classic description of *mujō* awareness:

The months and days are the travelers of eternity. The years that come and go are also voyagers. Those who float away their lives on boats or who grow old leading horses are forever journeying, and their homes are wherever their travels take them. Many of the men of old died on the road, and I too for years past have been stirred by the solitary cloud drifting with the wind, to ceaseless thoughts of roaming.[10]

Ozu's protagonist, Komajūrō, has grown old touring with his company. Surely he is, by virtue of that fact, more acutely aware of *mujō* than many of his coevals. And anyway, doesn't aging itself offer irrefutable proof that impermanence speaks for the human condition, no matter what manner of life one leads? The trouble is, Komajūrō is an actor, a man who has lived many lives on stage, a man of makeup and masquerade, a man peculiarly well prepared to deny the evidence of *mujō* in himself.

Floating Weeds is the story of a man in denial. Even as aging casts its spell on him, Komajūrō resists with all his actor's art. Ozu points to this conflict again and again. Komajūrō's age becomes a haunting image as various comments are made, sometimes by him, sometimes by others, sometimes by the camera's sly glance at the way he moves. He has not aged on stage, so why shouldn't his performance power carry over into real life and fend off this threat?

Any merit that argument might have is denied in no end of telling details we see quite clearly, even if he does not. Walking down the street he falls into a gait unmistakably true to what it is: the walk of an elderly man. One of the old folks in the town says that when Komajūrō was young, he performed in the best theater in Osaka. Two women watch him pass. One says to the other, "There's the actor, but he's an old man now." His common-law wife Oyoshi reminds him that she is just as old as he is. She does it by way of claiming to be too old to feel jealousy any more. Komajūrō looks at their son and says, "He's a big boy now." But he still insists on passing the boy off as his nephew.

Actually, age is the *idée fixe* of this film. Everyone seems preoccupied with it. An actor passing out handbills asks a child how old his elder sister is. Later he asks a barber's pretty daughter her age. Donald Richie sees Ozu using the question of age to build a case against Komajūrū. As the evidence mounts in simple, everyday increments, we come to realize that another more troubling question lies behind the fact of Komajūrō's age. We find ourselves asking, is Komajūrō too old to "change" in a changing world? Is he too old and set in his ways to transform himself into "a good father and husband"?[11] That same question in another form points to the central problem of the film: how does Komajūrō come to terms with a changing society?

He appears to have two choices: the uncertain, unsettling life on the road he is accustomed to or the settled certainties (such as they are) of domestic life he has never really known. Choice, of course, breeds moral conflict. Here, it pits the actor's easy come, easy go, career-centered life against the domestic obligations and anxieties of being a husband and father.

Ozu's familiar theme of dissolution of the family is doubly reinforced in this picture. Komajūrō begins and ends separated from his family. In the end, his troupe is disbanded, too. Fellow players have been another family. For years they were his best defense against harsh reality. But time takes its toll even on that side of the footlights. As the players age, their art seems dated, too. Even on this tiny coastal town, the troupe's last stop, the public's taste has changed. The audience no longer cares for the troupe's specialized repertoire of feudal themes. Komajūrō's son, Kiyoshi, advises him to try more contemporary pieces.

When Komajūrō arrives at his home place, he has no intention of retiring to family life there. He is a patriarch in his own right, as head of his troupe. His mistress is his leading lady, Sumiko. But then his troupe disbands. He and Sumiko break up. He is forced to face the idea of settling down.

Masterful Economy of Cinematic Devices

Ozu's gift for economy also shows in the deft cinematic touches he uses to convey shifting attitudes and relationships. Commonplace gestures take on a weight of meaning, especially shown in parallel or in rhythms involving repetition and hiatus. We see Komajūrō and his son Kiyoshi fishing side by side on the beach, bathed in welcoming sunshine. We know that they are father and son, and that Kiyoshi thinks they are uncle and nephew. That knowledge gains poignancy from an obvious resemblance in their posture and from a certain easygoing togetherness they clearly enjoy. A subtle change takes place as Komajūrō gives the young man a piece of avuncular advice: he should forget about running off to college in some big city; he ought to stay home for his mother's sake. Kiyoshi says quite frankly that he cannot wait to leave the island, adding that his mother has already reconciled herself to separation.

The camera studies the old man's back, inviting us to notice his elderly stoop. This hint of direction is typical Ozu. It is the kind of hint we take in stride throughout, thanks to his masterly light touch. We know at a glance what Komajūrō is feeling: old and alone and desolate. No close-up of his face is needed. Ozu has posed his figures with subtle art against a background of sand and sea in quietly moving counterpoint to what turns out to be the message of this scene. The old grow fixed in place as their time runs out, while the young grow expansive as the sea. A first-time viewer might look past the metaphor, but who could fail to share the old man's feeling of desolate isolation?

More importantly, scenes of father and son fishing side by side are a staple of Ozu's films. Critics have often taken note of the highly charged emotional and even philosophical nuances he catches in the simple, repetitive motions of casting a line. Shigehiko Hasumi claims that this rhythmical movement creates an impression of characters accepting the flux of time as casually as a breeze on the skin.[12]

The critic-filmmaker Kijū Yoshida invites us to reconsider the famous scene of father and son fishing in *There Was a Father* (Chichi ariki, 1942). In that scene, the father casts a line and the son follows the suit. Their unconscious, repetitive movements in the same manner, Yoshida argues, unmistakably suggest a firm bond between father and son. Yet when the father tells his son, now a high-school student, to move away from home and live in a dorm, the repetitive, synchronic action of casting and drawing lines is broken by the son's sudden halt. Yoshida shows how this shift foreshadows their inevitable separation and also illuminates the larger issue: the severe constraints implicit in the human condition. He relates this motif to Ozu's

Kiyoshi (l., Hiroshi Kawasaki) and Komajūrō (r., Ganjirō Nakamura) in *Floating Weeds* (1959). © Kadokawa Co., Ltd.

conviction that "human beings manage to portray themselves through repetitions and tiny differences with the passing of time."[13]

What we see in this scene of Komajūrō and Kiyoshi on the beach is basically a reconfiguration of a scene from *There Was a Father*. There the two are fishing a stream, not casting into surf, but dangling hook and line from a bamboo pole, waiting patiently for a bite. Here on the beach, action and implication are dynamically entwined. Just as Kiyoshi starts criticizing his father's old-fashioned repertoire, daring to replace it with more contemporary fare, Komajūrō reels in his line, only to find that he has lost his bait. This sudden break with father/son likeness, each intent on his long pole, clearly pinpoints their distinctive difference in values, foretelling their unavoidable separation at the end.

Ozu's superb control of parallelism and hiatus comes into play again when Sumiko arrives at the restaurant to confront Komajūrō. She has learned that he is visiting his common-law wife, Oyoshi. Ozu uses a stationary camera to take note of an exquisite compositional harmony as the quarreling lovers cross the screen in the same direction and at the same speed. Outside, Ozu makes use of close-ups (rare for him) to show Komajūrō shouting at Sumiko and vice versa. The camera cuts back and forth as their argument continues. This rhythmic device sets up an unmistakable linkage between these two lovers who have such harsh things to say. Komajūrō finds Sumiko's intrusion unforgivable. She has barged into his wife's restaurant and spoiled a happy family reunion. Sumiko feels betrayed by these old connections. This furious exchange depicts a breakup, yet it has the added narrative value of linking these two in a way that enriches the ending of the film.

Ozu ends this quarrel with a characteristic gesture: emptiness. A shot of the deserted alley in the rain serves as a hiatus, "a deliberately created break with a part missing—a kind of pause."[14] As Donald Richie notes, such a hiatus is similar to "a rhythmic point of division in a melody," and is used by Ozu most often to mark a change in the direction of the story.[15] In this case the empty alleyway marks a shift from outdoors to indoors, to the second floor of the inn where the troupe has been staying. Sumiko is persuading the young actress Kayo to seduce Kiyoshi. The girl is at first reluctant but finally agrees. As far as she knows, Kayo, now an orphan, is doing right by following her sense of *giri* (obligation) to the elder actress whom she considers to be "a big sister." But we know that Sumiko is getting back at Komajūrō, whose parting angry words are still ringing in our ears: "I don't need any help from a bitch like you . . . this is the end. Get out of my life."

Oyoshi's restaurant is the scene of two other dramatic hiatuses. The first takes place in her tiny backyard garden where red cockscombs (celosia) are in bloom. We recognize this as the scene of Komajūrō's reunion with her after a twelve-year absence. Now they sit quietly sipping sake, the picture of contented domesticity. At one point the camera glances over at the cockscombs from Komajūrō's persepective, when he says, "You planted nice flowers." This is another of the characteristic unobtrusive moves that give Ozu's work its quiet eloquence. The red cockscombs cannot escape our attention, yet they do more than add a note of naïve brightness to a commonplace garden. Ozu touches on them at just the right moment. His camera shift beckons to our awareness of their significance as flowers of summer at its height, blossoms setting seed in presence of this elderly couple sipping their tea contentedly. They could be any such couple resigned to the notion that for such as them "ripeness is all." But we happen to know the facts of this particular case.

Ozu has arranged these flowers and old folks with simple and meaningful cinematic art. We cannot miss the contrast between flourishing high-season annuals and all that we know about the failing energy and painful indecision of this superannuated actor. Equally unmistakable is Ozu's invi-

Komajūrō (l., Ganjirō Nakamura) and Oyoshi (r., Haruko Sugimura) in *Floating Weeds* (1959). © Kadokawa Co., Ltd.

tation to fit this vignette into the larger picture of *mujō,* where summer flowers and resigned old couples enrich our understanding of nature's ever changing cycle and the changeable nature of human destiny. Furthermore, the overall effect created by this tiny empty yard could be described as one of synesthesia. Its note of red (Ozu's favorite color) takes charge of the subdued surroundings, demanding commitment to meaning, much as William Carlos Williams does in his signature poem:

> So much depends
> upon
> a red wheel
> barrow,
> glazed with rain
> water
> beside the white
> chickens.[16]

Sight, sound, and smell respond in agreeable confusion to Ozu's vision of red cockscombs. We seem to hear their red and see the silence of a midsummer day whose emptiness they fill.

This scene of Komajūrō's visit ends with one more shot of the yard. Here too, as before, Ozu makes deft use of hiatus to signal a change in the storyline. The camera cuts to the exterior of the theater to show banners fluttering. Then it moves to the inside, where Sumiko is wondering aloud about Komajūrō's whereabouts.

A more complex use of hiatus/stasis occurs after the lovers' quarrel and Sumiko's plot to use Kayo to get even. Kayo finds Kiyoshi at work and, in effect, asks him out on a date. What will he do? Ozu refers our natural curiosity to an indifferent but significant object: a blue lantern hanging in an empty downstairs room of Oyoshi's restaurant. Ozu refers us to this image not just once but twice, first in close-up, then in medium shot.

A shot of the empty stairway leading up sustains this invitation by way of hiatus to contemplate the given human dilemma. A cut to Kiyoshi's room upstairs finds him wearing an expression of intense concentration. We can surmise that he is torn between his desire to rendezvous with Kayo and his sense of obligation to his mother. Sneaking around to flirt with an actress is not what Oyoshi would expect of him. His struggle ends when finally he gets up and leaves the room.

Ozu will return to the lantern once more later on. Just now, as the story nears its end, he uses hiatus/stasis to prepare a transition fraught with meaning. This climactic scene in Oyoshi's restraurant merits close analysis for two reasons. The first has to do with narrative. This highly emotional scene highlights the drama and offers a partial solution to the central problem of the film. The second reason is stylistic. This scene articulates Ozu's principle of simplicity through an effective single shot of hiatus/stasis.

The scene begins with Komajūrō and Oyoshi wondering about Kiyoshi's whereabouts. Earlier she told him that Kayo had come to get Kiyoshi for Komajūrō. Now, knowing that had to be a ruse, the old man is afraid that Kiyoshi might have eloped with the girl. Oyoshi does her best to reassure him. She insists that "their" son will soon return and life will go on as before. We know better, having witnessed the lovers' tryst in a previous scene. In it, Kiyoshi announced his intention to do the honorable thing. His mother will be the first to know that he has asked Kayo to marry him. The scene of the old folks waiting anxiously underscores the shift in Komajūrō's values. Now that his troupe has disbanded, he is all for settling into conventional family life. Oyoshi, of course, encourages him to do just that. A cut to the clock precisions their anxiety. It is nine o'clock at night. A young man ought to be home safe and sound in a little coastal town like this.

The camera shows Kiyoshi approaching the restaurant, followed by timid Kayo. The scene that follows goes from revelation to confrontation almost instantly. Komajūrō starts shouting even as they enter, accusing Kayo of seducing his "nephew." He slaps her, too. He occupies the foreground, facing away from the camera. Kayo is literally and visually overpowered by his show of authority. She stands in the middle ground, facing the camera. Kiyoshi comes to the rescue, pushing the old man to the ground. A reverse field setup gives foreground magnitude to the young man's muscular back as he stands over Komajūrō on the floor. Camera angle and posture capture the essence of this dramatic freeze, calling our attention to the old man's pathetic small size. What better confirmation of Komajūrō's earlier comment "How old he has grown!" This composition also underscores the dramatic revelation that comes in Oyoshi's outcry, reproaching Kiyoshi for showing such disrespect to his "father."

Up to this point, Ozu has been at pains to show how traditional values tend to vanish in a changing society. Kiyoshi has played a central, youthful role in this. As mentioned earlier, he is the one who commented on the lack of contemporary relevance in the feudal play Komajūrō brought to the village. He also stood up to his "uncle" on the subject of his desire to go to college far from home and an overprotective mother. And to top it all off, he has broken with the dutiful son tradition, asserting his right to elope with a girl of his choice.

Now, at this moment of climactic confrontation and revelation, he does not back down. His sense of entitlement here is poignantly expressed in his refusing to accept Komajūrō as his father. Even after Oyoshi speaks, Kiyoshi addresses him as "uncle." Worse yet, he goes on the offensive, daring to accuse the old man of being an unfit father and husband, too, a footloose egotistical performer who preferred his transient lifestyle to responsible home and family life. Komajūrō can hardly defend himself against charges fraught with so much truth, especially since this youthful prosecutor is assuming a form of authority that appears to speak for a new kind of world taking shape. What choice then does the old man have but to leave, hoping to pick up the pieces of his former life—but alone, so alone.

To his credit, he leaves on a kindly note, asking Oyoshi to take care of Kayo. As viewers, we are apt to recall a telling parallel expressed in Komajūrō's earlier remark: "Like father like son." Like his father, Kiyoshi has chosen an actress for a lover. Unlike his father, he thinks of Kayo as his wife, not his mistress. Ironically, marriage and family still matter to this young inheritor of the brave new world Komajūrō finds so hard to understand, for all its emphasis on freedom and self-assertion.

Oyoshi (l., Haruko Sugimura), Kiyoshi (c.l., Hiroshi Kawasaki), Kayo (c.r., Ayako Wakao) and Komajūrō (r., Ganjirō Nakamura) in *Floating Weeds* (1959). © Kadokawa Co., Ltd.

At the climax of this scene Komajūrō rushes out of the house. Kiyoshi tries to run after him, but Oyoshi holds him back, saying that Komajūrō will not return. She adds, "Nothing has changed. Everything is fine." Again this simple comment is charged with emotional overtones, suggesting Oyoshi's reticent acceptance of the changes that must come in all their lives. The last we see of them, all three are in tears.

A cut to the blue lantern now, Donald Richie notes, offers a moment of stasis meant for us, not anyone else. It is not, he explains, expressive of any emotion on the part of any character, or the director, but rather meant to generate complex emotions in us, the audience.[17] One might add that the lantern serves that complexity of emotion by focusing our attention on its character as a trivial, everyday object at this moment transcendently indifferent to the complex human transactions taking place around it. It is a point of sameness and indifference inviting us to contemplate the inevitabilities of change in human life. We are also predisposed psychologically to accommodate a shift to the concluding episode of this story. That change is signaled by a sudden break with silence—the whistle of the train in the distance.

The Final Sequence: A Simple Conclusion

Midway through the film Ozu sampled audience reactions to Komajūrō's troupe in this rural backwater. First we see Kayo and a little boy do a song-and-dance routine based on a song extremely popular at the time (sung by Peggy Hayama). The audience showers the performers with gifts of money. On another occasion, the troupe is offering a famous episode based on the adventures of Chūji Kunisada, a footloose gambler of the Edo period. Chūji has killed the state official, who made life a misery for the peasants he oppressed. As an outlaw on the run, Chūji roams the countryside with his faithful sidekick, Ishimatsu.

Sumiko is seen playing him on opening night. As she later mentions to Komajūrō, the turnout is good, but not as good as they expected. The number of empty seats is a clear index of a shift in taste, even out here in the boondocks. We cannot help recalling a comment overheard at the outset of the film. A clerk at the ferry landing says he prefers strip shows to feudal goings-on onstage—Kumajūrō's stock in trade.

The Chūji drama is thought to derive from the traditional *kōdan* tale, an oral genre featuring historical figures. Though popular for ages past and into recent memory, it now seems out of date and as such a clear indication that Komajūrō and his troupe are well on the way to becoming history. Thus, the final sequence of two brief scenes shows how a master of understatement uses simple means for complex ends at the conclusion of his story.

Komajūrō, entering the station, pretends not to notice Sumiko. A series of cross-cuts suggests, even so, that a bond still exists between this seemingly misfit pair. Ozu charges their most commonplace gestures with emotional overtones. When Komajūrō takes a seat nearby, Sumiko offers to light his cigarette. At first he refuses. Then he relents. The cigarette is lit; harmony is restored—all this without "outside" interference. These ordinary gestures on screen take place in our own dimension of "real time." Dialogue as simple and natural as the smoke they exhale reinforces the motif of bond renewed: "*We'll* work together one more time."

A cut to the passenger car sends them on their way, an elderly man and somewhat younger woman, an ordinary couple seated on a train. The film ends as it began, with a note on the weather. The opening sequence showed a steamship on the open sea. The troupe was on its way to a new engagement. The ship's whistle, boundless ocean horizon, and bright sunlight could be taken to correspond with their future hopes. Still, shipboard chit-chat was all about promise of sultry weather later in the day. No such outcome is mentioned in this final sequence, though we see Komajūrō accept a cool, wet towel for his head. The framing closes in on the nighttime discomforts of a dreary third-class carriage. Earlier the camera's casual look showed the door to the carriage with Chinese characters for "third-class" on it.

Shadows fall on this couple's future from every direction. We cannot help seeing that. This is the power of Ozu's masterful simplicity: it persuades his viewer to greater awareness of metaphorical nuance. And so we see in this dismal-as-usual third-class carriage scene the bond that lends this ill-assorted pair a kind of moral strength. Komajūrō is old and tired, an actor "all washed up." Sumiko is still young, a talented actress with a future. She will get work and possibly a "patron," too. But we sense that, come what may, she will stick by Komajūrō, even as he declines. Up to this moment, Ozu has reminded us of returning intimacy chiefly through physical placement. In the station they sat in separate corners before smoking brought them together. Now the crowded discomforts of a train bring comforts of reconciliation as Sumiko pours the old man a cup of sake.

We sense something new, however, even in this coming full circle. Komajūrō has resigned himself to life adrift after all—and we know why. Ozu's skill with circularity and repetition has done its work once more. The train moves away from the camera to vanish in a distant, uninhabited landscape. The clicking of its wheels call to mind an earlier ticking of a clock, always a favorite Ozu metaphor. Together they mark the passing of time no human can reverse.

Once more we have Ozu, this most Japanese of directors, closing with a shot entirely characteristic of the Japanese view of life as a matter of *mujō:* the impermanence of all that surrounds the living of our lives.

-6-
Eros, Politics, and Folk Religion
Kaneto Shindō's *Onibaba* (1963)

BORN IN 1912, Kaneto Shindō is one of Japanese cinema's most enduring masters. He is one of the most productive as well, with more than two
hundred scripts and forty-some films to his credit, the latest released in 2003.
The first film he directed was *The Story of a Beloved Wife* (Aisai monogatari,
1951). After his second, *Avalanche* (Nadare, 1951), made for the Daiei studio, he left the studio determined to work independently in every possible
way. He formed his own production company and never looked back,
going from strength to strength by dramatizing scenarios he wrote himself.

The first thirteen years of Shindō's career may be characterized as
devoted to social criticism, most notably in the quasi-documentary accounts
of events in recent memory. *Children of the Atom Bomb* (Genbaku no ko,
1952) recounts a teacher's experience of visiting former students injured by
the blast. *Lucky Dragon No. 5* (Daigo Fukuryūmaru, 1959) was based on an
incident still in the news, the 1954 hydrogen bomb test conducted by the
United States at Bikini Atoll. The crew of a Japanese finishing boat, the
Fukuryūmaru #5, were casualties of the blast.[1]

Many critics in the West agree by and large that *The Island* (Hadaka no
shima, 1960) is Shindō's best film from the 1960s.[2] It is a quasi-documentary set on a remote island in the Inland Sea. There is no dialogue, only the
camera's tenacious silent witness of daily life as lived by a family cut off
from every convenience of civilization. The film makes its point by way of
dutiful attention to the monotonous truths of such an existence. Time and
again the viewer is rowed back and forth to the mainland for supplies of
fresh water carried in buckets to the family's primitive shanty.

In 1964 Shindō changed directions, beginning with *Onibaba*. This story
looks back to the civil wars of the fourteenth century, a time of social dis-
integration he domesticates in a startling new way. His protagonists are not
the slashing dashing samurai of historic re-creation but two peasant women
struggling to survive, fighting against the odds with murderous intensity.

Even more shocking is the surcharge of erotic energy Shindō brings to his tale.

An auteurist view of a number of Shindō's films in the late 1960s and early 1970s would identify their thematic constant as one of persistent concerns with female sexuality. *Villain* (Akutō, 1965) and *Kuroneko* (Yabu no naka no kuroneko, 1968) share a central theme of woman using her sexual prowess to challenge feudal social structure. In *The Strong Woman and the Weak Man* (Tsuyomushi onna to yowamushi otoko, 1968), Shindō elaborates even more. Deploying three anecdotal stories very much like morality plays, he gives a comical depiction of woman's use of sex as a weapon. The plot shows how women leaving a coal-mining town to work in the city meet the challenge of survival with exuberance and vitality by taking full advantage of their sex appeal. *The Iron Crown* (Kanawa, 1972) extends the theme of *Onibaba* to a study of an abandoned wife's psychology. Taking its cue from the Noh play of the same title, the film probes various phases of timeless nature of female sexuality and jealousy.

Shindō himself has this to say about his treatment (view) of sex in these films: "Our human existence is rooted in sex. . . . It lies at the very heart of love. Though conservatives reject the very idea as dangerous, I would say that the way to save us from our own perversity is by confronting sex courageously. . . . Sex brings relief from tension and enmity and leads to harmony in human relationships—husband and wife, relatives and strangers."[3] In theory, Shindō would appear to be an idealist. In practice, he is more interested in the dramatic potential of sexuality gone awry, female sexuality especially. Most of his heroines are paragons of sexual frustration, not gratification. That thematic orientation still rules his most recent film, *An Owl* (Fukurō, 2003). Cast in a mold similar to *Onibaba*'s, the film shows how a mother and a daughter use their sexual prowess to survive in a remote region of western Japan.

Onibaba itself was the first in a long line of Eros-oriented films remarkable for their refreshingly innovative approaches to sexuality viewed as inseparable from the instinct for survival. Starting with that premise, Shindō weaves political and religious themes into his narrative tapestry. He shows how external forces such as the political ambitions of a ruling class and societal moral constraints distort the very source of human life.

Despite the complex interaction of its various themes, the film itself is quite simply patterned. The narrative develops around a single causal line related to the mother and daughter-in-law. Indeed, *Onibaba* strikes us as a kind of stage drama taking its cues from folklore. It exhibits the same economy, too, with a cast of a very limited number of characters, featuring two women and three men.

The initial causal line concerns the matriarchal bond that makes it possible for these two women to survive alone in war-torn medieval Japan. The bond is strained when the status quo is threatened by the arrival of a man. The story from that point on pursues the age-old motif of conflict as the old woman battles the threat posed by the younger woman's desire. Folkloric simplicity is suggested by the setting, too. The drama unfolds in the vicinity of a couple of shanties surrounded by a marshy wilderness of towering reeds. The film was in fact shot on location in Inba Marsh in Chiba Prefecture.[4] This filmmaking method came to be known as "Shindō-style," a fitting reference to a career-independent's dependence on economies of production. Thanks to his genius for filming on the cheap, Shindō ranged far and wide over the Japanese countryside, sometimes both shooting and camping out "on location."

Despite its economy of story and setting, this film's blend of sexual, political, and religious themes achieves a powerful dynamic, thanks to ambitiously stylistic embellishments. In this regard, *Onibaba* tends to be style-centered or "parametric," as David Bordwell calls it.[5] The camera's way of capturing the vibrant energy of the marshland reeds is central to the film's expressive patterning. Equally important are Shindō's borrowings from Noh conventions, especially the *han'nya* demon mask. Sound effects are shrewdly managed, too. All together, *Onibaba* shows how a master of dexterity such as Shindō orchestrates a number of expressive devices whose pattern creates a dynamic weave of interactive themes.

Historical Setting, Central Problem, and Choices of Action

Bits of information here and there add up to articulate the historical milieu of *Onibaba*. Our first glimpse of the two women at the outset piques our curiosity. Why are they alone in the middle of nowhere, in a marsh dominated by head-high reeds? How do they live? We barely have time to wonder. A wounded samurai comes staggering into the reeds. The women pounce. They grab his sword, stab him, and strip the corpse. They know the routine. We see that these women are doing what it takes to survive— but when? Selling their loot to a merchant, Ushi, they get an update on recent events. He says the two emperors have been fighting it out. One has fled from Kyoto to Mount Yoshino to set up a second imperial court. Ushi's peasant account sets the scene for us: the fourteenth-century civil war fought by rival Northern and Southern Courts.

A later sequence offers a more detailed description of the effects of this war on common folk. The young man Hachi returns to what remains of the village where the women are holed up. He and their husbands had been rounded up and forced to fight by the faction supporting Emperor Go-daigo, and they had been part of the rout that fled to Mount Yoshino. The emperor had been betrayed by his vassal Takauji Ashikaga. Hachi's account details the effect of this catastrophe on high and low. The women's husbands were killed. At this point we learn that the women are in-laws, not blood relatives. We never learn their names. They are the anonymous representatives of a portion of humanity of special interest to Shindō: "My mind was always on the commoners, not on the lord, politician, or anyone of name and fame. I wanted to convey the lives of down-to-earth people who have to live like weeds."[6]

Given the sociocultural milieu of the film, its central problem is readily identifiable: how are these two women to survive in a warring feudal society? Tilling the soil is no longer possible without their men. What can they do but take cover in the marsh and survive on the only resource available to them: samurai casualties of war looking for a place to hide in hopes of surviving their wounds. Two weak women are better than one at this dangerous work. This is the donnée of the film: that the struggle for survival has created this matriarchy, small but brutally strong.

The sudden appearance of a man cannot but threaten the women's bond. It is not a case of a male arriving to assert his traditional prerogative. Shindō evolves a much more provocative scenario. The threat comes from within. Like Emperor Go-daigo betrayed by his vassal, the mother sees her power threatened by the daughter-in-law's defection. The younger woman reverts to traditional type, and for good reason. A patriarchy has its ancient survival advantages: a physically stronger helpmate who can father a family. Given a man, a woman can hope for the future. With the help of husband and children, her life can return to normal after the war. And because Shindō sees sexuality as key, the primordial power struggle he depicts is driven by elemental carnality viewed with notable frankness.

The mother's struggle to retain her power is elemental, too. It borrows an ancient form of threat from folk religion. She warns her daughter-in-law that fleshly lust is punished with torment in the afterlife. When Hachi's male appeal proves stronger than imagined damnation, the mother resorts to dramatic actuality. She dons a demonic *han'nya* mask looted from a samurai general and lies in wait at night when her daughter-in-law sneaks out to join her lover in his hut. Ironically, the issue will be resolved by other means. Hachi will be killed by a samurai deserter, who happens on his hut. Shindō loses no opportunity to comment on the fortunes of war, especially as they affect common folk.

The end of the film is more problematic, playing on the theme of sin and retribution. The punishing mother is punished herself. The demon mask will not come off. The daughter-in-law must help with means so violent the old woman's face is left disfigured with leprous sores. What does this mean? The final scene is even more puzzling. Chasing after her daughter-in-law, the mother leaps to clear a hole. The two of them have dumped many a corpse in such holes. So now she takes a running jump. A freeze-frame catches her in mid-air. The end. Where does that leave her? Where does that leave us? As we shall see, Shindō invites us to analyze some complex evidence.

Stylistic Experiment and Interaction of Motifs

The opening sequence of nineteen shots establishes the basic canon for Shindō's well-measured expressive embellishment. The camera pans across the reed marsh, coming to a halt at a pit in the ground. The tall reeds rustle noisily, swept by the wind. An overhead pan looks down at the pit. Its pool of

Hachi (l., Kei Satō) and the old woman (r., Nobuko Otowa) in *Onibaba* (1963). © Kindai Eikyō.

water deep down reflects a pale circle of sky in stark contrast to the ominous blackness that fills the screen. A subtitle message reads: "A hole, deep and dark, a reminder of ages past." The film title appears, superimposed on a closer view of the swaying reeds. Loud drumbeats give their motion added life and energy. We sense that these reeds are a force to be reckoned with. That suggestion is reinforced by shifting perspectives on the restless marsh as credits flash on and off. The score by composer Hikaru Hayashi makes eerie good use of electronic instruments and folk music drums.

The windswept sway of the reeds is suddenly broken over yonder. A long shot looks for the source of this disturbance. It finds two staggering samurai pushing the reeds aside, one supporting the other. A series of rapid shots records their fate. This staccato burst does wonders for cinematic vigor. The weary death march of the pair on foot is suddenly interrupted by a shot of their triumphant enemy on horseback galloping across the field beyond. Even as the stronger of the two struggles to get a better grip on his comrade, an abrupt close-up shows the spear that strikes him in the chest. A cut shows where it came from: the two women seen earlier peering out of the reeds.

Another quick shuffle of action shots shows them stripping the corpses. The camera studies their backs as they drag the bodies through the reeds. Each woman is wearing an expensive kimono. The elaborate patterns show that they came from their victims. A still shot hiatus shows a crow perched on a snag. Its bird-of-ill-omen cawing drifts across the marsh. As each woman heaves her corpse into the pit, a sudden slowing in the shot conveys a sense of its ungainly fall. The edge of the pit is projected on the upper screen. As the corpse tumbles in an eldritch sound reverberates, something between a dying man's scream and call of carrion crow.

The opening sequence concludes with our first view of the life these women lead. A single long take of less than a minute and a half begins with a look inside their makeshift hut. We see right away that survival has brought these women to the brink of inhumanity. The hut is like an animal's lair. It bears no signs of comfort or security. There is nothing here beyond the basic, brutal energy it takes to stay alive. The camera closes in slightly as the young woman gulps water from a ladle. The old woman grabs rice and wolfs it down. They lie down to sleep. The camera tracks back to frame their brutish snoring. They have not spoken a word in all this time. The only human voice we have heard so far was the grunt of a murdered samurai. Our first glimpse of these women spoke true: two pairs of fierce eyes peering out of the thicket of reeds; two human animals preparing to pounce on their prey. The long take here of them sleeping is followed by a short still shot of the carrion crow outside.

Undoubtedly, these opening scenes strongly foster the thematic thrust the director himself mentioned: "Among these outcasts I wanted to capture their immense energy for survival."[7] The marsh itself becomes a natural and naturally expressive extension of that energy. The panning camera follows as the women push their way through the reedy wilderness. Even when it comes to a halt, the reeds keep moving. Their incessant rhythmic swaying speaks for the tireless predatory watchfulness of these fierce survivors. Time and again the camera takes note of the bestial degradation that is the price of survival here. Their conversation takes the form of greedy gulping and chewing. They eat with the rude haste of the habitually starved, as we see when the daughter-in-law attacks a skewered fish. Their makeshift diet scarcely lends itself to feminine delicacy. A series of rapid shots records their hunting skill as they run down a stray dog, snatch it up, and dash its brains out on the ground.

Both women's dormant sexual drives spring back to life when Hachi returns. The daughter-in-law's visits to him under cover of night are superbly rendered in fast-paced, liquid camera work. The moon is out the first time she makes her way to his shack. Some fifteen shots in rapid succession convey a sense of desperate eagerness. She runs toward the camera and across the screen to a sound of rustling reeds so hasty and insistent they appear to echo the beating of her heart. The effect is one of sinister, ghostly primal energy.

The second time she goes, the mother steals along behind. Crouching outside the hut, she peers in through a crack with glittering animal eyes. The tangle of limbs in close-up speaks for the old woman's awakening lust. A long shot finds her solitary outline in the looming darkness. She begins to massage her breasts. A medium shot shows her clinging to a tree, writhing lubriciously. The camera slowly pans up to show the tree in silhouette. It is a leafless dead snag. Carrion crows might perch on it by day. The barren tree confirms some earlier Freudian symbols of frustrated sexual energy. They range from beating straw with a sledge to pounding laundry with a log to grinding grain with a pestle. Even Hachi's brandished sword speaks of uncommon urgency when the daughter-in-law fails to join him one night.

The film's stylistic apogee comes in two highlights of the mother's attempt to keep her daughter-in-law away from Hachi by impersonating a terrifying apparition. The first begins with a few shots of waving reeds given foreground magnitude. A close-up of the daughter-in-law's determined face is followed by rapid shots of her running through the reeds, as before, moving across the screen and toward the camera. This time too, the sound of the reeds suggests a wildly beating heart.

The conventions of Noh are powerfully used in staging the women's encounter. Like a Noh performer on an outdoor stage, the mother appears disguised as a demon hag *(onibaba)*. She is wearing a demonic *han'nya* mask and a long, ornate kimono stripped from a dying samurai.[8] The simple convention of a quick zoom works a marvelous transformation, objectifying the horror the daughter-in-law experiences. Arms fully extended, the demon appears to be floating in air. To the younger woman, the *han'nya* mask, with its gaping mouth, lurid old eyes, and menacing horns, is the very picture of the horrors that await sinners like her in the Buddhist version of hell. She readily believes that this demon has come to punish her in the here and now, in advance of death and judgment. Schooled by her mother-in-law in a down-to-earth peasant version of Buddhist moral theology, she truly believes that sex outside of marriage is serious sin.

The viewer's reaction to this scene is of course more complex. The Japanese viewer comes to it prepared by culture and tradition to experience more than the thrill of horror anyone will feel in response to the image on screen. This menacing apparition is a familiar, highly aestheticized horror

The young woman (r., Jitsuko Yoshimura) in *Onibaba* (1963). © Kindai Eikyō.

of Noh drama. Here Shindō has brilliantly transferred the demon from the starkly artificial stage of Noh to this entirely natural setting in the marsh. Yet the demon's stage presence is richly apparent, too. The viewer acquainted with Noh will understand that the mother herself is indicted by the horror she summons up to punish her daughter. The *han'nya* mask in Noh plays such as *Aoi no Ue* (Lady Aoi) is used to demonize the sinful emotions of jealousy and its associative emotions.

The daughter-in-law's face, transfixed in terror, fills the screen as a drum beats a loud tattoo. She turns and runs shrieking back to the hut. A zoom back out to the marsh confirms the "reality" of the threat. The demon's ghostly apparition looms in reedy tumult as darkness blacks out the screen. This simple theatrical strategy returns for the second and climactic struggle between the two women. It begins with a structure parallel to the first: a close-up of the daughter-in-law's face yielding to several quick shots of her running through the marsh. This time, however, the desperate energy of her desire is suggested by a heavy thunderstorm. She is bolder this time, too. When the demon appears, she puts up a fight. Lateral pan and reverse-field shots join forces to provide a carefully measured rhythm to the movements of the two as they grapple. As Hachi appears, the daughter-in-law breaks free and escapes with him hand in hand. The demon, clearly overcome, staggers through the reeds.

The working principle here has to do with the evocative power of a Noh mask. Just as the Noh performer proliferates a range of emotions by moving in specific ways in relation to stage light, the mother's *han'nya* mask goes beyond its formal identification with explosive jealousy and rage. The old woman has ceased to perform, but the performance goes on. As she totters through the reeds, bolts of lightning now give a different stage light interpretation to her apparition. The viewer acquainted with Noh is prepared to take two basic movements of the mask into account. The actor portraying grief lowers the mask in a gesture known as *kumorasu,* literally, "clouding over." Joy is portrayed by raising the mask, a gesture known as *terasu,* or "shining out."[9]

In this instance, Shindō's manipulation of the mask is by way of a shot from a slightly lowered angle, a beautiful example of the subtlety available to Noh performance. Here the viewer alert to that range of nuance will see the *han'nya* mask's demonic expression of jealous outrage complicated, even somewhat mitigated; it comes to suggest the wearer's sorrow and dejection as the old woman struggles to make her way alone through the towering storm-lit reeds. Supernatural apparition has yielded this sorry commonplace: the vigorous, vengeful *onibaba* demon hag is reduced to a pitiful, defeated, old woman in a bad disguise.

The camera takes note of the lovers embracing, sopping wet and lightning lit, then returns to the crestfallen demon. There is a pause for the first time. She has lowered her menacing arms. She stands still, screened by toplofty reeds. Her posture speaks of defeat, of energy spent. Two close-up stills of reeds mark a hiatus, creating an exquisitely pictorial effect. The first shows the plant in the foreground, invigorated by the soaking rain. The second shows its black silhouette in stark contrast to a background of storm-lit white.

The Final Sequence

The final sequence of two scenes unfolds the apogee of dramatic action with an ironic twist. A long shot shows the daughter-in-law running through the marsh toward the camera. She has just been with Hachi. This simple shot speaks for the vigor and energy of gratified desire. The reeds themselves appear reinvigorated by the night's heavy rain. They add to our mounting sense of cruel irony since earlier we have been informed what the woman does not know: that her lover was stabbed to death by a wandering samurai shortly after she left him. She ducks into her own hut to find a shocking surprise. A close-up of her horrified expression yields to a line of sight shot showing what she sees. The old woman cowers in a corner. The camera closes in on the demon mask she wears. The rain has glued it to her face.

The women's struggle is central to this sequence, as is its increasing irony. The old woman begs for help removing the mask. Now their roles are reversed: the younger becomes the matriarch and makes the old woman promise not to interfere with her daily visits to Hachi. The camera studies the ensuing struggle in great detail, moving in for close-ups from every angle. The daughter-in-law pulls with all her might, but the mask will not yield. As a last resort, she wields a mallet. The sound of it striking the mask mingles with the old woman's shrieks of pain. The camera adds to the horror by enlarging the sinister mask to show blood running out of a crack.

Finally the mask gives way. A close-up of the daughter-in-law's face reads shock and consternation. A close-up cut to the old woman shows her face disfigured, covered in bleeding, leprous sores. At a visual level, this scene is in stark contrast with the earlier outdoor scene of the two women's struggle. This is the real-life counterpart, and consequence, of the demonic role she chose to play. The effect on the younger woman this time is all the more powerful for being a matter of fact so close. She sees not just a weary old hag worn down by life, but this horror of foul disfigurement.

What does this mean? The viewer's response from outside this drama partakes of two areas of understanding. The Japanese audience of 1963—like any serious student of cinema since—could scarcely miss the contemporary relevance. This is, after all, a film by a director who came to prominence in the 1950s documenting whole lives disfigured and sometimes lost outright to the horrors of atomic and hydrogen bombs. Adam Lowenstein has argued that the scars on the old woman's face are in fact meant to be seen as radiation burns.[10] Shindō himself is on record as saying he "based the make-up design for the brutal unmasking scene on photographs of maimed *hibakusha* [victims of atomic bombs.]"[11] Even so, a viewer concerned with all the possibilities here will look to the story itself and see what the old woman's disfigurement means in the feudal context of the film.

Joan Mellen locates Shindō's meaning in the class oppression represented by the samurai general the old woman murdered and robbed of his *han'nya* mask:

> The degenerative disease affecting him [the samurai general], as it did his entire class, was visited on the old woman when she took on his role, even if fleetingly and only to survive. It is not easy to remove the face of feudalism stamped on its victims. Even when they are successful, disfiguration will remain because the disease of the culture also afflicts its victims. Shindo does not condemn the old woman in so punishing her. The affliction is born of her momentary spiritual convergence with the repressive samurai role when she used the mask to coerce the girl into abandoning sexual joy.[12]

Mellen's Marxist reading is on the right track. However, her observation misses the religious dimension of the mask. The samurai *han'nya* with its horns, gilt eyes, and menacing gape embodied explosive "obsession," female jealousy especially. This accords with Buddhist belief that attachment to worldly desires is a sin. The samurai general who comes wandering into the wilderness is obsessed with unbridled political ambition. It is precisely this aberration that victimizes the masses like the old woman. As the old woman says, he is punished for his sins. When he falls into the pit to a terrible death, he is beyond redemption. The old woman's sin is jealousy, so she gets what she deserves.

At an elementary level, the tangle of samurai's corpses in the bottom of the pit is symbolic of Buddhist hell as the old woman sees it. She is guiding the general through the marsh at night, taking him, he thinks, to a place of safety. Instead, she brings him to the edge of the pit, where she takes revenge: "You deserve to die in this pit for all you've done." She speaks for Shindō's view that the war at hand will punish the oppressors, too.

Can there be more to it than that? A good many critics see horror films as ranging too widely for any single approach to "work." Yet Robin Wood has made this interesting observation on this genre: "The true subject of the horror genre is the struggle for recognition of all that our civilization represses or oppresses."[13] Certainly that insight accommodates a more complex working of the pit in *Onibaba* as it relates to the Freudian view of the womb as archetype of life force and sexuality.

That suggestion is reversed in the film, where the pit icon gets its negative magnitude from associations with death and decay. The worst crime committed by the ruling class is seen as reproductive oppression. War destroys the masses in a way more sinister than outright killing: the sexual drive itself is perverted when families are torn apart and peasant survivors like these women are driven from fields of honest tillage to lives of crime in marshland wilderness. The widowed mother's obscene embrace of the withered tree speaks to that. The tree itself adds emphasis, since peasant fecundity, vigor, and survival are tied to the soil.

As might be expected, the very last scene revolves around this complex

The old woman (r., Nobuko Otowa) in *Onibaba* (1963). © Kindai Eikyō.

central metaphor. The camera cuts to outside the hut. The old woman unmasked is such a horror that the daughter-in-law has taken flight. A series of rapid shots records her frantic progress through the marsh. She approaches the camera, brushing the reeds aside to leap across the fearful pit. A matching series of shots shows the old woman, equally frantic, running to catch up. A drum beats in time to her breathless haste. Not just once but twice she wails, "I'm not a demon. I'm a human."

Again, Shindō is bringing his political message home. The film concludes with the montage of the old woman's attempt to clear the pit. The final freeze-frame shot catches her in mid-air. Will she make it? Or will she fall into the pit? The film does not provide any legibility about her fate. Asked about the outcome, Shindō had this to say:

> Obviously the mother has done very cruel things, like preventing her daughter-in-law from finding another man. She is punished for these acts, but the punishment is an expression of the uncontrollable events which these people meet in their actual lives. My next suggestion is that the destroyed face is not the end of her world. The miserable face will dry later and she will find the day to live again.[14]

The pit in *Onibaba* (1963). © Kindai Eikyō.

To that he added emphatically that "the important thing" for her is to survive.[15]

If we accept Shindō's commentary at face value, a possible scenario takes us back to where the film began: the two women must survive, each counting on the other. Since the war is still ongoing, the daughter-in-law has no opportunity to seek the obvious, more promising alliance: marriage. For her part, the old woman cannot survive alone. Her crime is clinging to power. Her punishment is seeing her daughter-in-law get the upper hand.

No doubt about it, *Onibaba* offers a grimly ironic worldview. No matter what they do, the masses are at the mercy of an oppressive feudal system. Yet Shindō has shown how a director can transform a simply patterned folkish story into a sophisticated artifice rich in stylistics and complex in its themes.

–7–
The Age-Old Paradox of Innocence and Experience
Kōhei Oguri's *Muddy River* (1981)

CRITICS AGREE that Kōhei Oguri (b. 1945) is nothing if not independent. Between 1981 and 1996 he made just four films, all stubbornly his own, all free of the hassle and haggle of playing by studio rules. All of his films were funded independently. His first was underwritten by a "factory-owner film fan."[1] Gunma Prefecture funded his last. Oguri clearly prefers quality to quantity; his films suggest a correspondingly unwavering commitment to artistic integrity.

His first, *Muddy River* (Doro no kawa, 1981), was shot in black and white. Originally intended for a small screen, this neo-realist type film is considered "an anomaly amidst the Technicolor blockbusters" of the early 1980s, as one critic observes.[2] It is a resolutely stark reading of Teru Miyamoto's novel of underclass life, a story of boyhood friendship doomed by social circumstance.[3] It takes place in Osaka, one of Japan's largest, most remorselessly industrial cities, in the years just after the Korean War of the 1950s. Critical previews gave *Muddy River* rave reviews ahead of a number of prestigious awards at home and abroad. It won the Silver Prize at the 1982 Moscow International Film Festival and was an Oscar nominee for Best Foreign Film. Not surprisingly, *Muddy River* remains Oguri's best-known work in the West.

Hindsight suggests that *Muddy River* set the course for Oguri's artistic development by establishing two thematic characteristics that his next two films would define as peculiarly his own. *For Kayako* (Kayako no tame ni, 1984) and *Stings of Death* (Shi no toge, 1990) also deal with Japan's hard-won recovery in its early phase between the end of the Occupation in 1952 and of fighting in Korea in 1954. The economics of sudden industrial expansion form the background of Oguri's trilogy. Each film offers a searching, sometimes harrowing, critique of the dark downside of this prosperous new Japan. Oguri's foreground concern throughout is with the human cost and the fate of individuals left behind or even destroyed by this process of change.

Japan in these years was rebuilding its cities and industries at a hectic pace, with great success. By 1968 the world would be talking about a Japanese "economic miracle." The Korean War of 1951–1954 gave Japan's industrial base a major boost, thanks to America's procurement needs. Oguri's films show why he considered the mid 1950s of paramount importance to his boyhood, and especially to his developing artistic sensibilities and interests.

All of Oguri's films are peopled with casualties of interrelated social and economic forces. The boys in *Muddy River* are disadvantaged from the start. The parents of one run the poorest kind of eatery on the banks of a river as unappetizing as its name. The other boy's mother is a prostitute too poor to send her children to school. *For Kayako* shows the course of true love roughed up by differences of national origin: the boy Korean, the girl Japanese. The difficulties facing them are sadly familiar to parents of the girl, herself the adopted child of a Japanese mother and Korean father.

Sting of Death won the International Critics Prize at the 1990 Cannes Film Festival. It takes a somewhat different turn, offering a highly psychological rendering of Toshio Shimao's frankly autobiographical novel. Its mid 1950s protagonist is a former *kamikaze* pilot-turned-writer whose womanizing has cost his wife her sanity. The plot unfolds a six-month crisis of increasing social alienation as the husband moves his family around, seeking to cure the wife's disease.[4]

Oguri's most recent work, *Sleeping Man* (Nemuru otoko, 1996), is an exquisitely stylized film by a director "all too seriously engaged in creating Art with a capital A."[5] Its young hero returns to his mountain village where an accidental injury leaves him in a coma until he dies six months later. The story explores the effect of his cruelly suspended life on aged parents and fellow villagers.

Muddy River seems likely to remain the Oguri film most familiar outside Japan. Its theme is the universally accessible dichotomy between innocence and experience. Its sincere concern for the fate of children might interest viewers anywhere. The pity is that Oguri's treatment bears comparison with a Japanese master of films about children all but forgotten in Japan and known to very few in the West: Hiroshi Shimizu (1902–1956).[6] Admirers of *Muddy River* would do well to look into Shimizu's work. There they will find much to compare and admire to the credit of both directors.

Both directors deal with the age-old dichotomy between innocence and experience and with the difficult and oftentimes contradictory passage from childhood to adulthood. Both have a powerful grasp of sustained realism, especially when it comes to the highly focused child's view of the world.

Both find ways to skirt the obvious melodramatic dangers there, though both on occasion do come too near.

Their differences are instructive, too. Shimizu's approach is casual and spontaneous. Two classic examples are *Children in the Wind* (Kaze no naka no kodomotachi, 1937) and *Children of the Beehive* (Hachi no su no kodomotachi, 1948). Shimizu was famous for casting amateurs. Most of the time his camera keeps its distance, tagging along as children go about their lives, experiencing joy and sorrow, seemingly unaware.

Oguri's approach is carefully contrived. Unlike Shimizu, whose direction and story lines are simple and direct, Oguri makes powerful use of symbols and intricate causal relationships. *Muddy River,* as its title suggests, speaks in metaphor throughout. Some of his symbols are universally intelligible; others specific to the Japanese cultural context are apt to need explaining in the West.

A Time, a Place, a River, and the Central Problem

Muddy River is set in 1956, a time of rapid change in Japan. The post–Korean War boom economy, like any, had its impoverished underclass. *Muddy River* tells the story of the boy Nobuo Itakura's growing awareness of the kind of world he lives in. It is not a pretty one. His father sees things this way: "People are being carried away by the Jinmu boom. But we, the poor, have no share of the economic prosperity made possible by America's war with our neighboring country." (Emperor Jinmu was the mythical founder of Japan.[7]) Later, the camera takes ironic note of a newspaper headline announcing the end of the postwar period.

The river itself speaks for the downside of this economic upsurge. It is the muddy Aji, flowing through Osaka, a major industrial city, and muddy is clearly not the only thing this river is. Still, Oguri's aim is not that of a social or environmental activist. He had this to say about his film: "I belong to the generation that did not know the war nor anything of what our parents experienced during and after it. It is their bravery, their will to survive, that I wanted to discover."[8]

Donald Richie sees Oguri accommodating two familiar themes in Japanese cinema and narrative: a sense of the validity of the past and the dichotomy between innocence and experience.[9] This last theme relates to the central problem of the film: how does the innocent protagonist Nobuo come to terms with the world of the facts of life? He appears to have two choices: to grow up, or not to grow up. For him, agreeing to grow up means growing wiser at some cost of childhood innocence. Refusing to grow up means stagnation. Nobuo acts out this choice or nonchoice between progression and stagnation.

The boy Nobuo we see at the beginning is very different from the one at the end. His story asks hard questions about poor children confronting the world of adult knowledge. A child in better circumstances might enjoy some years of blissful delay. That is not a luxury given to boys of Nobuo's class—and even less to his poorer friends Kiichi and Ginko Matsumoto. Children such as these buy wisdom at some cost of innocence. Of course, the hardest question has to do with choice: how willingly does (or can) a boy like this trade innocence for survival?

No wonder Oguri looks for help from symbol and metaphor. He had this to say about his title metaphor:

> At the spring the water is pure, but as it descends to the sea, first as a stream and then as a river, it becomes more and more muddy. Yet this mud is also the essence of the river, which is, after all, made of both water and the mud. In the same way, though a child may be as pure as spring water, it is the mud of humanity, the experience of living, of knowing happiness and sorrow that nurtures him. This is what I wanted to celebrate in my film.[10]

Japanese literature and cinema are rich in river metaphors used to speak for *mujō*, the passingness of things, a mode of awareness deeply rooted in traditional Buddhist thought. Two classics in this vein are Chōmei Kamo's essay *Hōjōki* (An account of a hut, 1212) and Yasujiro Ozu's *Tokyo Story* (1953).

Oguri's river metaphor is somewhat different. It sticks to demonstrable facts, as befits a world aware of its manifold pollutions, most of them more like permanent than passing. His river is muddied in fact by flowing through a human landscape. Its metaphoric flow speaks for life itself, specifically the life of a child whose innocence is sullied by experience of the adult world. Yet his metaphor speaks for the age-old paradox of innocence and experience. As he points out himself, mud and experience both can enrich, even as they . . . sully.

Oguri's river is also an important player in the unfolding drama. Like any river flowing through a city, it draws life to itself. The Aji riverfront being what it is, the cast of characters here is underclass. The neighborhood is sordid, but not violently desperate. A certain social solidarity prevails, as we see at the outset when the driver of a horse cart and the boy Nobuo share a bowl of shaved ice. The river may be muddy, and may flow through a city remorselessly industrial, but it offers a very real sense of continuity to these people. Osaka's rampant modernization may be leaving them behind

—most of them have no stake in its economic miracle—but the river itself remains unchanged. The Aji has focused the everyday life and culture of these people for at least three centuries. Its Tenjin Festival dates back to the Genroku period (1688–1703), the era marked by a flowering of urban culture represented by kabuki, bunraku, and *ukiyoe*. The river still links the people on its banks with the lively spirit of the commoners who patronized those arts. It also bears the common freight it always has; its carriers still live nearby and eat at the little noodle shop run by Nobuo's parents. Another seventeenth-century survivor is the one-woman houseboat brothel that plays a part in Nobuo's education.

This is not to say that Oguri idealizes the Aji. He offers a telling contrast by way of Nobuo's father's yearning for the sea. It is rough compared to the river, he knows, but that, he says, is the price of its purity. His yearning connects to his past, to his youthful tour of duty in Manchuria, a soldier fighting for love of his country.

The Rich Texture of Symbols

Muddy River opens with credits passing in front of still shots of river and bridge and a bird's-eye view of the Aji winding to the sea. Oguri is showing us images and symbols he will manipulate throughout. What now is a bridge will come to resonate with meaning as we are led to think and feel in various ways about a young boy's journey to another side of life. These opening shots also sketch a vignette introducing us to Nobuo's world. We also hear a discreetly sentimental musical theme. It will return a number of times as a kind of leitmotif for a boy's growing pains. Oguri moves quickly in that respect. Our first glimpse of ten-year-old Nobuo shows him sharing shaved ice with the carter Shinoda, whose ear is hideously deformed. A close-up focuses on Nobuo's surprise and unease. He is too young to know about the war. Shinoda says he will give Nobuo his horse when he gets enough money to buy a secondhand truck. The boy is naïve enough to take this joke for a promise.

His childish trust is betrayed in a larger, more life-altering sense when he sees Shinoda crushed by his cart on the bridge. His mother has the presence of mind to clap her hands over his eyes, but the boy has seen what he has seen. Death is suddenly painfully real, and so is a childish nightmare suspicion that life itself is not to be trusted.

Oguri conveys all manner of messages symbolically here. The mother's hand is trying (and failing) to fend off experience too grown-up for one so young. The more complex psychological shock involving trust is conveyed by two close-ups of Nobuo gazing into the horse's eyes. The first of these shots is the real experience. The second is a flashback later that evening, a clear sign of innocent inexperience deeply troubled.

The film's rich texture of symbolic understandings reworks its materials a number of ways. In another kind of film, this process might have focused on the boy's parents—seen here as overly protective. Thanks to the novel that furnished his script, Oguri redoubles his young hero's troubles by making his mentor another boy, one even more disadvantaged than himself. Kiichi is ten, like Nobuo. He lives with his mother and sister in a dilapidated houseboat; the father is dead. We see at a glance that Kiichi is poorer than Nobuo and, worse, exposed to poverty's way of growing up too quickly.

They meet the day after Shinoda's fatal accident. Nobuo is in the state of pained uncertainty that lends itself to caution, so he is curious but wary of meeting this new boy. Earlier point-of-view shots spoke for Nobuo's interest in the houseboat newly moored in the river. He sees Kiichi standing on the bridge in the rain, then he sees him rummaging through the wreckage of Shinoda's cart, looking for something to steal. Nobuo cannot resist. He ventures onto the bridge.

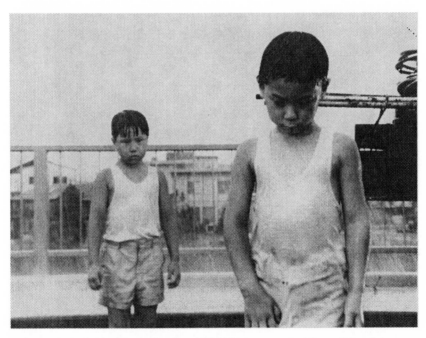

Nobuo Itakura (l., Yasuhiro Asahara) and Kiichi Matsumoto (r., Minoru Sakurai) in *Muddy River* (1981). © Kōhei Oguri.

The two become pals, not because Kiichi is grown-up enough to think of pilfering, but because he is a boy with a fantasy to share. He tells Nobuo about a gigantic carp that lives in the river. This, he adds, can be their big secret. (The carp, a bottom feeder, gets no respect in America, so viewers there may need to be told that Japanese hold this fish in high esteem. Children's Day [Kodomo no hi], May 5, is a national holiday decked out with carp streamers in celebration of boyhood virtues such as courage and bravery.) Nobuo is quickly drawn into Kiichi's world, though the difference in their upbringing shows in all manner of ways. As viewers, we are quickly aware of the symbolic import of Nobuo's forays into Kiichi's world. Crossing the river is itself a quest motif. The houseboat represents the dark side of that quest. It contaminates his innocence with experience of a world not just grown-up, but seedy and desperate as well. The contrast with his own loving, caring family life is painful, too. Every visit to Kiichi sends him home burdened with some disturbing secret he could never share with his parents.

The second time he meets Kiichi, Nobuo ventures across the bridge and down the stairs leading to the riverbank where the houseboat is moored. There, on the brink of new experience, he hesitates. Kiichi has to grab his

Nobuo Itakura (l., Yasuhiro Asahara) and Kiichi Matsumoto (r., Minoru Sakurai) in *Muddy River* (1981). © Kōhei Oguri.

hand and pull him aboard. That gesture is richly symbolic, too. Poverty has made Kiichi older than his years. The hand he extends offers guidance and protection.

A close-up of the hole in Kiichi's shoe is the first of many point-of-view clues to Nobuo's awakening sense of social inequity. A slow pan of the sparsely furnished galley speaks for his uneasy curiosity. Kiichi's older sister Ginko is kind from the start. She cleans Nobuo's shoes, soiled when he slipped in riverbank mud. Yet why, he wonders, is Ginko doing all the household chores? Why doesn't the mother come out of the back room to greet him? She calls out to Kiichi to give his friend a lump of sugar and tell him not to visit without being invited.

This visit gives Nobuo his first real taste of social discrimination. From this point on he will be haunted by differences of Us and Them. We as grown-up viewers can guess where desperate poverty has taken Kiichi's mother, and how her family will suffer socially as more and more local men find their way to the houseboat. We know what Shinpei, Nobuo's father, means when he says, "A baby is born into the world, unaware what its parents are!"

Another death exposes Nobuo to the complex workings of the adult world. He happens to see an old man fall into the river from a boat. Nobuo tells the policeman that he does not know what happened to the man because he was not looking. In all innocence, he adds that the river's giant carp must have eaten him. He is instantly aware of having broken his promise to Kiichi, telling their big secret, and to a grown-up. The policeman takes the matter lightly and only thinks the boy is joking. That too is upsetting, making Nobuo feel foolish. Luckily, his father is there to help. Smiling, he explains that his boy must have averted his eyes. Yet the harm is done. Nobuo sees that death is very real, an actual possibility, not something safely far distant in history or fairytale.

This theme returns when Nobuo is taken to the hospital to visit Shinpei's first wife. She is dying of cancer. Her hand in close-up reaches for Nobuo's. He stands powerless to move. Shinpei puts his son's hand to the woman's. This shot clearly speaks for the boy's pained acceptance of the reality of death. Here the father's guiding hand completes a kind of metaphoric transaction with the mother's hand at the outset, which covered Nobuo's eyes lest he see Shinoda die. That hand was protecting innocence by fending off information. This hand is guiding innocence on its way to experience, with parental love and understanding. The wistful theme music returns as if to end on an affirming note. Yet Nobuo is still troubled, and with reason. He does not know this woman. All Shinpei has said is that he owes her a debt of gratitude. And why is his mother weeping, begging this woman's forgiveness? The sequence ends with the family watching a street performance by some clowns playing flute and drums. Nobuo's look is withdrawn, distrait, even as a clown somersaults. Death is too real just now. It has robbed fantasy of its appeal.

Besides, another hand is guiding him along the way to growing up. He and Kiichi are now the best of friends. Nobuo is innocently impervious to prejudice. Even peer pressure fails to sever this bond with this boy from the wrong side of the river. A rich kid invites Nobuo and some classmates to his house to watch TV (still a luxury in the 1950s). Nobuo asks if he can bring his friend. Kiichi is dressed, as always, in shabby clothes. The rich kid, looking him up and down, says no. Nobuo says he will not be coming then.

As their friendship grows, the two friends cross the bridge both ways. Kiichi and Ginko visit Nobuo, too. They bring their "difference" with them—the look and manner of children made precocious by poverty and neglect. We see this at the meal they are served by Nobuo's mother. Kiichi is artless enough to say that Ginko takes care of him and does all the housework, too. Nobuo adds that their mother has nothing to do. He is too

Shinpei Itakura (l., Takahiro Tamura), Shoko Itakura (c.l., Yumiko Fujita), Kiichi Matsumoto (c.r., Minoru Sakurai), and Nobuo Itakura (r., Yasuhiro Sakurai) in *Muddy River* (1981). © Kōhei Oguri.

innocent to know whereof he speaks. Kiichi and Ginko know not to talk about their mother's profession. Kiichi also volunteers to sing the only song he knows. He says his father used to sing it. The song is about a soldier's experience on the battlefield—hardly fit for a childish treble.

Later, alone with Nobuo, Ginko says that even in the coldest weather, rice feels warm to her. She adds that nothing makes her feel happier than seeing a bin filled to the brim with rice. Nobuo says nothing, finding it that hard to imagine being so poor. Forgetting what Kiichi's mother said about not coming to visit uninvited, Nobuo comes to the houseboat looking for his pal. He finds the mother, Shoko, home alone. This first meeting contrasts Nobuo's guileless innocence with Shoko's corrupt experience. He is a "handsome young man," she says with a coquettish smile. He shows no sign of catching her drift. Asked if his mother is pretty, Nobuo says matter-of-factly that Shoko is much prettier. He goes on to invite her to visit his family. He is that artless, that uncunning, that primed for loss of innocence. But not quite yet.

Stylistic Devices

Oguri's choice of a leisurely pace is evident at the outset, in a lyrical slow tune that serves for a recurrent theme. The average shot length of fifteen seconds is unhurried, too, and serves its expressive purpose well, allowing the viewer to savor moments so formative in the life of this young boy. Oguri himself acknowledges the Polish filmmaker Andrzej Wajda's films, especially *Ashes and Diamonds* (1957), as a source of his visual inspiration for the film.[11]

Close-ups are freely used to study human emotions and their sources, often inanimate objects. This simple, legible device shapes and interprets narrative, as in the opening sequence where Shinoda shares a bowl of shaved ice with Nobuo. The situation speaks of easy familiarity, yet a close-up of the carter's deformed ear tells us that Nobuo is wondering how it came to be that way. Sure enough, later on we learn through his father that Shinoda was maimed in the war. Shinoda's joking promise to give Nobuo his horse returns in a haunting close-up at the end of the sequence, as mentioned earlier. Shinoda is dead. Nobuo is looking in the horse's eyes; a close-up studies his dismay and childish egocentricity. Death is not as real as what appears to be a broken promise—a recurrent motif used to mark this boy's progress in growing up. Similarly, a close-up of the hole in Kiichi's shoe marks an early stage of Nobuo's awareness of their difference. Small experiences like this are used to show how innocence is compromised by knowledge of the world. As mentioned earlier, Nobuo's growing awareness of mortality is conveyed through a carefully paced series of close-ups of hands in the hospital scene. The dying woman reaches out. The boy's hand hesitates, anxious and fearful. The father's hand reaches in to guide his son's, putting him in touch with dying.

Ginko's role is for the most part visual. She is kind and attentive in her actions, far too suppressed to display emotion, much less discuss her difficult life in words. The camera is correspondingly attentive. While she and her brother are eating in Nobuo's family's restaurant, a customer sees fit to mention in passing that Kiichi pimps for his mother. Kiichi hangs his head in silence. A close-up of Ginko tells us clearly that her impassive expression masks distress and resignation not to be spoken of. In the climactic sequence, the nature of the mother's business is conveyed in a succession of quick close-ups showing what Nobuo sees and how he reacts: Shoko's face, the hideous tattoo on her client's back, and the boy's shocked and stricken expression. These close-ups of the mother/prostitute's face and the tattoo work in several ways at once. Since the houseboat is small, they add to the trauma by giving us a sense of the close-up view that takes Nobuo by surprise. Just as shocking, we understand, would be the contrast between the impassioned grimace on this face and the gentle, though slightly coquettish, smile she greeted him with the day they met. That close-up emphasis also spoke for Nobuo's sense of the moment—the impression her beauty made on him. Nobuo, of course, is not of an age to accommodate this difference. Two more dramatic close-ups end this scene. One is of Kiichi, who bites his lip yet gives his friend an unmistakably defiant look. Neither says a word. Nobuo's tear-stained face speaks for his confusion, for our sense of innocence betrayed.

Muddy River also gains strength from the rare but effective use of extreme long shots. The most powerful shows Kiichi alone in the deserted school yard. The camera's distant gaze invites us to share his feelings of forlorn alienation. A closer shot reinforces that bond. Kiichi is filling his battered shoe with sand, watching it run out of the hole we have seen before. A few shots later, we learn that Nobuo shared our view of Kiichi's loneliness. A cut to the classroom shows the teacher scolding him for not paying attention.

The Climax and the Final Sequence

Oguri brings his theme of innocence betrayed to a climax in the ensuing closing sequence whose poignancy few viewers will feel inclined to resist, though a resolute critic might take note of a shade of excess. Here at the last he also makes use of a symbol requiring some explanation in the West: a crab. This animal has deep and rich associations with childhood in Japan. The crab is a beloved character in a number of children's stories, among them *Sarukani gassen* (Combat between monkey and crab). Every child knows this one about the good-natured crab who has found a delicious rice ball. A monkey comes along and offers a persimmon seed in exchange for it. The crab agrees and plants the seed, tending it faithfully for eight long years. At last the tree bears fruit—which the monkey kills the crab to get. There the story ends, having drawn a clear distinction between the crab's good-hearted, patient innocence and the monkey's selfish, impulsive wickedness.

The climax begins with Nobuo and Kiichi returning from a festival. Nobuo is deeply disillusioned. Shinpei had promised to take them, but never showed up. His promise was made "man to man," so the boys feel doubly betrayed, treated like little children. Worse yet, Kiichi lost Nobuo's money through a hole in his ragged pants. Kiichi suggests that they go to his place. It is after dark. Nobuo has promised his father he will not visit the house-boat at night. He breaks that promise now and goes to see Kiichi's treasure, a bucket of crabs. To his horror, Kiichi proceeds to dip his pets in oil and set them alight. Nobuo tries and fails to interfere.

In a sense, Kiichi's experimental cruelty is natural enough, especially in a boy whose upbringing has exposed him to the coarse and thoughtless side of adult life. Nobuo has heard his father talk about wartime experience, but Shinpei is a thoughtful, loving parent. Nothing he has said or done has prepared his son for this. We have seen enough to know why a boy such as Kiichi might play at war in his small way. The symbolism here is rich in such inference. These tortured crabs mark the end of an innocent friendship. Kiichi has muddied its clear stream with this cruel parody of adult knowledge.

Oguri drives the point home with a glimpse of the real grown-up thing. The camera follows Nobuo as he crawls out a window, reaching for a burning crab to save it. It drops into the water, leaving Nobuo outside, looking in another window. He sees Shoko having sex with a client. A close-up of a hideous tattoo identifies the man as a Yakuza. We see just enough of the brutish man and the expression on Shoko's face to know that Nobuo has suffered a complex traumatic experience. The camera scans it in a close-up of his tear-stained face. A cut shows Nobuo running across the bridge. He meets Ginko halfway. A close-up of Nobuo shows him weeping. One of her shows the mask-like face of a girl inured to knowledge that cannot be spoken of. They part without speaking. The sentimental musical theme returns.

A cut to the family's eatery introduces a final sequence that is somewhat anticlimactic. The focus of revelation shifts from Nobuo to us as the plot winds up. Nobuo finds his parents and diners celebrating the festival with sake. Shinpei explains that he missed the boys because he yielded to an overpowering desire to see the ocean. By the time he got back, the boys were gone. He makes light of a promise Nobuo took very much to heart. Shinpei has no way of knowing what happened to his son, thanks to promises broken on both their parts. He is too taken up with sake and celebration to wonder why Nobuo takes refuge in his room.

The noise of merriment follows him up the stairs, mixed with the soldier's song Kiichi had sung that time. The crowd downstairs is singing it in chorus now. A close-up of Nobuo's tear-stained face translates that noise to Kiichi singing. This simple transfer of reference fills us in on Shinpei's reason for that impulsive visit to the sea. Ironically, Kiichi's song awakened a host of painful wartime memories for Shinpei. The "singer" is a soldier on the Manchurian front. Surviving the hail of bullets that killed his buddy, he finds himself clutching a cruel souvenir, the fallen man's watch still ticking. Shinpei served in Manchuria too. Haunted by Keiichi's song, he had rushed to Maizuru, the port where he landed returning from Manchuria after Japan's defeat. Nobuo's face dissolves to the sound of Kiichi's singing. This shot suggests that a painful distance now separates the boys, that Kiichi's disembodied voice marks the dissolution of their bond.

The final sequence reworks the theme of innocence betrayed by experience. Here the motif of betrayal is doubly poignant, too. It is morning. Nobuo sprawls on the floor, refusing to go to the clown show. Here, as before, the world of fantasy has no appeal for a child withdrawing from the harsh reality of the world around him. We have seen Nobuo looking out windows any number of times, yearning for adventure into the unknown. Now it is his mother who looks out in time to see the houseboat leaving. Kiichi is leaving without saying goodbye. Nobuo, in a sulk, is getting even.

A cut to the outside shows that he could not go through with it. As he runs to catch up with the boat, the camera records every stumble and obstacle in his way. The effect is a bit too conscientious as the picture bumps along in tandem with this breathless, boyishly awkward, futile chase. The flow of the river, too, is glimpsed from a number of angles, a hectic effect in stark contrast to the stills that began the film. The river flows on down to the sea, taking the houseboat out of sight.

The ending credits flash in front of a fixed shot of the river flowing under the bridge where the houseboat was moored. Here at last, plot and symbols come to rest in this vanishing point—all the fantasies shared, promises made and broken, mishaps endured, and misunderstandings unresolved. This friendship was fleeting, but Nobuo has grown, nurtured by joy and sorrow. Like the old woman says of him, he is "a plant living in the water."

On the whole, *Muddy River* reminds us that the narrative and stylistic forms and formulae of Japanese cinema do not have to be innovative or experimental to command audience interest. Oguri works wonders with simple storytelling and conventional symbols that resonate with his native audience and arouse complex emotions. Given a modicum of exposure to Japanese culture, other audiences too can engage with the drama and nostalgia Oguri manages so artfully.[12]

–8–
Satire on the Family and Education in Postwar Japan

Yoshimitsu Morita's *The Family Game* (1983)

YOSHIMITSU MORITA (b. 1950) is known as a director whose success is based on sound commercial instincts. His first feature-length film was right on the money, and for good reason, or so he later claimed. "It's no good making a film the director just wants to make. I made *Something Like Yoshiwara* aiming at a box office hit."[1] *Something Like Yoshiwara* (No yō na mono, 1981) was a comedy celebrating youth's freedoms, aspirations, and boundless energy. Its odd-couple protagonists were in tune with the 1980s zeitgeist, too: she is an attendant at a Turkish bathhouse; he is an apprentice in the traditional art of *rakugo* comic storytelling.[2]

Like many of his generation, Morita edged into mainstream filmmaking by way of documentaries. His first was *POSI-?* (1970), a silent slapstick, twenty-minute short in 8 mm black and white. He went on to make twenty-one such films in the 1970s, all as an independent. The most highly acclaimed was the last, *Live-In Chigazaki* (Raibu-in Chigazaki, 1978). Morita brought a refreshing lively touch to this party film about youths savoring youth in Chigasaki, a coastal getaway far from the hectic metropolis. Morita's savvy subtitle hit the mark too: "A New Entertainment Film."

Morita's eighteen feature films since *Something Like Yoshiwara* testify to his versatility and creative acumen. *And Then* (Sorekara, 1995) and *Lost Paradise* (Shitsurakuen, 1997) are *bungei eiga* (adaptations of literary works). The former draws on the Meiji novelist Sōseki Natsume (1867–1916); the latter on Atsushi Watanabe's best-seller.[3] His two recent horror thrillers, *Copycat Killer* (Mohō han, 2002) and *The Black House* (Kuroi ie, 1997), are in line with major studio emphasis on staying in touch with shifts in audience taste.

Morita's gift for pleasing continues, though critics and the general public still give pride of place to *The Family Game* (Kazoku gēmu, 1983). Japan's prestigious journal *Kinema junpō* ranked it first on a list of that year's ten best pictures—not a bad outcome for a film shot in eighteen days by a thirty-three-year-old directing his fifth commercial feature. Morita's uniquely bold approach took the so-called family drama to a new level in the 1980s. In fact, any appreciation of his achievement must begin with a few examples from this wide-ranging genre.

A director such as Kōhei Oguri gives his somewhat idealized view of family life the benefit of a step back in generation. As discussed earlier, *Muddy River* (1981) is set in the post–Korean War period, which he considers most relevant to his own experience. His nostalgic looking backward celebrates traditional values of tightly knit family life poor in material goods yet rich in spirit and human affection.

Yōji Yamada's series of films titled *It's Tough Being a Man* (Otoko wa tsurai yo), commonly known as *Tora-san,* exhibits the same values in a comic setting. Begun in 1969, these features starring the good-natured protagonist Tora numbered thirty-six installments by 1985. (The series ended in 1996 with the forty-eighth installment.) Actually, the studio policy in this area is fairly restrictive, reflecting a longstanding commitment to the *shomingeki* genre of films depicting lower-middle-class family life. Within these constraints, Yamada manages to affirm values of familial solidarity still intact in contemporary Japan. Tora is a peddler, an antihero who falls in love with a beautifully new heroine in each episode only to find himself perpetually rejected. His family consists of a younger sister, her husband, and her child, along with an aunt and an uncle, all living in downtown Tokyo. He is cast back on the bosom of his family when the given romance does not work out. Here, family represents security, which even the scapegrace vagabond can count on when the chips are down.

Not so the hero of Mitsuo Yanagimachi's *Farewell to the Land* (Saraba itoshiki daichi, 1982). This young director presents a Japanese family in a state of total moral bankruptcy. Gone are all the relationships and values fostered by traditional Confucian virtues. One critic has observed that all the family moorings that should hold the hero Yukio in place "are torn apart by his compelling, if often incomprehensible, rage."[4]

We can be sure that family life is under siege when even gangsters lose control of their kith and kin. This happens in *Hishakaku* (Karyūin Hanako no shōgai, 1982), directed by Hideo Gosha (1929–2001). The hero here is a Yakuza boss whose authority is undermined by two rebellious daughters. It may be well to mention that the Yakuza genre film has had less reason than many others to strain for effect, since it continues to do well at the box office in a decade of diminishing returns for the cinema industry as a whole. Gosha's film, like many before his, is set in the early Showa period, though he distinguishes himself with this dynamic portrayal of Yakuza patriarchy on the decline.

The more timeless dilemma of old age is revived in *A Song about Flowers* (Hana ichimonme, 1985) by a veteran director from Tōei, Shunya Itō (b. 1937). The same theme was treated by Shirō Toyoda in *Twilight Years* (Kokotsu no hito, 1973) in a familiar vein, since taking in an aged grandparent presents ageless problems to the nuclear family. Itō, however, is less resigned in his approach, presenting a tragic ending more in tune with present-day doubts about the power of family to shield us from the horrors of final helplessness.

After a twelve-year absence, Yoshishige (Kijū) Yoshida returned to directing with a similar theme in *The Promise* (Ningen no yakusoku, 1986). This is a powerful study of senile decay and the anguish it engenders, which extends to two younger generations facing the terrifying dilemma of euthanasia.

Given such full measure of anxiety about contemporary Japanese family life, it is a relief to encounter the rich vein of comic satire on the subject found in Yoshimitsu Morita's *The Family Game*. Together with Yojirō Takita's 1988 slapstick satire, *The Yen Family* (Kimurake no hitotachi), which concerns a Japanese suburban family dedicated to aggressive materialism, *The Family Game* explores Morita's powerful satirical bent aimed at two issues in postwar Japan: affluent, middle-class nuclear family life in the city and nose-to-the-grindstone education systems generally. Let us see how he achieves this desired effect.

Morita's Satirical Tools: Icons and Ciphers

The Family Game takes its cues from ordinary life at home and at school, using sets and camera angles carefully arranged to produce caricature visions whose effect is laughably schematic and at the same time oddly expressive. This blend gains strength from the fact that family and education in postwar Japan developed a new and powerful interdependency. The anthropologist Ted Bestor explains it this way:

> Despite the ideological overlay of the idealized *ie* that the Meiji Civil Code imposed throughout society, in urban areas at least the reality of family life very quickly approximated the nuclear family. The urban family was smaller, it lacked generational depth, and it tended not to be a unit of production. Lacking property or an occupation that could be passed on, concern over inheritance and succession was lessened, but attention to children's education became paramount since education provided the only means for a wage-earner to invest in his offspring's future.[5]

Elsewhere, Bestor describes the tendency of the smaller modern family to intensify relations in new ways:

> [O]ne characteristic of nuclear family systems is that they heighten the emotional intensity of family life in part simply because each individual has fewer other family members with whom to interact. One consequence is that marital relationships become more fragile and divorce rates increase; another result where men work outside the home (especially true in Japan, where the "embrace" of the job is so complete) is that women's emotional lives become increasingly focused on their children and mother-child bonds become progressively closer.[6]

In order to pursue a satirical bent yielding a thought-provoking ending, Morita counts heavily on three powerful tools: rich icons of postmodern society, ciphering in the creation of his characters, and a parody of the classical Western narrative formula. Significantly, as we shall see, *The Family Game* generates a rhetorical stance directly opposite to the one we expect from satire. The definitive detachment of the mode is constantly undercut by direct emotional involvement of the viewer. Since the majority of Japan's theatergoing audience is quite young, *The Family Game* addresses problems with a high recognition value in the 1980s. Like Morita's earlier box office success *Something Like Yoshiwara,* this film puts the viewer within easy reach of individual characters instantly recognizable as present-day types in present-day situations. The satiric exaggerations never obscure that frame of reference, as we shall see.

From the outset, *The Family Game* is rich in icons of postmodern society. Morita's case-history family, the Numata household, is nuclear with a vengeance, consisting of father, mother, and two teenage sons living an almost schematically rigid and confining life in an atmosphere of heartless, high-tech get-aheadism. The opening scene shows them seated, all facing the camera, at a long, rectangular table. This piece of furniture could never yield the feeling of togetherness and intimacy of a more traditional round or square in Japan. Moreover, we see a family entirely absorbed in the business of eating. The sense that each is incommunicado is conveyed especially through the appalling manners of father and younger son. Their slurping and chewing take the place of conversation on the soundtrack, echoing the younger son's remarks with which this scene has begun: "The noise is too much for me; it shakes the whole house."

In a later scene, husband and wife are shown sitting side by side in the car, resolutely facing straight ahead. Again, their almost comical rigidity speaks of lack of communication and affection. When Mrs. Numata begins to reminisce about their carefree honeymoon days, her unresponsive spouse shuts her up.

The context of this family's life enlarges as we head for their apartment with the tutor, Yoshimoto. The camera surveys his route. A boat brings him across Tokyo Bay to a large middle-class apartment block *(danchi)* on reclaimed land out in the water. High-rises and industrial, artificial land-scapes define the environment—and the values—of this middle-class family.

At one point, the elder son, Shin'ichi, visits a girlfriend's house and comments admiringly on the industrial vista visible from the windows. Moreover, the brothers' appreciation of nature is only through the posters of scenic wonders that adorn Shigeyuki's room. The boy himself is most often seen (by the camera) partly obscured by a huge Spacewarp roller coaster model. At school he plays on Astroturf.

Throughout the film, these easily identifiable icons add up to an indict-ment of contemporary family life as foredoomed to fail, thanks to the "com-partmentalization" and "ciphering" they include. We see this, for example, in the food server being wheeled from one person to another at the dread-ful rectangular table, itself unmistakably analogous to assembly-line life in Japanese factories peopled by well-regimented automatons. Even the chil-dren's room is neatly divided by glass partitions. The effect is spanking clean, smart, abstract, and utterly heartless. Such a room is no more convincingly lived-in than a trade-show exhibit or model home module. Even an every-day apartment in a modern high-rise would offer more in the way of com-fort and humane clutter.

The tutor looking for the Numata household is led on a know-noth-ing chase by neighbors who clearly know one another only as apartment unit numbers, not actual people. In an interview, Morita has said that he deliberately made use of ciphers in creating his characters.[7] Thus the ency-clopedia of flora is a cipher for the tutor. The carton of soybean milk *is* the father, as the hobby leatherwork she does *is* the mother. This is civilization defined by its artifacts, not by its discontents. The eldest son, Shin'ichi, seems unnaturally defined by his telescope and cards for solitaire. His brother Shigeyuki is "indexed" by the Spacewarp model.

The Central Problem and Choices of Action: Morita's Characterization and Parody of the Classical Western

Given so many cartoon caricature cues about the impersonal, high-tech society surrounding the Numatas, we are anything but surprised to see them "realize" the title of this film by playing a game that Donald Richie defines as "an enactment the members agree to go through with, a set-up filled with tricks and dodges, a kind of gamble the results of which are not serious."[8] In this case, "not serious" refers us to the kind of world in which real choice is conspicuously absent. The very idea of being true to oneself is dismissed as wishy-washy fantasy in this "real world" of competitive drives and goals demanding absolute conformity to type.

This relates to the central problem of the film: how does each brother come to terms with his life as a student and son? The choice of action revolving around it is to be a model son and student, or to be a delinquent son and student. As mentioned above, the path to success means non-choice between them. Each brother is demanded to be an absolute cog in the system of get-aheadism with no derailment from the elite course whatsoever. However, the film's action charts out each brother's vacillation between conformity and rebellion, with emphasis on the reversal of roles, as we shall see.

Shin'ichi is initially presented as the model elder son, having made it into the best high school, one step closer to that "best" university. But there is the price to pay. The camera returns again and again to his telescope and games of solitaire. Clearly, this home, like his school, is so dedicated to competitive discipline that the boy seeks solace in the silent dialogue of cards and in nature in its remote, astronomical aspects. One might say that his world of featureless concrete high-rises built on the rubble of reclaimed land leaves him anxious to escape to the last frontier of nature as yet unravaged by man. His chances of communing with nature, even so, seem in doubt at the end of the film with its image of a helicopter fly-by, complete with whumping roar.

Yet Shin'ichi does attempt to rebel against his role as model elder brother. He comes home to find his kid brother comfortably ensconced with the tutor. The camera studies his reaction carefully, registering the older boy's longing for companionship. Inevitably, he seeks balance through a girlfriend—a classmate of poor academic standing. He quickly learns to play the truant. Shin'ichi finds little joy in this release, however. A close-up of his notebook shows that he is not focused. As we shall see, the final sequence shows his conversion to a cog in the strict educational system— the role assigned to the elder son.

Significantly, Morita's savage fun of role-playing is extended to the other members of the family. Each is also forced to enact a "model" role as it is understood in this world of hard-edged absolutes. Mr. Numata is your typical management-level white-collar workaholic. Next to his own suc-

cess he rates his son's. Absolutely required is a first-rate high school followed by a first-rate college. This recipe for success must be guaranteed by
hiring just the right tutor, who is given incentives in the form of a bonus
for improved exam scores in each subject.

The pace of Mr. Numata's work life is shown through his domestic life.
His wife begs him to come home earlier once in a while at least, but of
course working after hours is *de rigueur* for the competitive executive. What
connubial talk there is, is all business. Significantly enough, the venue for
confidential talk is not the traditional marriage bed, but the family car. All
of Mr. Numata's escape mechanisms are comically infantile and confining.
Relaxing at home, he soaks in a tiny tile tub, sucking his soybean milk from
a toy-size carton. He is even a confirmed sucker of eggs easy, sunny-side
up, berating his wife if her timing is off enough to spoil his slurpy fun. One
does not have to be much of an amateur psychologist to see the ready-made
formula here: hard-driving executive sublimating desire for escape into
infantile dependency.

Mrs. Numata, of course, is expected to function as wife, housewife, and
mother in charge of whiz kid educational outcomes in this ideal nuclear
family living on the hard competitive edge. She is notably ineffective in all
her roles. (Perhaps Morita meant to underscore a point by casting the thirty-
five-year-old Yuki Sayuri as mother of fifteen-and sixteen-year-old sons.)
Her very appearance is that of a mannequin. Certainly she shows no signs
of being the *"kyōiku mama"* fanatically dedicated to schooling. Aggressive
decision making is not her strong suit. Asked by Shigeyuki's teacher which
high school he should attend, she reaches for a name and ends up suggesting a second-rate one. Corrected by her husband later, she cannot bring
herself to tell the teacher that the family has made another choice. She
delegates the tutor to do this for her.

The younger son takes full advantage of his mother's fecklessness. He
gets out of going to class by feigning sickness. In any case, her interest in
his tutorial sessions is limited to serving refreshments. She falters even there
when his grades improve. She seems entirely unable to relate to her children, being too shallow and conventional. When the younger son asks a
question about menstruation, she cuts him off by saying, "Stop talking nonsense."

There is an odd moment of togetherness with the elder boy, Shin'ichi.
Mrs. Numata is listening to *My Fair Lady*. The song "I Could Have Danced
All Night" reminds her of the happy moment when she and her husband
were engaged and saw the film together. Naturally, the son does not know
old-timers like Audrey Hepburn, so the moment passes into the mainstream

of indifferent family feeling. It is interesting to note that the soundtrack does not pick up the actual music of *My Fair Lady*. This seems a good enough index of failed communication—even when the studious critic knows that Morita has admitted to saving money on the permissions this way!

Her family being such cold fish, one might expect Mrs. Numata to welcome a female friend when one appears. A neighbor lady tries her best, and is even invited in on one occasion. But she refuses to sit "in a row." For the first time, we see the Numata table line-up broken as the women sit opposite one another. The woman says that Mrs. Numata is in fact the only person in the building who has spoken to her, even casually. But a nodding acquaintance is all that ever develops. Mrs. Numata is too involved in the family game to have time for her neighbor's pressing problems—among them a crowded apartment shared with an ailing father-in-law whose prospective coffin, it is feared, may not fit in their building's small elevator. Mrs. Numata prefers her hobby of tooling leather to any friendly intimacy. We see how immune she is to fellow feeling: a thoroughly postmodern mother not bothered at all by the alienation and emptiness of her life.

Initially, Shigeyuki plays the role delegated to him: the student and son inferior to the elder brother. However, a similar transformation in the younger son takes center stage. His academic progress is charted through the shift from a delinquent to a model type then back to his initial status. Morita explores this in what amounts to a parody version of the classical Western picture formula. Films such as *Shane* (1953), *Dodge City* (1939), and *Duel in the Sun* (1946) feature a hero "who is somewhat estranged from a social group, but on whose ability rests the fate of that social group."[9] Shigeyuki's tutor, Yoshimoto, is that hero in this case. He is the stranger from out of town who plays his own game and gets the job done. He rescues the Numata family from the social and material disaster of having an unsuccessful son.

Morita makes clear use of a wilderness/civilization scheme of polarities to build this mock-Western pattern. The name Numata, incidentally, means "swampy field," or "marsh," surely the *locus classicus* for giving civilization its head start in soft and mushy ground. Modern developers understand these basics well, as witnessed by the landfill miracle in Tokyo Bay. The opening sequence shows Yoshimoto arriving from the sea. As he approaches this manmade island, a shot of him standing in the small boat takes in the natural landscape behind. He asks for the Numatas by name, with little luck, since residents of this area know one another only by apartment number.

Clearly, this stranger is out of place in this hub of impersonal, competitive, postmodern society. As it turns out, Yoshimoto is a clear instance of limited intellect, an undergraduate of a third-rate university still unable to graduate. He is obviously denied access to the material success and social status enjoyed by his pupil's father. His limitations are comically apparent at the outset, when he and Shigeyuki sit down to a standard text for classical Japanese at the high school level. Yoshimoto's progress through the opening passage of Basho's travel diary, *Oku no honomichi* (The narrow road of Oku, 1689) cannot fail to raise laughter from survivors of high school classical Japanese.

Yet Yoshimoto's limitations are powerfully balanced by the gifts this high-tech civilization has left behind. He combines genuine human warmth with old-fashioned physical discipline. He goes along with the family penchant for sitting side by side—a conformation expressive of their want of intimacy. Yet when Yoshimoto comes on the scene, he kisses his pupil on the cheek, sits close, and whispers in the boy's ear like an affectionate father might.[10] Morita himself has commented on this whispering as a deliberate effect. It is an apt device to convey that the tutor's wisdom is creating a "world of the two" for himself and the boy. As we see in the film, their course of study is a school of hard knocks, quite literally, but when time

Yoshimoto (l., Yūsaku Matsuda) and Shigeyuki (r., Ichirota Miyagawa) in *The Family Game* (1983). © ATG, Nikkatsu and New Century Producers.

comes for the exam, we see Yoshimoto giving his pupil a piggyback ride as students gather outside the high school they hope to attend.

Morita provides clue after clue to Yoshimoto's identity as a back-to-nature hero. He is seldom seen without his floral encyclopedia. And he knows how to deliver physical discipline. The camera captures Shigeyuki's surprised face with a bloody nose in close-up when he is first hit. This is not brutality so much as injury with understanding. Yoshimoto sees how Mrs. Numata's mollycoddling approach has not done the job. The bloody nose becomes badge of honor and success. Yoshimoto teaches Shigeyuki how to stand up for himself at school, where he has been bullied. We see him deliver a bloody nose there. And in a late scene, after his exam scores have improved, Shigeyuki jokes about not wanting to see his own nose bloodied again.

Though the immediate goal is passed, we see quite plainly the future of unrelenting study that awaits the student who seeks entrance into college. On his first day with Yoshimoto we see Shigeyuki ordered to copy out the *kanji* letters he is not sure of. He rebels, repeating two letters signifying *yūgure* (dusk). A series of close-ups views the evidence: literally thousands of letters filling page after page. The image itself will carry weight with all who remember the long, drawn-out purgatory of cramming and memorizing that awaits the aspiring high school student.

A more concrete image is the Spacewarp model featured in Shigeyuki's room. It is the perfect construct of the life mapped out for him. He must not be "derailed." All must go swiftly and smoothly along the given, if perilously "warped," course from elite schooling to college to status and security in the work place. Just as the Spacewarp ball returns to its terminal only to start up again, the endless circle of fierce competitiveness must be pursued without letup.

Without a tutor like Yoshimoto, a student might well fail to "win the game." Morita shows how this works outside the home in the academic context. A teacher returns exams to students, beginning with the lowest score. It is a girl, who covers her head with a paper bag. Several more bottom-ranking names are called as exams are tossed out the window. A high-angle long shot takes note of several male students retrieving them from the Astroturf of the playground. Oddly enough, they betray no signs of emotion at having failed at the game. In fact, we suspect that they accept their failure with a kind of relish.

Shigeyuki's teacher exemplifies the cold, impersonal world of the education system. Like Shigeyuki's father at home, he is a creature of rules and regulations, a stranger to kindness and imagination. Nothing could be further removed from the benevolent father/mentor figure, who might otherwise be in charge of a young person's future.

Some students, of course, rebel against this mechanical system of future-by-scorecard education. Shin'ichi escapes into fantasy-world drawings of trees—close contact with nature being denied these children of the high-tech world. Shigeyuki himself seems to play the role of underachieving younger brother without overt emotion. Yet as he toys with his ballpoint in class, the camera plays a close-up trick, which makes the point take on a fearsome hypodermic sharpness.

Yet thanks to his tutor, Shigeyuki learns to cope more actively with his unkind fate. During his fight with the bullying Tsuchiya the camera remains notably detached, letting the environment dominate the small combatants. Ironically they fight on honest ground—the dirt of a vacant lot, not the Astroturf of the playground. We sense, even so, that this land will soon enough fall prey to the city's building boom, as a bus running nearby suggests, and that these fighting boys are engaged in man-to-man combat that is nothing at all like a childhood game.

Shigeyuki's story also encompasses a sad little tale of childhood friendship spoiled by the fierce competitive drive nurtured in youths designed for elite schools. The bully he fights was Shigeyuki's best friend when they were small. By the time they reach high school age, rivalry has made them deadly enemies. Tsuchiya is the more aggressive, and apparently much more worldly wise: seeking to distract his rival at examination time, he sends Shigeyuki a bundle of X-rated magazines.

Morita's gift for sentimental shots is used to sketch the history of this lost friendship. As Shin'ichi explains it to the tutor in the house, a series of crosscuts alternates between the Numatas' repellently impersonal apartment and a landscape along a river bathed in the reflections of a beautiful sunset. The tiny figures of Shigeyuki and Tsuchiya stroll into this harmonious vista and blend with it as Shin'ichi's voice-over continues to describe the reasons for their rift. This scene is charged with sentimental overtones—a sense of nostalgia and of loss and rue for what might have been.

Thanks to Yoshimoto's tutelage, Shigeyuki emerges as a successful student, yet victory in the educational "game" does not mean capitulation on the part of this outsider. The final sequence of the film ironically affirms the syntactic functions shared with the classical Western narrative: the hero has been accepted by the social group, but leaves that society. Here the leave-taking is parodied by a farcical upset at the dinner celebrating Shigeyuki's success on the entrance exam. The tutor lashes out at the father and in the ensuing commotion sweeps away an expensive meal in what becomes a general free-for-all. Asked to explain this episode, Morita has said that the idea just suddenly hit him, that's all. Yet the critic, always rubbernecking for an answer, sees an internal consistency in this scene. Yoshimoto represents a hero plainly suggestive of Henry Thoreau's famous dictum that "in wildness is the preservation of the world." His disorderly conduct at the dinner spreads to the others, who for once in this brief melee allow their pent-up emotions to escape the rigidly compartmentalized limits of their postmodern society. In brief, they all yearn for return to childhood, and briefly act childish according to that wish.

Ironically, this farcical interlude works to bring the family together in a new way. They all end up on the floor, having left the rectangular table where so often we have seen them seated in a row. At the close of this scene we see them working together to clean up the mess. For the first time we perceive a significant small moment of physical intimacy as father and son *almost* touch hands reaching for the same beer bottle.

That charm is soon broken, however, as the camera cuts to the sunset over Tokyo Bay and Yoshimoto, like a departing gunslinger, turning his back on it and the surrounding high-rises in a mirror image of his arrival on the scene. The tutor's departure again opens up another crucial question:

Mrs. Numata (l., Sayuri Yuki), Mr. Numata (c.l., Jūzo Itami), Yoshimoto (c., Yūsaku Matsuda), Shigeyuki (c.r., Ichirota Miyagawa), and Shin'ichi (r., Jun'ichi Tsuchida) in *The Family Game* (1983). © ATG, Nikkatsu and New Century Producers.

how does the Numata family fare without some touch of wilderness in their lives? The central problem of the film is brought full circle in the next few scenes through a process of role reversal. A cut to the classroom puts Shige-yuki in a new context. His brother's English teacher is now his, but Shige-yuki is not doing well. He sits doodling in his notebook, reverting to the old days in junior high school when he played the sulking delinquent.

We know that his elder brother, Shin'ichi, is a rebel twice over, refusing to be a model son or student. His story now takes a different turn, beginning with a view of his bottoming out in sad isolation. The camera catches up with him at a karate club exhibition. The ranks of young men in uniform are seen engaged in regimented practice with perfectly timed precision. Shin'ichi crosses the background, alone, in casual clothes. The camera even takes him out of focus, as if to reinforce our sense of his solitary aloofness at school as at home. The following shot underscores this impression, coming to rest on an empty field and a bus.

That same shot also serves to mark a transition in Shin'ichi's decision making. The camera cuts to a karate practice room (dōjō) with club members clattering in the foreground. A gliding search singles out Shin'ichi in the background. For the first time we see him seated ceremoniously in front of the national flag. He has joined the club. This brings him full circle: the model student now belongs to the rigorously regimented elite. His future lies before him, mapped out precisely. Whether or not he will find the kind of camaraderie he desires is left open to question by Morita.

Stylistic Devices and the Final Scene

As mentioned before, Morita's mode of representation is highly satirical and cartoon-like throughout this film. Donald Richie claims that this thematic orientation, along with the extremely complex and stylized cinematography, creates a distancing "reminiscent of the Brechtian alienation effect" (Verfremdungseffekt).[11] However, for those like myself who have endured the punishing regime of the Japanese educational system, *The Family Game* evokes a rather ambivalent rhetorical stance. Call it emotional involvement combined with intellectual detachment—yielding a state of vacillation between the two. To begin with, Morita deliberately presents dramatic actions at a "technical distance." The Numata household itself suggests a model home display. In its confines, the characters do more role-playing than real "live" living. Mrs. Numata is more mannequin than mom. Even the children lack spontaneity. Shin'ichi and his girlfriend together seem oddly unsexed and remote from emotional involvement.

It is interesting, too, that Morita carefully avoids reverse-field setups. His characters are most often presented frontally, as they might appear to the audience in a theater. Scenes of emotional climax—like the one of the two boys fighting in the field—are seen from far away. Even the beautifully sentimental long shots of Shigeyuki and his pal Tsuchiya walking by the river are insistently artificial. The boys are in harmony with the scene, yet unmistakably detached, as if walking in front of a stage set or a huge landscape painting.

Even so, these theatrical artificialities are strongly counterbalanced by the universal emotional appeal of the characters, as one critic observes: "The basic distinction between the inside and outside view, then, is whether our attention is directed most strongly towards singularizing attributes or the universalizing problems of a character."[12] Their farcical or deadpan behavior is always clearly attached to a point of satire the Japanese audience can readily identify. Morita's critical jabs at family and educational systems provide ample reminders of the lack of warmth, individuality, and comradeship at home and work and school, so the evidence mounts in favor of empathy for his characters, however idiosyncratic their behavior. As a result, the film proceeds by way of constantly changing inside/outside views of the matter.

Perhaps the strongest evidence for this complex rhetorical oscillation between emotional and intellectual responses comes in the unpredictable, perplexing conclusion of the film. Morita prepares us for it with some carefully worked intermediate spaces for a three-stage transition. The first shot takes in the huge industrial complex near the Numata's apartment complex. A second shot studies two huge oil tanks rising above the industrial scene, as if in answer to apartment buildings as upwardly featureless in the human sense. The third shot takes note of a motorboat crossing the bay. The tutor's arrival and departure in such a small boat inevitably brings him to mind. Thoughts of him, and these other familiar sites reviewed, inevitably move the viewer to complex re-considerations of the matter at hand.

Oddly enough, the negative resonances here do not yield a feeling of unrelieved melancholy. They are introduced just after we see Shin'ichi give in and become a mere cog in the educational system. The first two shots echo his earlier remark (in his girlfriend's room) on the beauty of the industrial landscape in view from the windows. Morita's camera endows the scene with a picture-postcard appeal, so that we are eased perhaps more gracefully into accepting this boy's conformity, his "realistic" acceptance of the life that lies before him. What then of Yoshimoto, who has vanished from the scene, having helped Shigeyuki on his way to becoming yet another cog in the wheel? We can only watch the motorboat speed away empty and wonder how the Numatas will fare without this touch of "wilderness" in their lives.

As might be expected, the motorboat yields to a cut to the Numatas' apartment. The final scene consists of only two shots, the second being a long take of almost five minutes. First we are introduced to a peaceful domestic scene. The time of day is unclear, but Mrs. Numata sits alone with a piece of hobby leatherwork. She taps her shoulder with the little hammer, absent-mindedly, possibly out of boredom. A helicopter's whumping roar outside invades the room, drowning out the hammer's gentle strokes, breaking the woman's reverie.

Framing her, the next long shot follows her motions around the house. She opens the door to the children's room and asks if they want an afternoon snack. Both lie sleeping. So far so good. This final scene seems reassuringly like our own everyday life in the city. We begin to feel more at ease with the Numatas and their life. Our intellectual resistance to its limitations yields to a feeling of affinity that Morita has prepared us for with medium and medium-long shots, establishing us as invited guests, as it were, in this house. Then Mrs. Numata opens a window. The helicopter's noise roars in that much louder, and with it somehow a revived sense of detachment and critical scrutiny. She returns to her leatherwork, only to lean forward on the table and fall asleep. The camera backtracks to a long shot, then moves slowly around the kitchen, panning along the table. Our final glimpse of the Numata household consists of the mother asleep on the half-bare rectangular table stretching away screen right. The helicopter noise swells nearer, louder.

What are we to make of this, the helicopter especially? We feel our curiosity aroused and a vague sense of unease. Is this just a reprise reminiscent of the opening scene of the family glurping and slurping at the dinner table. Then Shigeyuki did say, "Everyday the noise is too much for us." Or is this a hovering, satirical reference to noise pollution? Another metaphor, this time and loud and clear, for the drowning out of human communication? That was a major concern at the outset of the film, and the likely success of the Numata children in this world seems unlikely to change it much for the better. Interestingly enough, scraps of dialogue from major scenes in the film are given in voice-over here, as if to offer a quick recap of the narrative, but then the sound of the "chopper" quite literally takes the dialogue to pieces, reducing speech—that most human dimension of all—to a helicopter roar.

If that interpretation seems too easy—even cozy—one might think of the helicopter as a poignant counterpoint to the Spacewarp model roller

Yoshimoto (c., Yūsaku Matsuda) in *The Family Game* (1983). © ATG, Nikkatsu and New Century Producers.

coaster. Our last glimpse of it was just before Shigeyuki's entrance examination. This mere toy is given foreground magnitude all out of proportion to its real size, so that tutor and pupil are blocked off behind it. A cut shows Yoshimoto behind it, playing its game. Yet another cut returns the toy to the wall. We are left with the sound of the ball speeding along the rails, as if to suggest a warped and empty velocity analogous to the vacuous, impersonal world in which Shigeyuki must play his "winning" game.

A Japanese audience will also inevitably associate the helicopter with Japan's Self-Defense Forces. Many there will also think of the Vietnam War and Tokyo University shaken by the radical student takeover of Yasuda Auditorium.[13]

Certainly this noisy piece of high-tech equipment hovering so near reminds us that the caricature makes fun of a game that is played for real. Those children asleep in their room are being fitted out for a kind of war in which even the fittest survive after a fashion that troubles us deeply. Thus, at the end of *The Family Game*, the temptation to lapse into easy fellow-feeling is withdrawn as we are stirred awake by intellectual alertness. Morita's cartoon comic book falls from our hands as we laugh uneasily, looking out again at a world of somber realities.

–9–
Defeat Revisited
Masahiro Shinoda's *MacArthur's Children* (1984)

THE NEW WAVE in Japanese cinema was more like a wavelet, a brief and loosely organized upset created by young new talent. They wanted to challenge the grand old masters with daring new treatments of issues faced by their postwar generation—the first to grow up in the shadow of Japan's defeat in World War II. Three titles and directors come to mind, all debuts at Shōchiku Studio: *A Town of Love and Hope* (Ai to kibō no machi, 1959) by Nagisa Ōshima (b. 1930), *One-Way Ticket for Love* (Koi no katamichi kippu, 1960) by Masahiro Shinoda (b. 1931), and *Good for Nothing* (Roku-denashi, 1960) by Yoshishige Yoshida (b. 1933).[1] Young as these directors were, it is no surprise that youth, sex, and identity topped their list of subjects in need of full, fair, and frankly shocking disclosure. More subtly disturbing issues came later, as each matured in his own way and the New Wave leveled out in the early 1970s.

Among the three, Shinoda has been most prolific, with thirty-some films to his credit. His most recent work is *Spy Sorge* (Zoruge, 2003), which concerns espionage during World War II. His mature career can be seen taking shape as early as 1969 with *Punishment Island* (Shokei no shima). This adaptation of the novel by Shintarō Ishihara (now the governor of Tokyo) probes the deeply damaging effects of the system on the young. The juvenile delinquents on a remote island are terrorized by a sadistic former officer of the military police. Among his victims is a boy whose family the officer had killed in the line of duty. This grimly forensic look at injustice foreshadows Shinoda's lifelong interest in films that explore his core conviction that societies victimize the individual.

Not surprisingly, he is drawn to scripts that explore moral dilemmas. Twice he has taken scripts from the classic playwright Monzaemon Chikamatsu (1653–1725): *Double Suicide* (Shinjū ten no amijima, 1969) and *Gonza the Spearman* (Yari no Gonza, 1986). Both these domestic dramas unfold the tragedy of a man and woman destroyed by the basic incompatibility between *giri* (social obligation) and *ninjō* (personal needs) in an oppressive feudal society.[2] *The Dancing Girl* (Maihime, 1989), based on Ōgai Mori's story of the same title, explores that dilemma in a Meiji-era setting. In this case, an intellectual is irreconcilably torn between demands of individual freedom and social norms still based on feudal moral absolutes.[3]

MacArthur's Children (Setouchi shōnen yakyūdan, 1984) updates Shinoda's concern in a drama closer to home in every sense. Born in 1931, he passed from boyhood to manhood at a time when Japan suffered not just war and defeat but peacetime recovery bought at a price of momentous change rife with peril for all Japanese, his own generation especially. This film can be seen as the first in a trilogy on its subject, the other two being *Childhood Days* (Shōnen jidai, 1991) and *Setouchi Moonlight Serenade* (Setouchi mūnraito serenāde, 1995).

Shinoda's abiding concern with his generation's struggle is addressed in a comment to an interviewer in 1986: "I was willing to sacrifice my life for the emperor. Ever since then I have wondered about the root of my patriotism. It is still an enigma to me. How can such absolutism take hold in any individual? Why did this moral imperative persist in Japan as a social phenomenon?"[4] *MacArthur's Children* asks those questions through a story set in a world Shinoda first learned about by being young in it. What answers did he find, looking back from the vantage point of maturity? How did he present them?

Central Problem and Choices of Action

The opening credits roll in front of a crowded schoolyard. The entire student body is listening to the emperor's momentous broadcast of August 15, 1945. Japan has lost the war.[5] The schoolboy Ryūta's voice-over speaks of this calamity. A rapid-fire montage offers an eclectic mixture of historical reference points to put this scene in context. Clips of actual newsreel coverage sample black and white images fraught with pain for Japanese of Shinoda's generation and older. We glimpse General MacArthur arriving in Japan, the iconic skeletal dome in Hiroshima, war orphans and repatriate soldiers loitering in a railway station, and the signing of the treaty of surrender on the battleship *Missouri*. This bleak historical scrapbook is relieved somewhat by a curious touch on the soundtrack toward the end: a jaunty mix of a Japanese popular song from the postwar years with Glenn Miller's wartime hit "In the Mood."

A dissolve trades that scattershot view of history for the sobering continuity of a schoolroom tour. These children of the occupation are busily crossing out all textbook references to Japan's prewar nationalism. Linda Ehrlich makes this insightful comment on the opening of the film:

> Covering such serious issues with a lighter tone, Shinoda presents an Occupation period in which war trials and executions are mixed with baseball tournaments and with the semi-comical loss of precious black-market rice. Underneath this deceptively smooth surface, however, *MacArthur's Children* stresses the essential role of the inner strength of the Japanese people in the success of the American Occupation.[6]

Ehrlich's view connects to the central problem of the film and the ensuing choices of action revolving around it. The majority of filmic actions are seen from the perspective of schoolchildren, often with voice-over narration by one of them. Still, the film has no hero or heroine, large or small. Its central "character" is collective; its view of the human condition in postwar Japan interweaves a number of individual histories in service of a central problem. That theme may be stated as the question Shinoda sees as haunting his generation still: how are the Japanese to come to terms with Japan's defeat and the ensuing Allied Occupation?

Shinoda's montage of case histories offers a sampling of Japanese society. The schoolchildren singled out for special attention are three war orphans: Ryūta, Saburō, and Mume, an admiral's daughter soon to be orphaned by his trial and execution for Class B war crimes. The schoolteacher Komako and the hairdresser Tome are war widows, though Komako's husband turns up later, a wounded soldier feeling inadequate in the confusion of repatriation. Though seen as representative, these are genuine individuals, not mere character types. Their histories exemplify different ways of coping with everyday workaday changes brought about, in part, by changes beyond their power to control. Shinoda offers them as "proof" of his considered opinion that their adaptability and ability to endure are irrevocably linked to "the inner strength of the Japanese people," as Ehrlich observes.[7] His eclectic method of presentation at the outset and throughout underscores another point, namely, that another measure of stress and success in this difficult time is flexibility—the need to assess and adjust to a changing society's changing values.

Shinoda was fourteen at the end of the war and well into middle age when he made this film in the prosperous Japan of 1984. Man and boy, he had seen the best of times and the worst of times. It makes sense that a hint of mellow nostalgia should find its way into this studied look back at a time he considered the most traumatic in his experience. That would explain the lighthearted tone of his film.

The story is set on Awaji, the largest island in the Island Sea (Setonaikai). Awaji itself was lucky, surviving the bombings virtually intact. Its people suffered nonetheless, survivors of war being never quite intact. The island has that to offer: a provincial small world seemingly unaffected, yet deeply affected, by turmoil in the world at large. This island community in a sea of postwar change is in no position to resist—though some on Awaji resist all they can. All must adapt. There is no other choice. Yet each and every individual must choose between two ways of adapting: that of the opportunist out for Number One or that of the moralist who values personal integrity and community.

Ironically, the latter choice is typified by the admiral tried and executed for his part in the war. Critics have given high praise to Jūzō Itami's portrayal of this stoic idealist. He is everything high-minded and good about a military man. He comes to the island to think and take stock, resigned to his fate. "I want to cleanse my soul in this idyllic place before I am tried," he says, and dies accordingly.

Komako's husband, Masao, the disabled veteran, is an idealist whose focus is on the future. He is willing to forget the past, transforming that bitter experience into purposeful action. He coaches a baseball team and lives in close communion with the earth. Awaji has always lived from the sea, but Masao sees that the future will be different, that the island must look to its hardscrabble land. And so, by force of hard work and ingenuity, he builds a new life in floriculture.

Barber-turned-hostess Tome (played by Shinoda's actress wife, Shima Iwashita) typifies the opportunist choice. Her gaudy bar takes full advantage of wealth soon lost by fishermen enriched by a quirk of the postwar economy. Jilted by a lover as heartless as herself, Tome leaves little Awaji in search of big-city money.

Saburō's brother and sister also leave the island, eager opportunists foiled by a black-market economy faltering in peacetime. Their outlandish Western outfits show what hicks they are, which is not to say they will not survive, maybe even thrive, in a dog-eat-dog mainland city.

There is nothing funny about Komako's opportunist brother-in-law Tetsuo. He is the polar opposite of his brother Masao. As far as Tetsuo is concerned, traditional values such as loyalty and filial piety are things of the past. When he cannot seduce his sister-in-law, he rapes her. That done, he joins the opportunist exodus.

Tetsuo's villainy is all the more odious because it violates standards of decency connected with Komako's immediate postwar dilemma. Her husband Masao has been given up for dead. Traditional family duty *(giri)* dictates that she marry his younger brother Tetsuo. Yet personal preference *(ninjō)* will not have it so. Tetsuo is a good-for-nothing, a man she knows she cannot love. Changing times and social mores and careers open to women all suggest leaving the family she married into in order to work and live as a single, independent woman. Reason and opportunity are on the side of this latter option; respect for tradition is against it. What can she do? Her dilemma is resolved by a convenience of plot: Masao, though disabled, returns, having survived the war after all. Yet Komako has a major part to play in this complex sampling of changing lives. Like her husband's, her vision of the future is rooted in sound traditional values and practical common sense. Like his, her sense of high moral purpose is expressed in work that aims to rebuild community.

At school, Komako is concerned with the welfare of three pupils most in need: Ryūta, Saburō, and Mume. How can she help them cope with so much change and feel hopeful about the future? She joins her husband in making baseball the medium for their message to this up-and-coming gen-

Teacher Komako (Masako Natsume) in *MacArthur's Children* (1984). © Asmik Ace Entertainment.

eration. Their coaching transforms the game into a major life lesson. Given the tendency to ironic self-awareness nowadays, this stratagem may strike us as simplistic, though Shinoda is perfectly serious about using baseball as the controlling metaphor for much of the film. He is also forthrightly schematic in his sampling of children orphaned by the war yet capable of survival, deserving of success in the end.

Ryūta, the head of his class, is from a solidly middle-class family. Having learned resignation from his grandfather, he seems able to let go of childish rage and fear. He burns his wartime drawings of battleships and fighter planes. They flicker in and out of sight as the camera pauses to study his face in a series of center front close-ups. He gives no sign of emotion. We are left to surmise what lies behind his look of sober reflection.

Saburō is the noisy, hyperactive one, a rebellious, mouthy casualty of poor background and wartime neglect. He is boyishly impressionable, too, open to every kind of change. Since he cannot become an admiral now, he tells Ryūta that he will be a gangster, a *baraketsu*. He quits school to learn from his brother and sister, both accomplished black-market cheats suspected of outright theft by the time they leave the island in a hurry. Saburō, deserted, returns to school. There he flourishes. Saburō is changed from juvenile delinquent to natural leader. He puts his knowledge of ill-gotten gains to honest, enterprising use. The baseball team needs equipment, so he spearheads the work it takes to pay for it.

Mume's future is the sad, uncertain one. As the daughter of an admiral, she has had upper-class advantages and it shows. She is also more mature in mind and body than the boys. (The camera takes careful note of actress Shiori Sakura's height and budding charms.) Yet she is more at risk for reasons of change. More will be required of her, as her name, "brave daughter," suggests. She measures up accordingly. Even though she is a privileged girl from Tokyo, she quickly gains acceptance in this insular community. Even after her father's trial and execution by the Allied Forces, she maintains a stoic equanimity. She does her part for the All Japan/U.S. baseball match.

Mume faces the future more resolutely than the others, too. When time comes to leave Awaji, she promises the grieving, uncertain Ryūta that they will meet again. Even if they do not attend the same college, she says, their work will help them keep in touch. Mume clearly speaks for Shinoda's social and political views on postwar Japan. Yet at times (as we shall see), his views partake of ambiguity, as when a brief montage uses a blown-up image of Mume's face to overshadow her father's ship.

Shinoda and Occupied Japan: Eclectic Ambiguity

Shinoda's backward look at occupied Japan seems fair enough and at times remarkably frank—the cinematic equivalent, say, of sorting through a box of family pictures or turning the pages of an old scrapbook. Here, the picture taker and scrapbook maker is present and accounting for his vision of the past. Sharing just naturally shades into reinterpretation, in this case, of the world of Shinoda's youth.

MacArthur's Children combines straightforward life histories with vignettes rich in signs of social, political, and cultural change. It also makes some use of studied ambiguity, as befits, since Shinoda is re-viewing (literally) what might be called a crisis of healing in Japanese history. No wonder viewers in the West need help catching his drift at times, as do some Japanese viewers now too young to have known such a different Japan. Shinoda mixes signs of change of every kind. Some are as momentous as footage of U.S. troops arriving to "occupy" Japan. Others are everyday trifles, like the surprising thing it was in those days to see lovers actually kissing in a film.

Shinoda's eclectic approach to crafting a scene results in a blend that allows us to share his sense that the past is present in us—the minute we see it "realized" on screen. He, of course, is in control of that realization. At times, as we have seen, his constructs may seem simplistic. At his best, however, Shinoda brings a light, forgiving touch to matters otherwise apt to be fraught with bitter memories.

His use of the soundtrack is especially delightful. American big band favorites such as "In the Mood" mix and mingle with Japanese popular songs. One of the latter was a golden oldie by 1984: "Apple Song" (Ringo no uta) was the guy-loves-gal hit sensation theme of the 1946 film *Breeze* (Soyokaze). Its simple, heartfelt lyric sent a message of hope to Japanese at a time when despair came easy. Shinoda uses it in three radically different contexts. The first involves the village's welcome reception for occupying American soldiers organized by Komako's father-in-law. When sinister, no-good Tetsuo rapes Komako in her room, a close-up of her tearful face is accompanied by the cheerful singing of guests in another part of the house. Later Tetsuo whistles it in the schoolyard, hoping to attract Komako's attention. During the village festival, Ryūta croons it to himself, waiting for his dear friend Mume to finish her business.

Tetsuo gets his satirical comeuppance in a play cobbled together by the hairdresser Tome's new beau, an actor who spent the war entertaining the troops overseas. Awaji's little theater is packed with eager locals. They get something like Kabuki set in feudal times, but no female impersonators. The heroine is played by Tome; the treatment is broadly comical. The plot takes its cues from village gossip, referring unmistakably to rumors that Tetsuo is out to seduce his sister-in-law Komako. As the actor onstage enacts his lover's declaration, the camera cuts to Tetsuo and his henchmen in the audience. He leaves amid riotous laughter. Here too, Shinoda cannot resist melding East and West, giving this stage performance music played on traditional *samisen* and a phonograph recording of Robert Schumann's "Träumerei."

The Japanese title *Setouchi shōnen yakyūdan* (Setouchi boys baseball team) clearly would not serve in the West, though something is lost in the "translation" to *MacArthur's Children,* namely, Shinoda's use of baseball as a controlling metaphor. On the most obvious level, baseball lends his theme of postwar change an instructive irony. After all, wars, like games, are won and lost, and in this case we have the inventors of baseball not just winning the war but coming to occupy Japan, which is to say, help the Japanese learn the rules of a "game" that will change their culture in a number of important ways. Linda Ehrlich reminds us that baseball "exemplifies the merging of Western technology and Japanese spirit that Japanese authorities had been espousing since the mid-1800s."[8]

The history of baseball in Japan dates back to 1877, when it was introduced by Hiroshi Hiraoka, who had returned from Boston. Two years later he established the Shinbashi Club Athletics, which was composed of railway workers and their American advisors.[9] Baseball quickly became a popular sport in Tokyo, as exemplified by the formation of college baseball teams. Professional baseball came much later, after an American Major League tour in 1934 exposed the Japanese to the likes of Babe Ruth and Lou Gehrig. By the time Shinoda made his film, Japanese baseball was "major league" in every way. Thanks to the boom economy, teams could compete with the large sums it took to fill in gaps with stars from the United States.

The value-added effect on goal-oriented youngsters East and West is too obvious to need comment. Non–Japan specialists, however, may need some help with cultural specifics. What, for example, does a rival coach mean when he says that Masao "made it to Kōshien" in his high school days? Every Japanese knows instantly that Kōshien is the stadium near Kobe that hosts the All-Japan high school tournament.

It goes without saying that the Japanese did not need baseball to teach them about team spirit. (By the time this film was made, the American automotive industry was learning new teamwork production techniques from the Japanese competition.) Values related to community solidarity run deep in Japan; in many respects they held fast, even in this time of radical post-war change. What baseball had to offer was a sporting chance to look ahead at the serious business of life in a more competitive world, a ritual enactment that had much to teach everyone concerned.

All of Awaji pitches in to help with the game. Here too, Shinoda takes full advantage of the eclectic possibilities. Male spectators cheer the team on with the help of drums used for local religious festivals. Dressed in gaudy Western outfits, Tome and her barmaids razz the men about the sexes being equal now. By the time the U.S.-Japan game is played, Mume's father has been executed. Saburō is willing to see it as a grudge match, but he is in the minority.

The game ends in a tie, another metaphorical clue to Shinoda's view of Japanese/American relations. The lighthearted, even comical tone of this episode speaks for his belief that relations between these former enemies were essentially harmonious. He spoke of this in an oft-quoted interview: "The children playing baseball with the American soldiers in this film has nothing to do with revenge. It was not the Americans who killed the father [the role played by Itami], but rather it was we who were responsible for his execution. Back then, we thought that we were to blame, not our enemy, and I still think so."[10]

Masao (c.l., Hiromi Gō) in *MacArthur's Children* (1984). © Asmik Ace Entertainment.

Shinoda's balanced view of the war does not get in the way of his concern for the plight of children during the Occupation. *MacArthur's Children* in rich in heartfelt instances, such as Ryūta burning his drawings of Japanese planes and battleships. Shinoda does contrive to send one notably ambiguous message, which comes by way of a montage lasting just several seconds midway through the film. Ryūta in voice-over asks Mume, "Do you know your father's ship was used as a target vessel during a recent U.S. atomic bomb test at Bikini Atoll?" Mume's face in close-up is superimposed on the battleship. The soundtrack records dead silence. What can this mean?

Rob Silverman is surely right in pointing out that Shinoda uses children as "vehicles for political commentary."[11] That being the case, the viewer needs to be aware of contextual details already vanishing into history at the time the film was made. Shinoda's troubling montage cries out for intelligent response. Yet any such response must be based on some knowledge of postwar events. The essential facts of the matter here begin with two treaties signed in 1951. The San Francisco Peace Treaty ended the Occupation by restoring Japan's national sovereignty. A separate U.S.-Japan Security Treaty formalized that aspect of alliance between these former enemies. The strength of that alliance was soon tested by events at home and abroad.

In 1954 the ruling Liberal Democratic Party established the Japan Self-Defense Forces. That decision was vigorously opposed by other parties on behalf of Japanese mistrustful of anything that smacked of the militaristic fervor they saw as leading to the catastrophe of World War II. That same year, however, the United States conducted a hydrogen bomb test on Bikini Atoll. The crew of a Japanese fishing boat, the *Fukuryūmaru #5,* were casualties of the blast. The incident is well-documented in Kaneto Shindō's film of 1959, *Lucky Dragon No. 5* (Daigo Fukuryūmaru), as mentioned earlier. Thanks to Hiroshima and Nagasaki, the Japanese were uniquely qualified to lead the world in sensitivity to nuclear issues, so the Fukuryūmaru accident returned to haunt negotiations for the renewal of the U.S.-Japan Security Treaty in 1959. The treaty was renewed despite a series of violent student demonstrations still fresh in the minds of Shinoda's generation, who came to see *MacArthur's Children* in 1984. Given the benefit of hindsight, we can see how events inside and outside Shinoda's work reinforce one another in service of his lifelong view of the individual's relationship with society as that of victim and victimizer.

Mume's role is tragic throughout. She is the stoic victim of forces beyond her control. In a few brief seconds Shinoda makes this point by enlarging her blank expression to cast its shadow over an entire battleship—

the ship of her defeated, executed father, a ship now blown to atoms by a bomb far more powerful than those dropped on Japan. Mume's expression speaks for stoic acceptance of individual fate at the mercy of historical progression. An alert viewer will connect this close-up with an earlier one of her face composed against a background of cherry trees in bloom. The cherry blossom traditionally associated with the samurai speaks for *mujō*, the passingness of things and, more specifically, human existence. This earlier shot is a clear index of the fleetingness of Mume's girlhood swept away by larger societal forces.

The Final Sequence

Shinoda's parting glance at his children confirms our sense that a deft eclectic touch has served him and his viewer well throughout. This last sequence takes us to three locations. The first is a classroom echo of the opening scene where Komako's students are busily censoring their textbooks, crossing out wartime nationalist exhortations to loyalty and self-sacrifice. Now we see them learning English, a subject banned before. "I am an American boy," they chant. The assertive first person speaks for the thrust of postwar change. The Japanese under the Occupation are learning to replace their native feudal collectivism with individualism from abroad.

A ship's horn reminds everyone that Mume is leaving the island. Ryūta in close-up registers bemused awareness tinged with resignation. He fidgets, fighting the urge to see Mume off. Saburō, predictably, yields to that impulse. His run for the harbor takes us there. A series of cross-cuts and pans conveys a sense of we share of youthful, painful, hopeful parting. Mume's future is left in question. How will she, an orphan, fare in war-torn Tokyo? Earlier she has promised Ryūta that they will meet again, but can they possibly? Shinoda's 1984 audience could be counted on to guess at that likelihood and whatever else they needed to bring closure to his film. That audience had forty years of experience to go on, a story of postwar recovery and change that could well afford to be optimistic. Five years later, when the bubble suddenly burst, viewers might well have adjusted accordingly.

Today, of course, *MacArthur's Children* must be viewed as part of cinema history. Critics have their work cut out for them, doing their best to cue viewers in to bits of historical evidence vital to understanding and enjoying a film of this kind. One such bit appears to have been overlooked thus far. It is a song whose tune we first hear Saburō's older brother humming. He sings it later on. The words explain its function in the film. "Returning Ship" (Kaeribune) was a postwar *enka* (popular song) in a nostalgic vein. It tells of a man returning home from somewhere far away. His ship sails slowly through hovering mist so he asks the gulls to fly ahead fast and tell his sweetheart he is coming home. Mume of course has no one to "fly" to in devastated Tokyo, so the burden of our sympathy is unresolved here at the end —though again, audiences in 1984 had reason to imagine a good outcome for her.

Shinoda turns back to Awaji for his final note of uplift and textural grandeur. A cut to Masao's nursery shows him surveying his crop. The foreground is flush with red flowers, echoing two earlier memorable shots of bold summer flowers (*manjushage,* genus *Papaver,* commonly known as wild poppy) growing wild near the fort. The first is a close-up of a single flower interspersed by shots of American soldiers destroying cannons at the fort. The second, also a close-up, shows Mume's hand crushing a poppy as she remembers her father's letter announcing his trial in Singapore.

Shinoda's worldview leaves room for attenuated romance mixed with irony. He is more apt to wed passion to purpose, as in the case of Komako and Masao. Their selfless devotion to children is its own reward though the drift of social change appears to be moving in the opposite direction, toward aggressive self-interest. The fate of these children hangs in poignant balance at the end. Shinoda is not about to abandon his conviction that individuals

Mume (c., Shiori Sakura) in *MacArthur's Children* (1984). © Asmik Ace Entertainment.

share in the fate of whole societies at the mercy of forces beyond their control.

That note of dogged reservation explains the mood of uplift at the end. Shinoda clearly means to praise the Japanese people after all. Thanks to their combination of strong willpower and superb adaptability, the nation had used defeat and occupation to lay the foundations of a new Japan. Better yet, by 1984 its "children of MacArthur" had grown up to be citizens of a major world power—Shinoda among them.

-10-
Satire on Contemporary Japan
Jūzō Itami's *A Taxing Woman* (1987)

JŪZŌ ITAMI'S acting career, which began in 1960, is well documented.[1] So are the fifteen years Itami (1933–1997) spent making films before his suicide in 1997.[2] His breakthrough year for both acting and directing was 1983. Audiences loved him in the role of the workaholic father in Yoshimitsu Morita's *The Family Game* (Kazoku gēmu). His own debut film, *The Funeral* (Osōshiki), was voted 1983's best picture by *Kinema jumpō,* a distinction followed by more than thirty awards at various film festivals at home and abroad. Itami directed seven films, all dealing with present-day issues of life in Japan. Again and again, in various ways he asks a basic question: what does it mean to be Japanese?[3]

Since marriages and funerals are the most definitive and expensive events in the lives of most Japanese, Itami could hardly miss the mark when he chose to parody the ritual ideal of a proper funeral. His second film, *Tampopo* (1984), parodies his countrymen's ritualistic obsession with food and sex.[4] *Tampopo* is Japanese from start to finish, though it takes its shape from an antic look back at classic Westerns such as Howard Hawks's *Rio Bravo* (1959).

Itami's next target could pop up in any country rich enough and bureaucratic enough to tax and hound taxpayers large and small. He himself grew from small to large overnight, when his first film's box office success hit him with a tax bill in the 250 million yen ($2.25 million) range. He hit back with *A Taxing Woman* (Marusa no onna, 1987) and *The Return of a Taxing Woman* (Marusa no onna 2, 1988). Both anatomize the postmodern big-money fixation keeping pace with Japan's postwar "miracle" economy. When that miracle redefined itself as a bubble by going bust in May 1991, captains of industry and gangland crooks retrenched and restructured with equal dis-ease. Itami skewers both in *Mimbo,* aka *The Gentle Art of Extortion* (Minbō no onna, 1992). This hilarious send-up of industry bigwigs in cahoots with lowlife Yakuza nearly cost the director his life. He was knifed by hoodlums thought to be members of a Yakuza gang. As Mark Schilling says, "Itami's brush with death—and his outrage at what he considered as an assault on the right of free expression—inspired him to make *Marutai*."[5] The title of this 1997 film, *Marutai no onna,* translates as "woman of the police protection program." Its heroine is an aging actress who witnesses a murder by members of a violent cult. The film looks steadily at a life changed overnight by happenstance as the killers stalk this woman.

Critics content to peg Itami as a maker of social comedies may be over-looking signs of underlying earnestness. Twice in the 1990s he tried his hand at serious social drama. *The Last Dance* (Daibyōnin, 1995) brings Itami's gift for satire to bear on a topic as sobering as terminal cancer. *A Quiet Life* (Shizuka na seikatsu, 1994) is based on the novel by Itami's brother-in-law, Nobel laureate Kenzaburo Ōe. This exploration of the life of a mentally retarded teenager is in line with Japanese society's growing sensitivity to the handicapped.

Critics at home and abroad have taken Itami seriously as a director, though the early success of *The Funeral* and *Tampopo* persists in shifting atten-tion to them at some cost to our sense of his work as a whole. For exam-ple, Itami deserves to be better known as the creator of a remarkably mod-ern type of female lead played by his wife, Nobuko Miyamoto. That and his gift for social satire should earn his brief career a place in cinema history. Though Itami's inventive use of the Japanese cultural context is rather easy for non-Japanese to appreciate, it still needs some cultural footnotes—all the more reason to show how much a film such as *A Taxing Woman* stands to gain from a critical "reading."

Central Problem, Issues, and Thematic Progression

A Taxing Woman is set in the 1980s, when the Japanese economy was the envy of the world. The country was awash in money, obsessed with get-ting and spending. Tax evasion kept pace accordingly as rich and poor and companies large and small looked for ways to limit the government's take. Itami had his own direct-hit tax experience to pique his interest in this phe-nomenon, as mentioned above. He also knew a timely issue when he saw it. The question was how to target the widest possible audience. He gave an interviewer this account of his strategy:

> What I do feel, though, is that Americans are the best in the world at writing scripts. The worst are the Japanese. They write stories that only they them-selves can understand. Also, there's no structure. I use the three-act structure of Western drama. In the first act you develop the incidents that bring the

hero into the drama. At the end of each act you have a climax and, in the third act, the climax for the entire film.[6]

Itami's working title for his script, *Marusa no onna: Nikki* (Diary: A Taxing Woman) adds that telling word "diary" *(nikki)*.[7] It speaks for his clear intent to script a story any audience anywhere can follow. Introduction, three acts, finale—each begins with a timely cue flashed on the screen. Each title resets the narrative clock, like a diarist does by heading each entry with some reference to time.

The film begins with a screen-size quote from Japanese Tax Law, Article 12: "A tax office shall take all steps necessary to prosecute when it discovers that an offence has been committed." Clearly, this is not going to be a film about law-abiding, tax-paying paragons of civic virtue. And sure enough, the story begins with Hideki Gondō, the villain in the piece. We see right away that this guy is some kind of crook in a mood to celebrate having just outwitted the tax man bigtime. We shall get to know Gondō better by and by—as an enterprising crook who steals a dying man's identity, using his name to front a dummy corporation to cover all manner of ill-gotten gains. We will see how he launders money in cahoots with a Yakuza organization. But first we need to know that the tax man can be a woman. The title *A Taxing Woman* opens the main part of the film, introducing Gondō's antagonist, Ryōko Itakura, the tax office investigator to be assigned to his case. We see her and another woman in a coffee shop. As far as the proprietor knows, they are just two women meeting for a coffee klatch. Ryōko is in fact training a rookie investigator. She explains that the way the shop owner handles his or her receipts is a dead giveaway. He or she is cooking the books.

This film tells Ryōko's story, exploring its central problem: How does this heroine achieve a holistic vision of life? Put another way, it concerns Ryōko's search for a self-image she can live with. Two basic choices revolving around the central problem are bondage and independence. The first (only to be implied) is the circumscribed life of a housewife, and the second is the more freewheeling life of a career woman. Ryōko chooses the latter and follows through relentlessly. Japanese audiences in 1987 would have been familiar with her Western prototype in films and television: the ambitious, careerist woman facing the gender challenge. She has to prove herself capable of doing what is seen as a man's job in a man's world. Proof on the job front is easy enough to plot. Proof of character is more difficult, as witnessed by the numbers of tough-gal roles that do not get beyond the action figure stage.

With Ryōko, Itami gives a woman's double burden of "proof" a double dose of challenge. She is not just a woman; she is a Japanese woman, a divorcée with a small child. The man's world she inhabits, personally and professionally, is far more predominantly male than its British or American counterpart in 1987. As we shall see, throughout the film Ryōko's workplace is portrayed idealistically with a benevolent boss and a sense of collegiality: it is far removed from the real business or bureaucratic world in Japan. One sociologist has this to say: "Japanese women have serious difficulty in securing managerial posts in companies. Only a quarter of Japanese firms have female managers at or above the hancho (section head) level, and 73 percent of those who have attained managerial positions have not borne children."[8] Ryōko has to do more than catch her crook: she has to bear creditable witness to a new kind of Japanese womanhood. Itami's concern to script a film intelligible at home and abroad adds to the challenge. He meets it with straightforward narrative structure and characters whose humanity is universally intelligible.

Like any good scriptwriter, Itami knows how to gain strength of character from complications of self-doubt and identity conflict. In Ryōko's case, this means reconciling all the usual womanly variables with her chosen way of life. She has turned her back on a woman's "place" in traditional Japanese society with its measure of security bought with housewifely thrift and subservience. In its place she has put a professional career. Her choice defines her as an interesting new kind of woman, a deeply human individual with a role to play in this edgy, thriller-type satirical comedy.

The script is notably reticent about Ryōko's background. We know that she is divorced, but not when or why. We do glimpse her showing her five-year-old son how to heat his supper in the microwave. Like the long, late hours she works, this scene suggests that career and conventional family life proved incompatible.

The nature of Ryōko's work may have come into it as well. We see her threatened repeatedly. A Yakuza boss aims a thinly veiled threat at her son. An oversize close-up takes note of her anxiety in the latter case. Still, Itami approaches the question of Ryōko's motherly instincts by shifting focus from her son to the son of her sworn enemy Gondō. This economy of script enriches the plot in surprising ways, as we shall see.

The main thrust of plot and action follow Ryōko where careerist ambition leads her. Itami builds suspense by presenting her with an obstacle course of steadily increasing complexity. It begins with her netting small-time cheats such as a grocery shop owner. Ryōko, a quick study, proves shrewdly observant, resourceful, decisive, and gutsy, too. She goes from strength to strength—as do the cunning villains she is assigned to outwit. Itami knows how to structure climax. His first "act" ends with a breakthrough case for Ryōko. A criminal mastermind named Gondō needs to launder a lot of money. Can Ryōko catch him at it?

The second act title sets the time: "Spring." Ryōko and her team go after the so-called love hotels used as fronts by Gondō and his Yakuza pals. The stakes are high, so danger is in the air. Ryōko is harassed, even threatened with bodily injury. She scores a kind of antic victory when the gangsters crowd into her office. Refusing to be intimidated, Ryōko pours their boss a cup of coffee laced with salt on the sly. When he throws the cup across the room, she nails him on a technicality: destroying government property. Even so, the end of act two suggests a draw. Ryōko knows how Gondō's operations work but she cannot prove a thing. He has outwitted her, cheated her of a professional coup.

Act three, "Summer," opens with a pleasant surprise. Ryōko has been promoted after all. She is now a member of Marusa, the special investigation branch of the national tax office. Membership in this elite group is proof that her skills have been noticed at the top. Also telling is the fact that she is the only woman on the team. Ryōko's response to promotion is predictably careerist. The plot winds up predictably too. By the end of act three, her

Ryōko's supervisor (l., Shūji Ōtaki) and Ryōko (Nobuko Miyamoto) in *A Taxing Woman* (1987). © Itami Production.

team gets their man. What is surprising is how the film gains strength from two innovations Itami uses to balance one another: a new type of heroine and a brave new world of ideal bureaucrats.

Ryōko is about as far as it is possible to get from Japanese cinema's most famous female archetype: Mizoguchi's silent sufferer so touchingly submissive to the system that exploits her. One classic instance from the prewar era is the geisha Umekichi in *Sisters of the Gion* (discussed in chapter 1). Another is the lowly housemaid Otoku in *The Story of the Last Chrysanthemum* (*Zangiku monogatari*, 1939). Otoku dies as she has lived, entirely devoted to advancing the career of a wholly self-involved aspiring Kabuki actor. She lives offstage, in the commonplace obscurity of unquestioning servitude. Mizoguchi makes brilliant use of the contrast between her selfless suffering and the actor's triumph in the histrionic irreality of the Meiji world of Kabuki, with its all remnants of feudal social structure.[9]

Mizoguchi's favorite women are geisha and courtesans doomed to make good on youth and beauty while they last. No amount of cultivated charm can halt the fearful progress of that vanishing economy. Itami's Ryōko could not be more different. She is a new kind of woman working in an entirely new economic model. Her new breed of professional woman is empow-

Ryōko (l., Nobuko Miyamoto), Ryōko's colleague (c., Fumiake Mahha), and Ryōko's supervisor (r., Shūji Ōtaki) in *A Taxing Woman* (1987). © Itami Production.

ered. She has a self that has a future: independent, self-sufficient, competent, and highly motivated. She sets goals. She achieves. She holds herself to the highest standard of excellence on the job.

As movie heroines go, sex appeal is not Ryōko's forte. She is that near to being a somewhat "caricaturistic" creation of Itami's desire to satirize the Japanese postwar obsession with money and success. One could say that he skirts that problem by down-sexing Ryōko. She competes with men by being more like them than the women they expect to dominate. She appears to wear no makeup. Not just once, but three times, her boss tells her that she has a cowlick. She wears pants and is the only woman seen smoking. She downs whole beers—alone.

Yet Ryōko is easy to look at and identify with. Prettily freckled Nobuko Miyamoto sees to that. She gives Ryōko the unstudied appeal of a self-confident woman whose focus is on matters outside herself. She is more than merely confident when the chips are down. She can be downright aggressive. We see her jerk a male colleague to his feet and give him what-for in no uncertain terms. She is the one gripping the handlebars in a motorcycle chase. Her male supervisor rides behind, hanging on for dear life.

Ironically it is Gondō, her sworn enemy, who helps awaken Ryōko's motherly instincts. He is a commonplace money-hungry philanderer but devoted to his boy, confessing to Ryōko that his goal as a tax cheat has always been to leave young Tarō a fortune. The setup for this plot detour is typical of Itami's fondness for building a scene around a given motif. Ryōko is sitting alone in a cafe, drinking a beer, looking distrait. A woman with a baby catches her eye. She makes funny faces at the baby. Gondō happens in. He joins her. It is his birthday. Ryōko salutes him with her mug. Something else clicks between them. Gondō's confession ends the scene. He wants her advice but she excuses herself in something of a hurry. We sense that something more is at stake than her fear of being professionally compromised. Two later scenes (as we shall see) suggest that Gondō's revelation touched a nerve. Ryōko's concern for her own son extends to Gondō's boy, Tarō.

Ryōko's emotional development helps explain Itami's somewhat surprising decision to idealize the tax office bureaucracy, the elite Marusa branch especially. She goes from being one of a handful of women in the tax office generally to the only woman on a team where unit cohesion is a must—yet she fits right in. Itami wastes no time on gender politics. It helps that both divisions are run by benevolent father figures. The first compares her to his daughter. When she is promoted, he feels like he is giving his daughter away in marriage. The head of Marusa addresses her as "Ryōko-chan," a term of endearment.

In the rougher, tougher world of scripting since, Ryōko might fight on both fronts. Itami is satisfied to give her the supportive bosses and peers she needs to realize her goals. The opposition is on the outside: the real world of ice-cold clear distinctions between his and hers. There, like Gondō's mistresses, she is an object of male desire—leered at, harassed, insulted, and, if need be, assaulted. Ryōko learns on the job how to handle herself. It is not always easy. Gondō himself sees the woman, not the professional. Early on, he interrupts her audit of his office by pushing her onto a sofa, throwing sheets of various colors at her—linens for his love hotels. He also has things to say about her personal appearance. She meets these affronts with increasing confidence conveyed with subtle skill by the leading lady Nobuko Miyamoto.

Itami's Cinematic Devices

Itami came on the scene at a time when the major talents such as Yoshimitsu Morita (b. 1950) and Kichitarō Negishi (b. 1950) were making films whose cinematic sophistication was hard to match. Itami had no such flair. Instead, he made vigorous, well-crafted films based on familiar techniques. An Itami film is action-packed and fast-paced. Characters tend to act decisively, with little time out for brooding introspection. Plots unfold quickly, too, with help from nimble camera work. Brief shots and plentiful cuts and close-ups take note of characters and situations. The effect is one of speed-reading efficiency, not leisurely, much less playful, study.

The soundtrack has the same jazzy verve. In *A Taxing Woman* a jaunty tune makes the rounds with Gondō as he moves from cheat to cheat. It also serves to underscore surveillance and pursuit. But it is Gondō's tune we know. It comes with our first view of him—the introduction's glimpse of the clumsy dance he does to celebrate a money laundering coup. It makes an ironic return at the end when he shuffles off in sad defeat.

Point-of-view shots have lots to do in a plot driven by surveillance. Sometimes we share the monitor's view from inside a stakeout van. More often a shot gives us an inside track on the focused alertness of pursuer or pursued. For example, we share Ryōko's view of a parking lot belonging to a love hotel. She just happens to duck in out of the rain. It just happens to keep her there long enough to notice a telltale pattern of motion. The hotel is serving more customers than its books are likely to show. We have seen into her way of thinking—officially. This glimpse moves the plot forward accordingly.

Itami uses a series of rapid-fire cross-cuts to convey the speed and urgency of a major bust. More than a hundred agents converge on Gondō and his associates in a number of locations—a simple but effective use of this basic technique.

Though fluid, rapid shots prevail, there are a few instances of "settled" camera work. The most memorable occurs when Gondō's son Tarō runs away from home after a scolding from his father. Ryōko catches up with him at a railway crossing. She is breathless with anxiety, thinking he means to throw himself in front of a train. A next shot lasts some minutes. The camera follows Tarō and Ryōko walking down a path, moving and pausing as they do. Their talk is free and easy. Tarō describes his boyish trades at school. This rare lyrical moment reveals the depth of feeling concealed by Ryōko's tough-gal style. She sees her fall quite naturally into the role of surrogate for this boy whose mother has died. This moment of harmony finds its echo in nature all around. Ryōko seems more at home here than in the world of her successful career—the hard-edged confines of cityscape and Gondō's well-guarded compound.

The next scene reinforces the irony implicit in this shot of Ryōko and Gondō's son. We have every reason to believe that this gangster kingpin's admiration is based on Ryōko's professional qualities. Yet here we learn that what he values most is her motherly affection for his son. That fact lends the plot an even richer irony. It turns out that Ryōko, without meaning to at all, has softened Gondō up, making it easier for the tax office to nab him after all.

The Final Sequence

The camera's settled gaze takes in a final scene surprisingly rich in sentiment. Has Itami's admiration for his creation—this new kind of Japanese woman—won out over his intent to satirize his money-hungry countrymen? Has Ryōko softened her own creator up? Has she taken him in, like that weary old gangster Gondō? This scene takes its cue from one last item of unfinished business: a billion yen still missing. Without it, Ryōko's success is not complete. Here it turns up in a way that can only be called romantic.

The finale title flashes us ahead to spring. The soundtrack takes us back to the softly lyrical opening of the second "act." This theme belongs to Ryōko. There she appeared in pants, the tough gal on the job. Here quite another Ryōko approaches the camera, dressed in a full-length skirt and rather fashionable long spring coat. She is dressed for a rendezvous—personal not official—with Gondō! They meet as friends, discussing mostly family matters of family solidarity. She tells Gondō that his son is worried about him. Her advice to him, as a friend, is that his legacy to Tarō should be his inner strength and perseverance, not money.

All this while the camera is settled on Ryōko and Gondō in a medium shot, the former facing the camera. Their conversation takes place in real time. In subsequent shots, we see that Ryōko's advice has been persuasive enough to help Gondō change his mind. This is conveyed through the important recurring image of Ryōko's handkerchief. Our first glimpse of it came in the café scene, which also focuses on the family bond motif. There Gondō finds Ryōko drinking alone from a larger mug of beer. She is the very picture of a tough-minded, independent career woman, yet here she is, toying with her beer and making playful faces at the baby in a woman's arms nearby. Gondō cannot wait to share his latest bright idea. He has figured out a way to leave his son a billion yen tax-free. Alarmed that this confidence might compromise her professionally, Ryōko hurries away, leaving her handkerchief behind.

Now Gondō takes out the handkerchief. He opens it, gashes his thumb with a penknife, and writes something on it in blood: the number of the safety deposit box where he has stashed the billion yen. As in so many cultures, this gesture is rich in references to classic oaths of loyalty and allegiance. The definitive Japanese instance is found in the classical *bunraku* play *Chūshingura* (Forty-seven loyal retainers), later adapted for kabuki. The loyal samurai from the Akō clan swear to avenge their master's death, signing their oath in blood. Gondō's dramatic gesture is an unmistakable reference to that exalted moment. Ryōko can be safely assumed to make that same connection when he returns her handkerchief.

Here again, the sanctity of family life is clearly encoded in the scene. Not just once, but twice, the overhead pan takes pointed note of a playground visible from where they stand. The children playing happily speak clearly of yearnings we know these two grown-ups share, however differently. Gondō says outright, "The sight of those little ones eases my mind."

Still, Gondō is who he is. He urges Ryōko to work for him. The camera rests on her impassive face. The interval seems long. Finally she shakes her head no. A number of critics interpret this scene as proof of mutual sexual attraction; surely that is misleading. Just as Gondō's writing in blood is sincere, so his offer is in earnest. It is clearly a case of worthy enemy seen as even worthier ally. The camera watches with Ryōko as Gondō moves away, a dejected, awkward parody of the dancing, jubilant gangster we met in that introductory scene. That jaunty tune returns now to add its note of irony.

The film ends with Ryōko's distant view of the metropolis spreading far and wide. Clearly we are meant to see that she will meet this world of men on her own terms, as a woman who can count on her own strength and resourcefulness—a woman who has earned the respect of her peers. It is easy to see why Itami went on to direct and produce *The Return of a Taxing Woman*.

–11–
Animation Seminal and Influential
Hayao Miyazaki's *My Neighbor Totoro* (1988)

THE ANIMATION FILM known as *anime* in Japan has earned the respect and admiration of viewers worldwide. Two examples—both science fiction—come readily to mind. Katsuhiro Otomo's *Akira* (1988) created a sensation in the West, especially in the United States, where it edged out *Return of the Jedi* at the Oscars. Mamoru Ōishi's *Ghost in the Shell* (Kōkaku kidōtai, 1995) was a bigger popular hit in the United States than in Japan. Its debt to Ridley Scott's *Blade Runner* (1982) helped give it instant status with *anime* lovers in the West. The appeal of Ōishi's work has much to do with its "technically sophisticated computer animation" in service of a complex storyline mix of biblical, Shinto, and Buddhist sources.[1]

More recently, *Spirited Away* (Sen to Chihiro no kamikakushi, 2001) by Hayao Miyazaki (b. 1941) went right to the top, becoming the biggest box office hit in a hundred years of Japanese cinema history. It also cut a wide swath through the awards at a number of international film festivals, among them the Berlin Film Festival's Golden Lion for 2001 and the Best Animated Film Oscar for 2002.

Many in the West think of animation as a Johnny-come-lately film genre from the 1930s. Animation got off to a somewhat earlier start in Japan, thanks to a few stray shorts imported from, ironically, France and America as early as 1909. Japanese audiences were entranced, creating a demand for some homegrown equivalent. The earliest known result dates from 1917, *A New Picture of the Mischievous Boy* (Chamebō shingachō).[2] Communications being what they were, the renowned cartoonist Bokuten Shimogawa had no idea how Western animators worked. The best he could think to do was draw, photograph, erase, and redraw image after image on a chalkboard.[3] Primitive as it was, Shimogawa's innovation led to the far more serviceable idea of drawing characters on preprinted backgrounds. By around 1929, drawing directly on celluloid became standard procedure.[4]

Noburō Ōfuji (1900–1961) was an influential figure in early animation. He is credited with developing the *Chiyogami eiga* color-paper film, so called because its technique grew out of the traditional art of shadow pictures on rice paper. His representative works included *Whale* (Kujira, 1927) and *The Thief of Baghdad* (Bagudaddo no tōzoku, 1929). Ōfuji's updated remake of *Whale* in 1952 won a prize at the Cannes Film Festival.

With few exceptions these early animations were the brief, low-budget products of small independents. The first full-length feature was Mitsuyo Seo's *Peach Boy's Sea Eagle* (Momotarō no kaijū, 1943). The year explains its patriotic potboiler character and the reviews dutifully lauding its depiction of the attack on Pearl Harbor as launched by the hero of a popular children's book. Wartime propaganda spawned any number of such films, among them Sanae Yamamoto's *Children's March* (Kodakara kōshinkyoku, 1942) exhorting women to do right by population growth.[5] It would not be the first time in history that government subsidy failed to discredit an art form. Japanese animation quickly outgrew its wartime compromises, becoming a major box office draw by the 1960s and the amazing commercial success it is today and looks to be for the foreseeable future.

Miyazaki's achievements as an animation filmmaker/producer have been widely discussed.[6] Undoubtedly, his current success owes much to his distinctive achievement back in 1988 with *My Neighbor Totoro* (Tonari no Totoro). He wrote both the original story and the screenplay for this animation film. It was voted best picture of 1988 by *Kinema jumpō,* Japan's most prestigious film journal. That same year, *Kinema jumpō* gave sixth place to another *anime,* Isao Takahata's *The Grave of Fireflies* (Hotaru no haka). Those two awards were remarkable for two reasons. First, no *anime* had enjoyed such critical acclaim in the history of Japanese cinema. Second, the awards that year included two films devoted to the heavily charged issue of antiwar sentiment in Japan. Kazuo Kuroki's *Tomorrow* and Kaneto Shindō's *The Death of the Cherry Blossom Troupe (Sakuratai chiru)* both depicted traumatic wartime experiences. Takahata's *anime* did the same, in fact. The difference was in his choice of genre, one whose readily accessible entertainment value made the message more accessible to general audiences.

Miyazaki's film (his third feature-length film) could not have been more different. *My Neighbor Totoro* might be called an idyll. It takes a longing look back at the 1950s, when some rural and suburban communities still offered refuge from the throes of transformation run amok in the name of postwar recovery. Though the film focuses on children free to live in a fantasy world, it appealed to adult audiences as well. Obviously, nostalgia had something to do with it. But so did the fact that Miyazaki, like Takahata, used the conventions of animation to address issues deeply ingrained in the social fabric of contemporary Japan.

Oneness with nature, for example, has long been considered part of the Japanese national character. By 1988, parents had reason to be concerned that their children were losing touch with nature. Urban sprawl was partly to blame. So was an education system so demanding of achievement that children were, in effect, held hostage at home as well as at school. Family life had suffered, too. The competitive pressures of the workplace took much of the blame for dissolving family bonds. Overworked fathers had little time for family life. Mothers, forced to take charge at home, became overachievers of another, dreadful kind. Social anthropologists dubbed her the *"kyōiku mama,"* the mother obsessed with her children's education to the exclusion of almost everything else.[7] Miyazaki's film "animates" all these very real concerns.

Still, *My Neighbor Totoro* gets its power not from weighty social critique, but from its melding of two worlds: the real and the imaginary. David Bordwell has suggested an interesting way to approach a mass-entertainment film. He urges us to "look for a tension between spectacle and narrative."[8] Let us see how that approach explains Miyazaki's success in this *anime*.

Historical and Geographic Settings and the Central Problem

My Neighbor Totoro tells what happens when nine-year-old Satsuki and her four-year-old sister Mei move to the country with their college professor father. The film is frankly informative, beginning with the idyllic opening sequence. Miyazaki plays no games with withheld information. We know early on why the mother is missing. She is ill, hospitalized. We see the central problem that will move the plot: how will these little girls cope without her, brought to a strange new place? We quickly learn that they feel lost in these unfamiliar surroundings and that they miss their mother keenly, little Mei especially. Worse yet, their father, Tatsuo, has to leave them alone for hours at a time when he goes into town to teach his classes.

The children do what children have done in so many classics: they balance fact with fantasy. Grownups would feel obliged to manage that dichotomy by drawing clear distinctions between what is real and what is not. These children manage, as children do. They switch back and forth between confronting reality and escaping into the imaginary. They do this freely, naïvely. It follows that they do some mixing and mingling of the two as well. But first, like us, they have to meet the given, unknown real world. We see them enter it as the film begins. A man is pedaling a tricycle van down a country lane. The van is packed full with the two little girls and all manner of things. They pass through lovely, unspoiled countryside. The music we hear is lively and reassuring.

A scene this lovely could be a dream. As Miyazaki explained in an interview, he is showing us a faithful depiction of the countryside as it was in the 1950s.[9] Since then, that enchanting landscape has evolved into the cityscape that gives the area its present-day name and fame as Tokorozawa, a city whose busy prosperity has done more than gobble up its share of green and pleasant countryside. Tokorozawa in Saitama Prefecture is synonymous with urban pollution.

Various images seen in passing and in intimate detail offer important clues to definitive change taking place in the childhood years of these two girls. The tadpoles that fascinate Mei in her new surroundings clearly indicate that the family has moved to the country in the spring, as does a later view of farmers wading in a paddy, sprigging rice. Toward the end of film, the calendar in the mother's hospital ward tells us exactly when the children's adventure is coming to an end: Thursday, August 21, 1958. The calendar's sunflower picture is telling, too.

Those familiar with postwar Japanese culture will pick up on a number of culturally specific details harkening back to the late 1950s. Kanta is seen making a model airplane the old-fashioned way, using strips of bamboo. Ready-made kit models did not come on the scene till late in the decade. An American director seeking the same effect might have shown a kid making a soap box derby racecar out of an orange crate.[10] Another end-of-era detail is the female ticket taker on a bus driven by a man. Still another is the scolding Kanta gets for doodling in imitation of *Magic Ninja Boy Jiraiya* (Shonen Jiraiya), an enormously popular comic book by Shigeru Sugiura (1908–2000). Sugiura comics with titles such as *Ninja Sasuke* (Sarutobi Sasuke) were entertainment mainstays in the 1950s.

Miyazaki clearly intends to focus our attention on a family bond significantly stronger in August than it was the April before. His careful attention to seasonal detail is typical of his storytelling method, which enriches a painstakingly evocative naturalistic setting with the free play of fantasy possible with *anime*.

Needless to say, the *anime* fantasy enrichment is set against a realistic backdrop throughout. Miyazaki takes full advantage of naturalistic detail, as in his careful attention to seasonal detail. He also makes sure that pictorial effects evoke a specifically Japanese response by dwelling on the surviving evidence of the country lifestyle.[11] Rice paddies, an unpaved country road, a roadside bus stop—details such as these, familiar for time out of mind, speak for the director's childhood memories of 1950s country life. Japanese Miyazaki's age and younger understand the rustic simplicity implicit in artifacts such as the *Goemon-buro,* a kind of cast-iron tub with a wooden base.

Miyazaki also invites the viewer to share his nostalgia for a lovely human harmony engrained in rural communities now rapidly disappearing. We see everyone turning out to welcome the professor and his girls. They are offered food and any help they need to settle in. There is one notable holdout: Kanta. Yet we soon discover, like the girls, that his unfriendliness is all bluff, a mask for painful shyness.

From this point on the plot is led by these two little girls. They meet and overcome one obstacle after another with the verve and enterprise of innocents who turn out to be quite capable of managing this new life on their own terms. They move into a house they find mysterious and strange, intriguing and somehow scary. Their lively imaginations take it from there. Dust bunnies turn into tiny black spirits haunting the house. They struggle to balance fear and curiosity, little Mei especially.

Their father is a paragon of the affectionate common sense that knows how to nurture imagination by playing along. He says these dust bunny spirits are not that scary. Not if they can be scared away—with laughter. And so they laugh for all they are worth, father and daughters together, soaking in that rustic tub, the *Goemon-buro.* The water rocks and spills over as they laugh so loud. All the father-daughter bond that any child could wish for is conveyed in a few simple shots.

The next shot takes us outside the house in time to see what look like black dust bunnies floating out of the chimney and vanishing sky high. True, it could be smoke or floating soot. This *is* country life in the 1950s. Or it could be childish fantasy. The engaging, easygoing music suggests that it does not matter which. And so this simple scene takes us in. We share the children's sense of being pleasantly reassured.

This is the first (if minor) instance of tension between "spectacle" and "narrative." According to David Bordwell, a mass-entertainment movie, like a musical prototype, often contains "those moments when the story seems to halt and we are forced simply to watch and listen." Such a moment of "spectacle" or "splendor" may insist on itself at the expense of the chain of cause and effect, that mainstay of narrative.[12] As we shall see, the parade of spectacles becomes increasingly dominant in the sisters' world of imagination and fantasy. After all, as an *anime* director, Miyazaki's concern is with sustaining our indulgence in a world he has endowed with such a wealth of "convincing" effects.

Thematic Progression and Miyazaki's Creation of Furry Totoro

The dust bunny sequence introduces Miyazaki's concern with the deeper psychological issue of abandonment/substitution. Like Frank Baum's *The Wizard of Oz* and Lewis Carroll's *Alice's Adventures in Wonderland,* his film creates a new context that itself explains the childhood strategy of dealing with hardship and fear by imagining and entering into a world of fantasy. Any amateur psychologist could state the formula: once a given harsh reality is sublimated into (lodged in) the unconscious, the conscious mind attempts to reassure itself by acting out "wish fulfillment."

Elsewhere, Miyazaki has this to say about Mei's sensitivity: "Undaunted by strange creatures, Mei opens up her heart to them. This shows that her world is not yet contaminated by the commonsense cautions of grownup life. Yet it speaks of her loneliness as well. . . . A mother's absence is no small matter for a four-year-old."[13] This happens first to little Mei. Even though she has her sister, her father, and a kindly neighbor "granny" to serve as mother substitutes, she sometimes finds herself left to her own devices. Her first encounter with Totoro occurs on one such occasion. Satsuki is off at school. Her father is preoccupied with his books. Mei sees and follows tiny, furry creatures down a "long tunnel" entered through a hole in a huge camphor tree. The tunnel leads to a gigantic Totoro, sound asleep.

Miyazaki gives the child time to adjust to her discovery. She soon adopts a playful, mischievous attitude toward the furry giant. She scratches his face, pulls his whiskers, whispers "Totoro!" in his ear. The scene ends on a second instance of "spectacle." Totoro, sound asleep, brings the action to a halt, in effect redefining the terms of the fantasy. We see little Mei enlisted in a mood of soothing harmony. She falls asleep on the Totoro's comfy belly. A long shot takes note of details that show how fantasy has eased this child back into a natural world that is safe and secure. A butterfly flutters over the sleeping giant and child. A snail comes creeping near. A viewer alert to similarities will not miss the impish contrast between Totoro's plump, owlish face and the professor's skinny, bookish face, complete with horn-rimmed spectacles. The transition from this world of make-believe to reality is conventionally abrupt. Satsuki and her father, out looking for Mei, find her asleep under a bush.

Mei's need for a mother substitute enlivens the plot with a chain of events that link the worlds of fact and fantasy as one problem solved leads to the next. Thus Granny finds she just cannot cope, so little Mei is taken to school where Satsuki, her classmates, and her teacher become her "babysitters." One day, heading home, the sisters are caught in a heavy downpour. They take refuge in a wayside temple. Kanta, the country boy whose painful shyness hides behind a show of ruffian unfriendliness, happens to see them there. He cannot bring himself to rescue them outright. Instead, he hurries up, hands them his umbrella without a word, and then runs off into the pouring rain. Satsuki, in the meantime, has shown herself to be a kindly older sister anxious to mother Mei all she can. Their very names in Japanese encode the strength of such a bond. Satsuki in classical Japanese denotes the month of May, as does Mei in the vernacular.

Miyazaki's choice of a girl *(shōjo)* as a main character has been discussed by a number of critics. Susan Napier observes that such devices came to the fore in Miyazaki films of the 1980s: "In contrast to the armored *mecha* [disordered] body, the *shōjo* exhibits strength plus vulnerability in a way that is intriguingly feminine."[14] Elsewhere, she adds, "In contemporary Japanese society, girls, with their seemingly still-amorphous identities, seem to embody the potential for unfettered change and excitement is far less available to Japanese males, who are caught in the network of demanding workforce responsibilities."[15] She instances the girls in *My Neighbor Totoro* (and in *Kiki's Delivery Service* [Majo no takkyūbin, 1989]), where the narrative premise of family loss is "defamiliarized through the use of the *shōjo* characters, whose curious, assertive, but still feminine personalities add fresh notes to classic stories."[16]

This is definitely true of Satsuki. She has her mother's slight build but her behavior is that of a girl endowed with courage and strong will. We see this in the way she faces up to hardship. She suffers, but shoulders responsibility with patient endurance. We see this clearly as the sisters wait for their father at the bus stop. The bus arrives without him. Rainy darkness falls as they wait for the next. Satsuki stands bravely with sleepy little Mei on her back. The moment is ripe for rescue. We feel it coming and sure enough, for the first time ever, Satsuki sees Totoro. Suddenly there he is, standing next to her. Miyazaki uses more "padding" than "spectacle" to develop this episode. Again, he takes his time establishing intimacy. The camera lingers on the sight of gigantic Totoro standing tall in the rain. Satsuki offers him an umbrella. Shot by shot, we see Totoro react to this new toy, this real-world artifact. He does the natural fantasy thing, acquainting himself with playing. Mei wakes and shares this fantastic encounter with her sister.

This scene confirms our growing sense that Totoro does more than serve as a parent substitute. A number of clues have pointed to a more comprehensive role. The earliest grew out of Mei's first encounter with him.

Her sister's reaction is to pooh-pooh the idea that such a creature could exist. Their father settles the issue by referring it to the reverential awe the three of them feel for the gigantic camphor tree *(Cinnamomum camphora)* that looms over near their new house. As the three of them stroke its velvety bark, the father uses the indisputable fact of this giant to explain the existence of the other. He assures the children that Totoro does exist—suggesting, in effect, that to be seen Totoro must be imagined. He adds weight to this proposition by calling the tree "the king of the forest," mentioning that it is the only reason he purchased this old house.

Miyazaki offers us no end of visual cues in support of the father's message. The camera follows Mei being led by the tiny creatures to the hole and tunnel in the camphor tree. Panning in close, it takes note of a sacred rope, the *shimenawa,* encircling the bole, marking the tree as one set apart for special reverence. Later, as the father and girls approach, they pass a little *torii* gate that marks the entrance to a shrine. The shot of their admiring gaze at the tree's immensity is carefully framed. We clearly see the sacred rope. It evidently serves a deeper meaning: the father's desire to teach his daughters something about Shinto, namely, its awareness of the divine presence in nature. The scene ends with the three of them offering prayers to the ancient tree.

The Japanese audience is prepared for this reverential attitude by any number of traditional instances. The one most familiar in the West would be Mount Fuji, originally immortalized quite literally as the mountain of everlasting life. Japanese poetry offers no end of elevating views, as in this classic by the eighth-century poet Yamabe Akahito:

Along the Tago Coast	*Tago no urayu*
We come out into the open and see it—	*Uchiidete mireba*
How white it is!	*Mashironi zo*
The lofty cone of Fuji sparkling	*Fuji no takane ni*
Beneath its newly fallen snow.	*Yuki wa furikeri.*[17]

Totoro's place in nature is affirmed by the umbrella Satsuki offers him. Rain is wetting him, like them, yet she has to show him how to take shelter under this human artifact. His response is telling, too. He gives the girls a packet of seeds. Thanks to Totoro's magical powers, the girls are put in touch with a freewheeling fantasy mix of nature and divinity. They plant the seeds he gave them and then wait, as children will, impatiently. The camera hovers, offering a faithful record of their naïve anticipation and anxiety. Finally, the seeds sprout. The long wait yields a dramatic highlight as Totoro and tiny furry creatures appear, unfolding a musical spectacle rich in effects of sympathetic magic. Seeds sprout all around in response to Totoro's touch. Mei and Satsuki join in a dance shared by creatures and growing plants alike. The effect is that of a fertility dance, an easygoing, modern version of ancient ritual celebration of the ties that bind the farmer to his land. Also unmistakable is the suggestion that these little girls have achieved true oneness with nature's immanent divinity. Lest there be any doubt about that point, the spectacle shifts from earth to sky. Totoro and the girls take off in a motion the camera shows as an effortless glide up the camphor tree to soar above its canopy.

The episode ends with a shot of the professor working late into the night. His contented smile yields to a final shot of an owl perched in the camphor tree. The connection is obvious. He feels that he has done right by his daughters. We are inclined to agree. We have seen the larger, more spectacular picture, the fantasy world the girls have shared. Even more to the point is Miyazaki's expressive intention to alert his audience to a danger: that the hustle and bustle of contemporary Japan may work to suppress one of childhood's greatest gifts, namely, the innate awareness of something inspiriting in nature.

The disappearance of the Shinto god in contemporary Japan is more poignantly suggested in *Spirited Away*. The bathhouse and the polluted river offer a simple analogy for the rift between Shinto divinity and humanity. It is also plainly suggested by the sadly forlorn, ghost-like god craving for human companionship. Add a state of nature too foul for the divine presence to manifest itself as immanent and you have the image of a river god making do by resorting to the bathhouse for frequent ritual cleansing. It follows that Chihiro's four-day journey to the other side is what it takes to restore values missing in her life, namely, a sense of family solidarity and belief in the divine presence.

The Climax and the Final Sequence

The climax of the film is built on a synthesis of style and theme. The bonding motif is strengthened with telling details. Hearing that her mother cannot come home soon, little Mei sets out to visit her with a gift that speaks for itself: an ear of fresh corn. She is soon missed. A frantic search ensues with predictably sentimental results. Shy Kanta does all he can to help, acting as a kind of wise older brother to Satsuki. But of course his bike will not save the day, not in a film with Totoro in it. Satsuki turns to him.

This section takes full advantage of narrative/spectacle tension. Narrative prevails in the ground-level search for Mei, but the minute Totoro comes to the rescue, visual splendor tells the tale. The cat skybus Satsuki rides is an obvious bow to Lewis Carroll. Miyazaki rounds the image out by showing it from every angle—a creature whose very strangeness speaks for a child's uninhibited imagination. It is not just a twelve-legged cat, but cat and mice combined. The soaring fantastical freedom of that ride makes a commonsense narrative landing when Mei is spotted down below on a lonely country path. Her rescue continues the joyride. That, too, makes sense, given the premise of the film, namely, that the world has much to gain from children free to indulge their vivid imaginations.

Girls in fantasy flight is in fact a notable element in many Miyazaki films, among them *Nausicaä of the Valley of the Winds* (Kaze no tani no Naushika, 1984), *Kiki's Delivery Service,* and *Spirited Away.* Susan Napier observes:

> Flying is a major symbol of empowerment for [Miyazaki's] *shōjo* characters. In flight the girls transcend the strictures of the real, be they the expectations of society or simply the limitations of the body itself. Flying also adds a carnival or festival element to the narrative. . . . Most important, however, the image of the flying girl sends a message of boundless possibility in which emotions, imagination, and sometimes even technology (for example, *Nausicaä*'s soaring glider) combine to offer a hope of a potentially attainable alternative world that transcends our own.[18]

Obvious but significant too is the image of flying free on the wind—itself symbolic of natural energy and refreshing purity. Miyazaki is in every way devoted to images whose motions are charged with meaning. In his view, details as commonplace as rice and wheat swaying in the wind speak of nature's power to nurture spirited children like Satsuki and Mei. He is a master at persuading grown-up viewers that we have much to gain from sharing a child's spontaneous and highly imaginative delight in nature as yet unspoiled. The pity is that his films also serve to remind us that the solid, stolid grown-up world has a way of cheating future generations of children of nature's freedoms and formative delights.[19]

Worlds real and imaginary converge to end the film. They are "in fact" distinct, though they touch at important points. We see this family's bond affirmed and strengthened as they, seated on a tree, watch their father beside their mother's hospital bed. The children's gift of an ear of corn communicates across all boundaries. It does not matter how it got there. Neighbor

Granny taught them earlier to see it as a gift from heaven. Here, given to their mother, it speaks for the enduring earthly abundance of loving togetherness. The engaging theme song returns to bring that message home.

My Neighbor Totoro does more than celebrate wholesome bonds and the power of nature to inspire and heal. It praises in order to warn. Miyazaki invites our admiration of gifts that come naturally to children: curiosity and openness to nature, a lively sense of adventure, the power that comes of trusting imagination. Yet these, he insists, are gifts that can be snatched away by grown-ups unwise enough (and forgetful enough) not to recognize their value. He himself has often expressed his belief in the limitless potential that children possess.[20]

In *My Neighbor Totoro* he uses the childlike freedoms of *anime* fantasy to "send that message home" to adult viewers. This film, in effect, urges parents to help their children naturally. Miyazaki also clearly worries about the future of traditional Japanese childhood. Is the nation's push for "progress" threatening to destroy it?

–12–
Cultural Responses to Simplicity
Akira Kurosawa's *Madadayo* (1993)

AKIRA KUROSAWA'S great achievements in his fifty-year filmmaking career have already been summarized in chapter 2. *Madadayo,* made five years before his death, was this great master's thirty-first and last work. However, the film received a rather lukewarm response in both the East and the West. Critics and audiences regard it as lacking the energetic charge and tightly knit structure for which his best films, such as *Seven Samurai* and *Ran,* are famous. Nonetheless, they agree in seeing *Madadayo* as a "self-referential" statement about his own life.[1] They suggest that the film is about Kurosawa's reflections on change and death by way of a nostalgic harkening back to the good old days before the war, when students and teachers forged a lifelong bond. In fact, the first draft of Kurosawa's script was dated August 15, 1991, to commemorate the forty-sixth anniversary of Japan's surrender to the Allied forces.

A number of critics have offered insightful examinations of Kurosawa's approach to the universals addressed in this film. Donald Richie, Stephen Prince, and Mitsuhiro Yoshimoto come to mind. Here I would like to add my observations on this subject and the methods Kurosawa uses to generate complex emotions in his audience.[2] This is important to do, since *Madadayo* is the kind of film that makes considerable demands on its viewer. As I will show, this film requires a keen, "intuitive" sensitivity to specific cultural cues ranging from the boldly elemental to the subtly sophisticated.

Let us begin with Kurosawa's assumption that his viewer will have some general knowledge of Hyakken Uchida (1889–1971), a writer who has been called "the paragon of stylish essayists in modern Japanese literature."[3] After graduating from the German Department of Tokyo University (then known as Tokyo Imperial University), Uchida taught at the Army OCS, Hōsei University, and the like for eighteen years before deciding to become a full-time writer. In his youth, his love of haiku put him under the spell of the Meiji master of that form and fiction, Sōseki Natsume (1867–1916). Though his earlier novellas such as *Meido* (Styx, 1921) were highly acclaimed for their surreal depiction of the human mind, Uchida's name and fame are now most closely associated his best-seller of 1934, a collection of essays on various subjects published under the recondite title *Hyakken zuihitsu* (Essays on the garden of a hundred devils).

The film owes much to his life and works, especially his diaries and essays. A student of modern Japanese literature also knows that throughout his career Hyakken was obsessed with the idea of death. He made his will before he began to work on his diary at the age of twenty-nine. His love of cats and birds is also well known. Two important episodes in *Madadayo* concern the stray cats Nora and Kurz, written about by Hyakken in a number of essays devoted to his pets. One of those essays is titled "Nora ya, Nora!" (Oh, Nora, Nora!), "Nora" being an abbreviation of "Noraneko" (stray cat).[4]

Even though Kurosawa holds his viewer accountable for important amounts of literary information, most of his film's essential cultural specifics lie at the surface, readily available—at least to the Japanese audience. Most of these references are simple and familiar, the commonplace stuff of Japanese childhood. What Kurosawa does is energize these childish icons with emotional and philosophical complexities appropriate to grown-up inspections at the end of life.

As a native Japanese myself, I agree with my countryman, the critic Yoshimoto, who takes note of the importance of various kinds of songs used in the film. "They are all simple and uncontrived," he writes, "naturally expressing human feelings."[5] I only wish he had made more of this valuable observation. Let's consider two important questions this film poses: what are these simple references doing in the film, and how does the old man, this director at the end of his career, make them work?

Kurosawa's Use of Cultural Icons

Madadayo offers too many "leads" to follow up. Especially noticeable are a few important cultural icons readily accessible to the Japanese general audience. I have chosen these few examples because they speak to the central problem that lies at the heart of *Madadayo*, namely, how does the protagonist come to terms with his changing world? His choices of action revolve around that central problem. What will he do? Will he accept change as a necessary condition of life? Or will he refuse? We see the professor protagonist accede to change and to passing time, and in charge of this deeply human drama we have that other old man, Kurosawa, the canny old master who knows exactly how to manage the complex flow of cultural icons so meaningful to him and his audience.

The narrative itself spans nineteen years in the professor's life, from 1943 to 1962. Those years are rich in notable upheavals for him and his countrymen. Social and political changes combine with purely personal ones to bring him to the state we see him reach in old age. The narrative counts on the viewer to fill in most of the obvious historical detail. We are expected, for example, to know about the Hōsei incident that forced Uchida to retire and of course about the war itself.[6] We see no actual air raids, only the massive damage done by them. A glimpse of an American military policeman speaks for the era of the Occupation.

The personal changes in the professor's life evolve into a pattern of repetitions marked by differences of circumstance and outlook. This pattern begins with a clear reference to the Maadakai game of hide-and-seek. The Japanese name for this universal children's game is used as a Buddhist pun I'll elaborate on by and by. This childhood connection takes on a special poignancy at the time of the seventeenth reunion of the old professor with his students. On that occasion he suffers a minor stroke, that harbinger of old age and its sometimes puzzled relationship with the world around—a kind of second childhood game of hide-and-seek.

The theme of reunion extends to the professor's relations with two stray cats. The first to appear is the one called Nora. When she disappears, another stray appears to take her place, the cat named Kurz, which also disappears. A later shot of burial mounds dedicated to them signals the old man's acceptance of his pets' mortality.

Even more pervasively suggestive of that central theme is Kurosawa's use of the waxing and waning moon. That simple, obvious icon is seen and sung about too, as it is in childhood in every culture. Here it is introduced when several students, now middle-aged adults, come to visit their teacher after the war. He is living in temporary shelter, little more than a shack. The old man and his visitors stand outside, looking at the bombed-out city bathed in full moonlight. They revisit their days of childhood innocence by way of a song they sang together then. This song, "Deta deta tsuki ga" (The moon is out), is one every Japanese child learns in kindergarten. The opening stanza compares the rising, round full moon to a tray in the sky. Dark clouds in the second stanza take it away. But lo, in the third stanza the moon tray reappears, sailing out of the clouds. What better metaphor for Kurosawa's theme? What better expression of progress from innocence to experience?

The Japanese cultural context is rich in metaphors expressive of the impermanence of earthly things. As discussed earlier, the Japanese word for this awareness, *mujō,* means literally "nothing is constant." It is a staple theme in many classical pieces of Japanese literature, as witnessed by this ninth-century poem by Ariwara Narihira:

Is not that the moon?	*Tsuki ya aranu*
And is not the spring the same	*Haru ya mukashi no*
Spring of the old days?	*Haru naranu*
My body is the same body—	*Waga mi hitotsu wa*
Yet everything seems different.	*Moto no mi ni shite.*[7]

As any Japanese survivor of high school classical Japanese knows, this poem first appeared in *Ise monogatari* (Tales of Ise), a ninth-century compendium of 125 stories and 209 poems. This particular poem also appeared in a later, equally famous compilation, *Kokinshū* (Collection of old and new poems), an imperial anthology of a thousand *waka* poems compiled in the tenth century.

Earl Miner invites us to consider that poem's ironic contradiction between philosophical reality and human feelings. If the moon changes according to the law of mutability, then surely mankind, being part of ever-changing nature, should follow suit. The trouble is, human nature has its own contradictory tendency to cherish youth—yes, even the youth that cannot outlast its own growth and change[8]—hence the suffering done in verse on behalf of all of us by poets in every culture. In this case, we might add that Narihira was a nobleman at court, a student of everything exquisite and beautiful and elegant—all of it *mujō* doomed to pass away.

Kurosawa's *Madadayo* doubly reinforces the moon image. It returns during the first Maadakai reunion between the professor and his former students. Here, he gives the moon song image a fuller measure of cinematic time in the musical skit the grown-up students perform to act out the changes of the moon. This moon song quite clearly links with another important song, "Aogeba tōtoshi" (Farewell song). The title literally means "looking back at those years, we revere our teachers." As may be expected, this song is a staple of graduation ceremonies in Japanese schools. Just as he does with the moon song, Kurosawa uses it twice in *Madadayo*. It is sung the first time by boisterous students leaving the professor's postwar shack, where he has contrived to host a banquet. We hear it again on a different note at their seventeenth Maadakai, the one marred by the old man's stroke.

As he leaves the hotel, the students and their families send him off with a poignant rendition of "Farewell Song."

Needless to say, this song goes to the heart of the Japanese audience. Any explanation of its complex cultural resonance would have to touch on matters like fond regard for years of learning in school and gratitude to teachers. In a culture so *mujō*-aware, teachers are apt to be seen as guides past *and* future. Certain teachers, such as Kurosawa's professor, may be seen as guardians of lifelong moral development. The reunions seen in this film speak for the value of that relationship, both to the students and to their teacher as he learns his own last lesson about life: the lesson of *mujō* itself, the lesson of acceptance and resignation to things "past and passing and to come" (as the poet Yeats put it so beautifully).

Kurosawa gives the simple moon image another equally important function. He uses it to map out the underlining "thematic" pattern of appearance/disappearance and submergence/emergence. Its most obvious human equivalent is the game of the film's title. As we see, Japanese children playing hide-and-seek use three key expressions: *"Mādada kai?"* (are you ready?), *"Mādada yo"* (not yet), and *"Mō ii yo"* (I'm ready).

Our first experience of the game in the film suggests the obvious link between teacher and childhood innocence. Kurosawa's professor, in fact, is seen by his grown-up students as a man whose essence is a kind of innocence. They compare him to "pure, untarnished gold." Gradually we see how the game of hide-and-seek is more deeply symbolic here. It speaks for the professor's approaching rendezvous with death—the ultimate, most difficult life lesson. And since he is a teacher, it is important for his students to see him learning that lesson, becoming the epitome of *mujō* awareness.

In this way, the teacher plays the role of haiku poet, the man with a gift for telling insights into questions as difficult as death itself. (Hyakken was an acknowledged master of haiku.) The haiku poet's mastery of awareness teaches him that nature and man (as part of nature) are bound by the same laws of change. An interesting side effect of the poet's mastery is a kind of keen, almost vulnerable, affinity with the life around him. We see this in the professor's attachment to his pets, which at times verges on the ridiculous.

One might say that a side effect of that side effect has to do with eyeing death more calmly. There is, in fact, a strong Buddhist tradition of detachment and transcendence expressed with a touch of light-hearted good humor. It would be entirely within the Japanese cultural tradition to think of death as a waiting game, a game of hide-and-seek. The Buddha calls out,

"Are ya ready ta kick the bucket?" And you, poor, wavering mortal, shout back, "Noooooooooo! Not yet!" This brings us to the Japanese grown-up equivalent of end-time hide-and-seek. This more elaborate game takes the form of a Maadakai annual reunion celebrating the long life of a beloved teacher. One of the students in the film refers to the complex pun involved. The opening shout of Japanese hide and seek, *"Māda(da) kai"* (are you ready yet?), rhymes with the Kanji letters associated with two Buddhist deities. "Ma" suggests "Daruma," the saint who attained enlightenment by sitting in meditation until he lost both arms and legs. The letters "Ada" recall Amida Buddha, the dispenser of infinite compassion.

The first such Maadakai reunion in the film takes place in 1946. Kurosawa gives a good twenty minutes to this boisterous celebration in the shadow of wartime death and destruction. He gives that much time again to the seventeenth reunion in 1962. This time, however, change and thoughts about change take on a more sobering tone. All the participants have grown noticeably older. The old professor has grown sadly frail as well. Kurosawa shows us that evidence, leaving his audience to fill in the actual historical blank: the momentous (some would say relentless) social and political changes at work in Japan since the war. Still, each of the professor's rendezvous with death retains a certain playfulness appropriate to *mujō*. Each reunion returns him to "this world."

Amaki (c., George Tokoro) in *Madadayo* (1993). © Kadokawa Co., Ltd.

For actual real movement in and out of it we have his pets. The entrances and exits of these two cats offer a telling counterpoint to the *mujō* pattern of the film. A Japanese viewer cannot help but notice that the stray tabby, Nora, enters the professor's life through a small hole under the willow that shades his garden. She becomes a part of his life then vanishes forever, back through the hole. The other cat, Kurz, comes by way of the hole as well. The symbolism here is obvious to the Japanese viewer, who naturally and culturally knows of the link between willows and the world of ghosts. Buddhist folktales abound in ghosts appearing near willows, restless souls of the dead not yet worthy of entry into heaven.

Kurosawa's Further Exploration of *Mujō*

My own apparition here as restless ghost–critic has to do with arguing for a closer look at Kurosawa's valedictory film. I would like Western viewers to see how he uses the professor's life to express his own deeply ingrained awareness of *mujō* at the end, with all that means for poignant, and in some respects reticent, acceptance of change. The film achieves a brilliantly effective scene evoking that philosophical attitude. It takes place after the war. Since their house was bombed, the professor and his wife have taken shel-

Amaki (l., George Tokoro), Sawamura (c.l., Akira Terao), Takayama (c.r., Hiroshi Igawa), and Professor (r., Tatsuo Matsumura) in *Madadayo* (1983). © Kadokawa Co., Ltd.

ter in the equivalent of a garden shed on a nobleman's estate. When former students come to visit, he lectures them on one of his favorite books, *Hōjōki* (An account of my hut, 1212). The author, Chōmei Kamo (1153–1216), was a Shinto priest turned Buddhist hermit.

Any survivor of the Japanese equivalent of high school English knows *An Account of My Hut* and *Heike monogatari* (The tale of the Heike) as classics of the so-called literature of *mujō*. Both books begin with the obligatory disquisition on the laws of mutability at work in the human world. Kurosawa honors the time-honored educational commitment of the genre by fixing the camera on the professor in a medium shot lasting some four minutes. Could anyone doubt that he means to move the viewer to the head of the class? Certainly many of the more incorrigibly well educated in the Japanese audience will be mouthing the famous opening lines the professor intones, "The flow of the river is ceaseless and its water is never the same. The bubbles that float in the pools, now vanishing, now forming, are not of long duration: so in the world are man and his dwellings."[9] Here too, the professor's discourse on *mujō* refers us to two of the songs used to such effect in the film: "The Moon Is Out" and "Farewell Song." The scene clinches its point at the end with four rapid shots depicting seasonal change. What better counterpoint to scenes of man-made change by way of destruction seen in deep focus as the professor lectures amid the ruins of war?

Chōmei saw something of the same in his own twelfth century. The great fire of 1177 destroyed the capital. Famine, earthquake, and a variety of natural and man-made calamities spoke to him of *mujō*. He also saw them as heralding the last degenerate phase of Buddhism known as *mappō*, the last Dharmic law. Chōmei saw no apocalyptic vision of purposeful destruction, only the prelude to utter chaos. He wrote, "All is as I have described it— the things in the world which make life difficult to endure, our own helplessness and the undependability of our dwellings."[10]

The professor's world is not so hopelessly fragmented. This four-minute scene conveys his commitment to important moral questions posed by Kurosawa's films early and late. Professor and director both want to know if the better world we envision really *can* come to pass. Both want to know where we should look for sources of socially redeeming value.

Early in his career, Kurosawa showed himself a moralist eager to persuade his audience that society can be improved by individuals motivated by compassion—altruism deeply rooted in Buddhism and consonant with Bushido as well. Here we see the professor's benevolence reciprocated by the loyalty of his students, and how this teacher/student bond is of lasting importance. We also see evidence that the professor's simple probity influences others as well. The man who sold him the plot of ground for his tiny house was a complete stranger. But later that same man turns down a hugely profitable offer for land adjacent. The mansion a Yakuza boss wants to build there would block the sunlight, casting the professor's house and garden in shadow.

Kurosawa's sense of moral imperative finds ways to speak through no end of telling details. The trouble is that many such details "speak" only to viewers familiar with the Japanese cultural context. One example is the song the professor sings at the seventeenth reunion party. On the face of it, his choice of "Daikoku-sama" could pass for a generic gesture of forward-looking hopefulness suitable to the occasion. Daikoku-sama, one of the five ancient celestial deities, is the god of wealth or good fortune in Japan. And so the professor sings. Apart for a few quick cuts to his audience, the camera frames him in a medium shot, giving full cinematic time to his rendition of all three stanzas. (That other old master, Ozu, often did the same.)

This song's significance is immediately apparent to the native audience. Most Japanese know the story it refers to, a famous episode from Japan's first written history dating back to 712, a book titled *Kojiki* (Records of ancient matters). This compendium of creation myths, imperial genealogies, and folktales contains this story about Daikoku in the mythical days when the world was young. Then, as the teacher's song says, all of creation lived in harmony. But then one day sharks attack a rabbit, leaving him badly injured. Ōkuninushi no Mikoto, a kindly god, passes by and teaches the sufferer how to heal his wound. (The name of this god as written in Chinese characters can be construed as "Taikoku," hence the later conflation with Japan's own god of wealth, Daikoku.)

Some Japanese audiences are also famously receptive to moralistic input in every medium, even cinema, so Kurosawa can count on his countrymen to catch the professor's drift here. He is, in effect, suggesting that any act of kindness "shines like a good deed in a naughty world," whether that world is the ancient mythical one or the rapidly changing modern one of postwar Japan. By this point in the film we know that the professor practices what he preaches. And knowing Kurosawa as we do, we might even see unmistakable traces of an ancient deity in this frail old modern man, filled as he is with compassion for fellow humans and stray animals.

Where then, would analysis of its important cultural icons lead us in this film? Syntagmatically, they must be related to the final scene that depicts the professor's dream. A number of auteurists relate it to Kurosawa's 1990 film, *Dreams* (Yume). Yet no critic thus far has pointed out an important connection between this closing scene and its source in Hyakken Uchida. A quick glance of that writer's representative works shows how dreams furnish important material throughout. Many, such as *Styx,* explore the narrator's vision of death in terms of his dreams.

The Final Scene

Kurosawa's lyrical final scene consists of six shots. It opens with an extreme distant view of a group of children playing hide-and-seek. They move screen right. One boy seems to harken back to the professor's childhood. This boy has the old man's air of unsullied innocence. He goes off by himself, looking for a place to hide. The next two shots follow him. He finds a pile of straw. He seems about to enter it when the other childish voices off-screen call out, *"Mādada kai?"* (are you ready?). Yet the boy doesn't hide. The fourth long shot takes in the boy at the foot of the hill and his companions at the top. The boy says loudly, *"Mādada yo"* (no, not yet). The same two shouts ring out between them again as the next shot pans up from the boy to meet the sky. What can this mean but that the old professor is not yet ready to die?

The film ends with a picturesque sky view richly tinged with color as the music soars to a climax. The scene is reminiscent of the Buddhist pantheon of Amida described in the last episode of *The Tale of the Heike.* Colorful clouds descend to lead the dead into the world to come. Here, of course, the vision is Kurosawa's, his dreamlike attempt to lend meaning to life's full circle.

We know that the professor will wake from his dream—his subconscious mulling over questions about death—and return to the world of reality. We make that guess based on our knowledge that Hyakken died in 1971. If we are right, the professor will survive his lovely reverie for another eight years. Then finally, playfully (we think), he will say, *"Mō ii yo"* (I am ready).

I do think viewers East and West can see (as many have, in fact) that Kurosawa's last film is a meditation on change and death. Those who view it from the "inside," from the vantage point of personal experience of Japanese culture, will also find themselves nodding in assent as the grand old man looks backward with some degree of sweet sorrow and yearning for a somewhat different Japan now lost in time.

In fact, this film struck just such a chord with Japanese audiences still populated with those of Kurosawa's age. The critic Nagaharu Yodogawa (1901–2000) found himself responding to its story of teacher/student bonding by dissolving in tears.[11] Taking his point of view, we might well feel entitled to mixed emotions—sweet nostalgia for the past and some bitter judgments too, seeing as how prosperity gives so much, even as it takes away much whose loss we live to regret.

Surely there is a telling irony in the fact that this film was released in the 1990s, a decade marked by a new social phenomenon in Japan: teachers assaulted by students. No wonder many Japanese are beginning to ask questions about the true worth of material prosperity, even as the media celebrate the latest manias related to life at the luxurious "top." The pet craze is a recent example: the upscale dog bathed in its own upscale shower, pampered even postmortem, in a luxury pet cemetery plot.

The old professor's love for his students and pets seems a world away from all such extremes. Kurosawa's film seems a worthwhile invitation to consider the values of that world. Maybe we should not be shy about joining in its naïve "Farewell Song":

> We look up to our teachers,
> We think how much we owe to them
> In the garden of learning they tended.
> And now so many years have passed,
> It's time to bid them a fond farewell.

–13–
The Danger and Allure of Phantom Light
Hirokazu Koreeda's *Maboroshi* (1995)

HIROKAZU KOREEDA (b. 1962) is one of a new breed of director, one whose interest in social issues has a strongly documentary bent. In 1987 he joined TV Man Union, a production company, where he made documentaries such as *However* (Shikashi: Fukushi kirisute no jidai ni, 1991), *Another Type of Education* (Mō hitotsu no kyōiku, 1991), and *August without Him* (Kare no inai hachigatsu ga, 1994).

Koreeda gained international recognition in 1995 when a number of festivals singled out *Maboroshi* (Maboroshi no hikari) as the first feature-length film of a promising new talent and tendency. Makoto Shinozaki's *Okaeri* shared in this triumph, and rightly so, since both newcomers offered a confident, thought-provoking approach to a familiar subject still relevant in Japan today: the breakdown of an ordinary family. *Okaeri* studies a young couple's helplessness in face of the wife's decline into insanity. *Maboroshi* explores a young widow's growing obsession with death.

Koreeda's next two films continued to probe the subject of death through its dynamic interaction with memory: *After Life* (Wandafuru raifu, 1999) and *Distance* (2002).[1] *After Life* revisits the theme of an earlier TV documentary, *Without Memory* (Kioku ga ushinawareta toki, 1999).[2] A group of individuals, recently deceased, is asked to describe the cherished memory they would take into eternal life. Also shot in a documentary style, *Distance* connects death and memory in a story directly related to real-life events. After the notorious sarin gas-attack carried out by members of Aum shinri-kyō in 1995, the perpetrators were executed by others in the cult. Koreeda's film bears documentary witness to a visit by friends and relatives to the execution site. A convoluted "plot" evolves as the film shifts back and forth between past and present as survivors confront and interact with their individual and collective memories of the deceased.

Koreeda's output to date has been limited, but his thematic orientation seems clearly set on an intensely personal path, especially compared to the youthful New Wave directors making their marks the year he was born. Asked to comment on his own New Wave generation, he said, "The current New Wave is quite different from mainstream filmmaking. Directors seem to be focusing more on personal issues, less on themes like Japanese politics or history."[3]

Among those feature films of a rather apolitical nature, I think Koreeda's debut feature-length film, *Maboroshi,* is by far the best and also the most accessible to a general audience. The film has been widely discussed since it won the Golden Ozella, the prize awarded the third best picture at the Venice Film Festival.[4] As so often is the case, the discussion has bred its share of questionable critical observations and assumptions. Some of them, I think, stray into errors damaging to appreciation of this significant work. For example, it is generally assumed that the first two segments of *Maboroshi* are set in Osaka, when they are in fact set in Amagasaki, an industrial city associated with the steel industry. The film encompasses three locales, each in its way important in relation to Koreeda's exploration of the central metaphor of his title, *Maboroshi no hikari,* literally, "phantasmal light."

Several critics have made much of Koreeda's stylistic forebears, most notably Ozu and Mizoguchi.[5] Any such resemblance is at best superficial and potentially deceptive. I would argue (and in fact will) that Koreeda's mode of representation differs radically from those two great masters. Setting the record straight on that point will give us a chance to explore related issues. We will find much to praise in this new director's synthesis of thematic thrust and expressive devices in support of it. We will see how he experiments with color and pervasive use of the long take and long shot. Study of his remarkable camera work will show us how to read "on sight" the cues he offers by way of taking us into the protagonist's unspoken thoughts and feelings.

Narrative Progression: The Prologue and the Second Segment

The central problem of *Maboroshi* has to do with the heroine Yumiko's coming to terms with her life after loss, with finding a way to go on living after the death of loved ones. Will she seek comfort in the past? Or will she learn to trust in the future? Those are the choices open to her. They make for a straightforward story whose complications are all about anguished hesitation as the grieving Yumiko finds a way to live.

The screenplay spans about ten years in three parts with significant narrative ellipses between. The opening sequence serves as a prologue, setting the stage for the drama that follows. We first meet Yumiko at twelve years of age. We see why she feels responsible for her grandmother's disappearance and, presumably, death. A blackout takes us from that childhood trauma to the second segment, where she is a happy newlywed mother in her early twenties. Still, she is haunted by that childhood grief. Now suddenly her husband, Ikuo, for no apparent reason, commits suicide.

A fade speeds us forward about six years to the third and longest part of the film. Yumiko and her boy, Yūichi, take the train to remote Sosogi, a small coastal town near Wajima in Ishikawa Prefecture on the Sea of Japan. A matchmaker has arranged a marriage with a widower, Tamio. His daughter, Tomoko, is a little older than her son. The rest of the story takes place in Sosogi, except for one brief shift back to Amagasaki, where Yumiko goes to attend her brother's wedding. In both places Koreeda counts on his powerful cinematic rubrics to convey a sense of Yumiko's pain as she is torn between claims of past and future lives. Her conflict may also be seen in Freudian terms as the classical dichotomy of Eros and Thanatos, love and death.

Brief as it is, the opening sequence of the film provides its *donnée*. Here Koreeda introduces motifs, imagery, and stylistic devices he will return to throughout. The scene depicting the grandmother's disappearance is seen from afar. We have seen the child Yumiko run down the dark tunnel of an underpass, hesitate, and race up onto a noisy overpass bridge to catch up with the old lady hobbling along. The camera holds us back. We see two figures in distant shadow profile, a child catching hold of a shrunken, arthritic old woman who seems scarcely larger than herself. We cannot see faces but we do hear voices clearly. The soundtrack brings them close, two voices raised above the din of traffic down below. The child's high-pitched, anxious pleading is answered by the old lady's softly weary declaration. She must go to Shikoku—to Sukumo, her native village. That is where she must die. The child argues in vain. We see the crooked old shadow free itself from the young one and hobble on into the distance. The young shadow watches her vanish.

We have not seen the old woman's face. It might have answered the obvious questions. How does she feel about growing old? About city life? The camera's gaze takes in the scene, suggesting answers to those questions. This is a noisy, crowded, run-down place. Yumiko's family lives nearby, in sight and sound of road and railway traffic. Their tiny house itself is buried in shadows cast by those same hectic arteries raised above their narrow street.

This is Amagasaki, the setting for the first two parts of the film. It lies between Osaka and Kobe. Amagasaki is a typical steel town, a dreary creation of the grit and grime and chaos of heavy industry. The grandmother's brief reference to her native place offers a telling contrast. Sukumo in Shikoku is a coastal village in Kōchi Prefecture, a place of idyllic scenic beauty blessed with abundant sunlight. What person, even with dying in mind, wouldn't prefer that openness and light to this narrow, dirty confinement we see the old lady turning her back on?

Her wished-for destination also connects with the central metaphor of the film's Japanese title, *Maboroshi no hikari*.[6] It is a pity that the film is marketed abroad as *Maboroshi,* period. That is somewhat misleading, since that word confines the title meaning to mirage, phantom, or illusion. The full Japanese title completes the film's controlling metaphor: Koreeda's counterpointing of *maboroshi* (illusion) and *hikari* (light). The phantom illusion is visible as light, though in the end we see the reality of everyday light triumph after all. Light is a theme right from the beginning. After the grandmother disappears, the camera invites discomfort as it moves among the glaring confusions of city light. It pauses to gaze up at a streetlight's gritty glare. Yumiko's little brother lights firecrackers.

The grandmother has turned her back on this hectic scene. We do not know it yet, but the title of the film anticipates the visionary gleam of phantom light we will see in its most sinister aspect: the light that lures a person into death's dark shadow. But even here, the grandmother's yearning for the sunlit village of her birth is couched in an express wish to die and be buried there. What better evidence for the death wish of Freudian Thanatos?

A number of critics have pointed to the grandmother's turning away as the first of many instances of a gesture/leitmotif expressing loss of a loved one.[7] We see it again when Yumiko's husband, Ikuo, comes home to fetch an umbrella. She in her fondness follows him downstairs into the street and watches him go. His gait is jaunty, nonchalant. She answers it with an endearing feminine motion of her own, rising on tiptoe as if expecting him to turn and return her little wave of everyday love. But Ikuo never looks back.

The next news she has of him is the worst. The policeman says that he ignored the train's warning whistle, the screeching brakes. Ikuo, the engineer said, kept walking down the tracks ahead, "never looking back." It is as if "lights" (possibly railway lights) looming out of darkness had beckoned him. Like Yumiko's grandmother, the manner of his going suggests that he answered the phantom light call of Thanatos.

In stark contrast to this movement is the act of "gazing into." We see this when the child Yumiko runs out of the house at night through dark and light of city streets up onto the overpass bridge in one last desperate search for her grandmother. She heads back home, downcast. Ikuo is seen with his bicycle on screen left in the foreground. He looks in her direction. The next point-of-view shot shows the object of his intent gaze: Yumiko's forlorn figure. That gaze will be seen again later at the height of Yumiko's happiness as Ikuo's wife and mother of their baby. She goes to his place of work and stands outside peering in through the window. Ikuo returns her gaze. This is the only time we see them as lovers looking in one another's eyes.

Here in the nighttime point-of-view shot, they are still children, cast in glaring light and shade of noisy cityscape. The prologue to Yumiko's story ends with a screen suddenly black. Sleepy voices of husband and wife tell us where we are now—with Yumiko waking Ikuo, wanting to talk about the troubling dream she has had, again, about her grandmother. Was that previous shot of their young love part of Yumiko's dream? Or did it really happen? Is it part of her waking recollection of that fateful night? It does not really matter which. What matters is what comes home to us now: that Yumiko is still tormented by feelings of guilt and loss.

Even so, the second segment proceeds with happy views of Yumiko's life as the wife of her childhood friend and mother of a baby three months old. She seems to have overcome her obsession with her grandmother's death. Ikuo seems good-natured, good-humored. So why did he suddenly choose to die? Yumiko asks to see the body. The policeman tells her there is nothing left to see. The story turns on this second sudden, mystifying loss. Koreeda orchestrates a powerful array of intricate stylistic devices aimed at showing how Yumiko struggles in vain to free herself from obsession with past loss.

At one point a long take shows her gazing into space. This simple composition speaks for her new condition, that of the widow bereft of her husband's gaze in return. Yumiko sits motionless near the window. She is seen in profile, in a medium shot. The camera keeps its respectful distance, denying our natural curiosity a closer look at her face. We can guess that it wears a blank expression. She shows no interest in her baby nearby. Her mother is bathing him and putting him to bed. Toward the end of the take, she announces her decision to move in and help her daughter and the child.

Ikuo's bicycle returns to play an important part as well. Earlier we saw them polishing it and then cycling through the city night, Ikuo pedaling, Yumiko riding behind. Rain was forecast that day he came home to get an umbrella. We saw how he parked the bike and left it there when he walked away so jauntily, followed by the loving gaze he did not turn around to see, much less return.

After his death, the bicycle becomes a poignant symbol of his absence and her sense of grieving emptiness. We see her use it in a series of telling shots. The camera takes note of her pushing the bike along alone, disconsolate. She crosses screen left. The camera follows. A long shot shows her turning her back on the camera, pushing the bike along a street in the distance. To the right, the busy elevated highway looms. We can scarcely miss its reference to the day her grandmother vanished, the same day Yumiko and Ikuo exchanged such a significant look right there. That gaze needed no words to explain it. Now the camera gazes in silence at Yumiko. We do not need words to tell us how she feels. Picture after picture tells us how it is with her. She herself feels lost and gone, a stranger in a world painfully familiar. The camera fixes its gaze on her in an extreme long shot, as she grows tiny in the distance, a lone forlorn figure taking its small place in the noisy heartless cityscape.

A fade marks a considerable narrative gap as the third segment opens on Yumiko about six years later. We are left to wonder how she managed to survive her grief, raise her son, Yūichi, and work to support them both.

Yumiko (l., Makiko Esumi) and Ikuo (r., Tadanobu Andō) in *Maboroshi* (1995). © TV Man Union.

Koreeda moves right ahead with her story. It continues with news of a major change about to take place.

The Suggestive Power of the Central Metaphor and Koreeda's Experiment with Colors

We have seen how the hectic glare of city life in Amagasaki served the title metaphor of phantom light in parts one and two. Part three quite literally sheds new light on that controlling metaphor as Yumiko and her son move out into nature in Sosogi. This little coastal village looks seaward, like the village her grandmother set out to find again the day she disappeared. However, it is far from an idyllic village. Hardly blessed with warm sunlight, it is noted for the long winter. As Yumiko's new husband observes, the landscape around Sosogi is "barren." Barren it may be, but in the spring the mountainside sweeping up behind the house is open to the sun, and Yumiko's new home hugs the sparkling blue shore of the sunlit, turbulent Sea of Japan.

Significantly, Koreeda symbolically links light imagery to color corollary in order to dramatize Yumiko's vacillating state. Though the series of everyday snapshots we see is sketching out the future life of wife and mother, Thanatos haunts her. Here in Sosogi we are (perhaps subliminally) aware of Koreeda's use of red to underscore it. We notice that Tomoko's backpack is bright red. The camera also takes note of red flowers blooming in the field. A red oil container sits in the corner of the kitchen. When Tamio and Yumiko visit the market the day after they marry, a red tent occupies the foreground.

More importantly, even songs are structured around light. Yumiko sings a song about a red flower compared to the shining sun. On their way back to Amagasaki, Tomoko and Yūichi sing a children's song about toys. Again it introduces a similar simile: "The toys are like twinkling stars." Red tends to be a stand-out color wherever it is, but here we catch notes of meaningful emphasis.

On the contrary, green, for obvious reasons, belongs to the young. Green is the color of simple hopeful joys: candy and carefree childhood play outdoors in the country. Some of these scenes related to green even aspire to the idyllic. One scene shows Yūichi and Tomoko's playful journey. They chase across snowdrifts and through green fields. True, given the tone of Yumiko's previous life, they cause us moments of anxiety, too. We see them enter the darkness of a covered bridge, a sinister reminder of that glimpse we had of the child Yumiko searching for her lost grandmother.

But at the end of this dark tunnel the children run into green light and more light. Yūichi leads the way, tiny arms swinging manfully, as they run the length of a very long dike that dams a pond high up in sight of the sea. The sea is too far away to fear, but here, so perilously near, is this pond. We see in a flash what we are meant to see: that these children, too, live on the edge of death's dark shadow, even on sunlit days.

The critic Kenichi Ōkubo claims that the outdoor sequence of Yūichi and Tomoko's playful venture is a manifestation of "Yumiko's subconsciousness hovering on the verge of life and death."[8] It is a valid interpretation. However, one can also argue that Koreeda simply contrasts the innocent children's life with the adults'. Throughout the film Koreeda keeps reinforcing "green" as an attribute of Yūichi. This color is suggestive of Yumiko's yearning for a better future. We have seen many instances of this earlier. The scene of Yumiko and Ikuo's last night out was suffused with green. When they came out from the coffee shop and walked down the street, the camera impressed upon us the greenish glow of street lamps.

The day Yumiko and Yūichi left the city, we saw the boy hold his first piece of candy up to passing window light in the train. Like Yumiko, we shared his childish fascination with its gem-like flash of green, answering the greenish light outside. Here in part three the same green candy returns.

Yumiko (Makiko Esumi) in *Maboroshi* (1995). © TV Man Union.

The scene of the children's game leads to another scene of their togetherness. Yūichi and Tomoko are riding home in the back of Tamio's truck. There he shares the last of his green candy with his stepsister. The candy was a goodbye gift from the old man next door in Amagasaki.

A viewer responsive to color cues will find any number of subtle emotional hints expressed that way. (We will consider more examples later on.) Koreeda works in silence much of the time, eliciting responses with many kinds of visual cues. Time after time the camera pauses, as if in contemplation of a room or scene. These are telling narrative moments, that we know. We are invited to take note of everyday details.

Sometimes Koreeda adds motion to these studies in the suggestive power of light. In one, the camera studies Yumiko as she cleans a short flight of stairs inside the house at Sosogi. Light floods in on her from an unseen source above. This shaft of light lends a hazy, conspiratorial atmosphere to the scene. It illuminates some surfaces and casts others in shadows darker by reason of brilliant contrast. The camera shifts its angle in relation to Yumiko as if to study her motions in greater detail. What is there to see? Is there something more than a woman scrubbing the stairs in her house? We notice that she moves with the vigor of someone working to banish a troubling thought.

Part three of the film draws us deeper into the drama of Yumiko's haunted inner life. Koreeda leads the way by showing us pictures rich in telling detail of everyday life troubled by hints and portents of "phantom light." Sometimes we get the briefest glimpse, as when the camera looks out at fishermen lost from sight, all but the twinkling lights of their boats in the restless darkness of the sea. At other times, we find ourselves gazing transfixed by a brilliant play of light and composition used to intensify our understanding of Yumiko's inner torment. The more actively narrative drive in this third part of the film exposes us to even more troubling aspects of Yumiko's suffering: the real and present danger to her life of this sinister trickster *maboroshi no hikari* (phantom light).

The Reality of Illusion: The Motif of Journey in the Third Segment

We should not be surprised to see part three of *Maboroshi* open with a change of scene. The journey metaphor is an age-old device for exploring the timeless question of individual survival in the face of mysterious and capricious human destiny. And so Yumiko and her son leave for Sosogi, for a change of place, somewhere the story can play itself out. She will make two other brief journeys en route to *dénouement*. The first might be called a straightforward, narrative, matter-of-fact event. Returning to Amagasaki for her brother's wedding, Yumiko revisits the past she has ostensibly left behind. But has she really? That journey opens up troubling possibilities of doubt. The other brief journey confirms and helps resolve those doubts. It takes her—and us—into another kind of narrative event, one whose matters of fact are in fact open to question. It is ostensibly a funeral procession she follows at a distance. This is Yumiko's own near-death experience, her direct encounter with the allure and danger of the phantom light itself. We will discuss that splendidly beautiful, deeply troubling scene when we come to it.

In the meantime, most of part three makes obvious narrative sense, though we must be visually active partners, too, willing to engage with Koreeda's carefully orchestrated cinematic rubrics. Clue after clue alerts us to Yumiko's continued silent suffering. Dialogue does play its part, but most of what we learn about this woman's emotional quandary comes by way of inference: "facts" of her case we get from watching pictures and gestures carefully composed.

One might say that Koreeda's camera takes us in hand, making us thoughtful witnesses of everyday life. We see this in the casual narrative flow of shots whose business is getting Yumiko and Yūichi from Amagasaki to Sosogi. Accompanied by her mother, they walk to the station. Guided by the camera, we take note of their silence, of Yumiko's air of restraint, of uncertainty. Her long, black dress looks oddly mournful for a woman on her way to become a bride. But mourning becomes Yumiko, tall and willowy, gracefully sad as she is. This will be her "look" for much of part three. It is especially noticeable when she returns to Amagasaki for her brother's wedding. Then we see her visiting these streets and rooms she is leaving now.

Here at the outset, two shots seem especially remarkable. One is a long take lasting over two minutes. Here cinematic time corresponds to actual time. Yumiko and Yūichi say goodbye to her mother and cross to a platform across the tracks. The camera watches from a distance, standing still. They move slowly down the all but deserted platform. A barge off yonder moves slowly on the dirty industrial river. Mother and son look as lonely and sad as their surroundings.

Later, aboard the train, Yūichi's childish energy shows itself in shadow play, holding the sparkling green candy up to the light (as mentioned above). He draws her attention to his feat. She smiles, clearly making an effort to change her train of thought. We can easily guess which way it runs. By and by a flickering sunlit country landscape floods the car with cheerful light.

Compared to industrial Amagasaki, the little seaside village of Sosogi looks like a promise of better life to come. Still, it will be the scene of a dynamic struggle between past and present, as the phantom light of grief and doubt threaten to destroy Yumiko. As she greets her new father-in-law, we hear this bit of news on the radio: "The industry in the area is on decline." Her new husband adds that Sosogi is shrinking in size, thanks to so many young people leaving in hopes of a better life in the city.

Almost ironically, the camera is generous in its appreciation of gorgeous views. True, the mountainsides are not majestically wooded, but they sweep grandly up behind the town. And while the Sea of Japan is famous for its wild waves and rough weather, it fronts the village with the deep, rich blue of endless horizon. Surely here Yumiko can find peace—in a place so much like Sukumo, the little coastal town her grandmother yearned so much to return to.

We do see Yumiko trying to adjust. She says to her new husband's daughter, "I will be your mother now." Her new husband and his family seem to take her in quite naturally. She says nothing about unhappiness, but time and again the camera catches her gazing off into space. The camera focuses our attention, too, on the color red, like a small red mailbox in front of the house. The objects themselves are in no way remarkable, but they do stand out. Like Yumiko's abstracted gaze, they seem to hint at thoughts of death.

Tamio (c., Takashi Naitō), Tamio's father (c.r., Akira Emoto), and Yumiko (Makiko Esumi) in *Maboroshi* (1995). © TV Man Union.

Yumiko's brief return to Amagasaki is for a happy occasion, her brother's wedding. The wedding, however, is not shown. Instead, we see Yumiko revisiting scenes from the past. We know enough to feel the weight they add to her secret burden. She peers in through the window of the factory where Ikuo worked. It is empty, motionless. We have our own investment of interest in this place, the scene of the only time we saw Yumiko and Ikuo gaze into one another's eyes. She walks their old street. A bicycle passes, tinkling its bell. We know that sound, for her, has something like the value of a knell. The next thing we know, we are studying her face as she stands in the door of their old apartment. Its empty gleam casts a glow. In its light we catch this rare close-up of her. In her face we see nothing. It is blank. But blank expressions can be telling too.

Finally, we hear someone speak about Ikuo's death. It is the master of the coffee shop where she and Ikuo sat in such a happy, teasing mood. Now the proprietor tells Yumiko something she did not know: Ikuo came in the day he died. There was nothing unusual about him then. We see Yumiko growing more pensive, absorbing this news in silence. Surely her question is as natural as wanting to know what it meant that Ikuo chose to die on that perfectly ordinary day in his life. Surely that is the haunting mystery that threatens Yumiko so.

She returns to Sosogi. There we see her anxiety grow. One especially dramatic instance concerns Tomeno, an old woman related to the family. Again a journey motif returns. She is going out to fish for crabs in spite of stormy winter weather. The wild sea wind whistles in a partly open window as Yumiko comes to look out. A shift in shot shows Tomeno outside looking up, asking how many crabs she'd like. A point-of-view shot from Yumiko's line of sight shows the old woman turning her back on her and heading out to sea. We do not need to be told what that departing likeness means to Yumiko.

We see Yumiko's emotional tension build as the storm gathers strength, darkening the house. We sense that hours have passed. The family gathers in the kitchen. A cut to the outside shows a raging snowstorm in progress. And still no sign of Tomeno. The family refuses to share Yumiko's concern. Her father-in-law says, in effect, that Tomeno is a tough old bird who knows the sea so well she could swim her way back to shore if need be. Yumiko tries to light a kerosene stove. The fuel can sits off to one side, insistently red, a reminder of that color hint throughout signifying death.

Another shot shows Tamio lounging at ease in the foreground and Yumiko in the background, sitting upright, facing the camera. Even at this distance she conveys a sense of being rigid with anxiety. Tamio gets up to answer a loud knocking at the door. Yumiko sits alone. Could she be thinking of that other dark night when she sat up waiting for Ikuo? That night she fell asleep, only to wake to the policeman's knock, to ride through rainy darkness to the station. Tamio enters with Tomeno. She who turned her back on the safety of the shore was not lured to her death.

From this point on, signs of her unease proliferate as scenes from her everyday life continue. She goes to the market, still wearing the long, black overcoat that adds such a note of mourning to her graceful young figure. The bicycle theme returns. Yūichi runs to look at bikes for sale as Yumiko talks to Tomeno in her market stall. The old lady asks how old the boy was when his father died.

That commonplace question leads to a logical poignant scene. Back at the house, Yumiko opens a drawer and takes something out. The way she handles it suggests a memento. And sure enough, we see what it is: the bicycle bell key she gave Ikuo. She cradles one hand in the other as she holds the bell key in her palm, then closes her fingers, hiding it from sight. She hears someone coming and moves quickly to put the bell key in the drawer. Tamio, coming in, glimpses that motion and asks, "What are you hiding?" "Oh, nothing," she says. Tamio accepts her response. Still, that scene between Yumiko and Tamio has its jarring inference. How could a woman so locked up tight in tormented grief have explained this memento to her new husband?

Koreeda has enriched his narrative with a parallel scene that offers an oblique answer to that very question. It also heightens our sense that Yumiko is on the brink of an emotional crisis. Here we see her sitting upright at the kitchen table, facing the camera. Tamio, still in his overcoat, sprawls dead drunk in front of her, supported by the table. Her complaint about having to wait and worry all evening long is couched in terms of harm to him, not her. She says that driving drunk is "dangerous." This long take gives us time to sense her building frustration as he continues to lie there in a slump. We see that at some point while she waited she opened that little drawer again, because now she occupies her hands with Ikuo's bell key. As she fidgets, it tinkles. That erratic, arrhythmic sound adds its nervous counterpoint to the steadily regular tick-tock of the kitchen clock. Suddenly Yumiko breaks. She moves closer to Tamio. She questions his past, not Ikuo's, now. Her tone is shrill, despairing, as she asks him in plain words, "Why did you leave Osaka? Why did you marry me?" Did he come back here to marry *her*, she asks. She has crossed that perilous line, raising the ghost of the previous wife.

Suddenly we are aware of something else new. Can Yumiko be suffering jealousy? Has her blank expression all this time concealed more attachment to her new life than we were led to expect? Has she in fact fallen in love with Tamio? A viewer alert to the complex tension built into the narrative thus far will know that this director is not about to take the easy way out.

Climax and Resolution: Life in the Light of Death

Yumiko's outburst is left unresolved. In a scene depicting marriage as usual, Tamio's drunken stupor might serve as an excuse for letting the moment pass into long-suffering silence of resentment common enough. But this is the story of this woman's state of mind. Thanks to Koreeda's eloquent silent treatment, we know a fair bit about Yumiko's inner imbalance. We have seen the peril in her conflicted sense of having to choose between Eros and Thanatos.

Koreeda approaches her moment of climactic choice in deceptively casual fashion. He has done this often enough for us to be on the alert for hints of danger lurking in everyday events. A glance at Tamio and Yūichi playing catch ends with the father asking his stepson a perfectly ordinary question: "Where's mommy?" The camera answers his question. It shows us Yumiko at some distance, sitting at a bus stop. She is wearing the long, black overcoat so oddly familiar now, mournful as it seems, like her air of being lost in thought. We see that now, too. The bus pulls in, blocking our view of Yumiko. As it pulls away, the camera clearly takes note of its flashing red caution lights. Black coat and red light interact. As so often before, we sense some connection with Yumiko's inner turmoil.

Previous shots of Yumiko in transit lead us to expect a view of her inside the bus. But the bus passes on out of sight. We are left with the camera's thoughtful pause on the bus stop shelter. A rectangle of solid black shadow all but fills the doorframe. This, too, seems like an obvious, ominous hint. This moment of stasis, however, delivers a startling surprise. Yumiko steps out through that dark shadow into the light. Here she is after all! What on earth is she up to? Even as we wonder, we hear a tinkling sound she must be hearing, too. Could it echo a bicycle bell?

A shift to a medium shot answers that question with a matter of fact even more ominously pertinent to Yumiko's state of mind: two mourners in a procession are seen striking a funeral chime. A long shot enlarges our view as the sound of wind merges with the notes of this funeral knell. We have a sense of sharing Yumiko's view. Then a shifting high-angle shot shows the procession advancing slowly toward the camera. This shift in perspective itself might cause us to take in breath, a response well nigh guaranteed by another surprise in a sequence whose visual mystery and splendor grows more breathtaking with every shot. It begins here, as we see the procession advance through a drifting veil of white—hard to tell which it is, snowflakes or shattering blossoms of cherry or plum. The funeral knell is joined by simple folk music featuring bamboo flute.

Delightful as this vision is, there is something uncertain in it, too. Is it real or surreal? Is it a matter-of-fact coincidence with what we know to be Yumiko's troubled state of mind? Or is it in fact a delusion, a projection of that state of mind? A syntagmatic view of the sequence argues for illusion. Certainly any Japanese viewer versed in the Japanese classics will catch the allusion conveyed by this picture. A famous example would be these verses by Ōtomo Yakamochi, the eighth-century editor of *Manyōshū* (A collection of myriad leaves):

What is this fallen in my garden?	*Waga sono no*
Blossoms from	*Sumono no hana ka*
The courtyard plums?	*Niwa ni furu*
New snow scattered	*Hadare no imada*
Lingering on the ground?	*Nokoritaru ka mo.*[9]

On screen, as in the poem, we see an effect of heightened consciousness, possibly Yumiko's. We cannot feel sure, but already at this stage we sense the possibility that Yumiko's agitated imagination is the source of this solemn celebration of the end of life. That likelihood grows stronger as we watch the scene grow steadily more splendidly ominous. A shift to extreme long shot reframes the procession. It now moves slowly from right to left along the beach. This framing confines the human figures to a narrow band between earth and sky. That band is close to the bottom of the frame. The slow motion of figures seen in black profile creates an effect of solidity shared with the earth. But the frame is heavy with sky as well. These tiny figures appear to bear the weight not just of a single corpse, but of an immense horizon weighing down on them. The music adds its rueful tone to this scene, which empties as slowly as it was filled. The camera's transfixed gaze shows Yumiko's lone figure, black like the rest, trailing some distance behind. When the last of the mourners vanishes off screen to the left she is left alone, briefly centered on the screen before she, too, vanishes slowly. This magnificent slow shot lasts a full two minutes and eighteen seconds. As mentioned earlier, several critics see the influence of Mizoguchi in this long take. I would argue that the resemblance is far less illuminating than a radical difference in approach.

Let us look at the old master, whose famous long take in outdoor scenes relies on two different uses of the camera. In one the camera is fixed in place. In the other, its movement may be described as liquid. In either case, the Mizoguchi long take is also a showcase for masterly performers doing their best for a director whose drive for perfection was commonly considered "diabolical."

Two boat scenes from two Mizoguchi films are justly famous for their dramatic use of the long take. The first is in *The Crucified Lovers* (Chikamatsu monogatari, 1954). The gentlewoman Osan and her servant Mohei have fled a false suspicion of adultery. Their boat scene is intended to dramatize a shift in psychology from constraint to freedom. In place of Koreeda's long-distance framing, here we are given a medium shot, and for good reason. Thanks to Mizoguchi's exquisite attention to detail, his accomplished actors use gesture and dialogue to bring a wealth of subtle detail to this shift from suicidal resignation to enraptured desire to live and love.

This is no easy transition, since more is involved than overcoming a shared death wish. The director's task is to present a plausible victory over formidable social and psychological forces opposed to the socially unacceptable decision they reach by the end of the scene. Since both of them are products of a rigidly hierarchical society, those same forces are at work in the lovers themselves.

Mizogochi's brilliant solution depends in part on his camera's steady gaze on the couple. The resulting shot is very long in cinematic time. It lasts several minutes, long enough for the movements of these talented actors to create a system of connotations. Though the shot framework is open all that time, the lovers in their boat are enveloped in dense fog. That effect echoes the psychological contradiction in process of being resolved. It also adds a sense of enclosure, adding to the feeling of rapt attention we share, thanks to the camera's studious observation of the slightest visual alteration in this scene. We cannot help but be drawn in by its beauty of texture and composition: dark water and ghostly fog in harmony with Osan's black kimono and Mohei's striped garment.

Mohei's first motions speak for the difference in rank that lies behind their tragedy. He stops rowing and kneels to bind Osan's ankles in preparation for her suicide. However, with death so close, he forgets who he is.

He confesses his love; he even places his hands on her knees. Osan, suddenly waking to love herself, abandons her death wish; she asks Mohei to hold her tight.

Next we see them standing close, a clear sign that difference of class no longer matters. Music of drum and bamboo flute grows more insistent. He sits down. So does she. When she throws herself on him, the boat turns suddenly ninety degrees. This dramatic shift has the same effect as the sudden halt, or *merihari* device, of classical Japanese theater. The actor uses it to signal action leading to decisive outcome. Here, it signifies that Mohei and Osan are now man and woman, not servant and mistress; they have resolved to live and love, even as fugitives, social outcasts.

This scene is one of the best examples of Mizoguchi's tenacious perfectionism. He brought out the best in talented performers by rehearsing tirelessly till they got it "right." In this case, he rivets our attention on drama realized not just in words but through gestures eloquent down to the last detail.

Like Mizoguchi in *The Crucified Lovers,* Koreeda directs a steady camera at his virtuoso long take. But there the similarity ends. This young director sets his sights on characters much farther away; they are in fact reduced to distant silhouettes. Mizoguchi would not have done that. He was too much the connoisseur of eloquent body language, especially in women.

This is a difference of approach, not a critic's discounting of Koreeda's method. It might be seen as more spontaneous, for various reasons—casting could be one. Mizoguchi had seasoned veterans such as Kyōko Kagawa (b. 1931) and Kazuo Hasegawa (1908–1984) to work with. Koreeda's heroine is the fashion model–turned–actress Makiko Esumi. She is still at the early stage of her career, so it makes sense to make allowances. That is done shrewdly here. She has no lines to speak; the composition speaks for itself. Like a model, she can move through it somewhat mechanically and with dramatic effect.

This long take gets its power from Koreeda's distant, painterly depiction of disturbed imagination.[10] Though shot in color in broad daylight, his composition harmonizes elements that suggest a funereal monochrome. The black-clad figures are all of a piece with the turgid gray-blue sky and ominous black beach. As we watch the procession move on left, beach becomes jetty pointing out to sea. And there, at the end of it, we see Yumiko's destination: a funeral pyre of red flames licking up at a rising pall of thick black smoke. This shot confirms our surmise that what we are witnessing is Yumiko's dramatic projection of her death wish. This funeral is her own. We see it as she imagines it, complete with the burning pyre that Eros and Thanatos together might well envision. We also realize that Yumiko is in real danger here. This is the *maboroshi no hikari* of the title, the beckoning dark light of illusion.

The spell cast by Yumiko's delusion is broken by our clear insight into its meaning and natural anxiety for her safety now. A sudden shift to narrative action and suspense begins with a cut to the beachfront road. We see a speeding white car that looks like Tamio's. The sound of its reckless haste blends with the folk music residue of the phantom funeral. A series of quick shots confirms our guess that this is Tamio coming to the rescue, even as Yumiko walks out onto the jetty toward the burning pyre.

The camera's hasty resketching of the scene has the effect of increasing our sense of urgency, even as it banishes illusion by acknowledging real-life details. The funeral music melts away. The ocean roars in its place. True, the fire still appears to burn. Its drifting dark smoke adds a note of fitting ambiguity to a scene whose best outcome is still as unsettling as any near-death experience must be. But the fire, we now understand, is part of illusion's dark light. Yumiko's death must come by way of water, in rough seas waiting at the end of the jetty.

Tamio sees that danger too. Here, Koreeda slips in another reference to death as a passing to "the other side": Tamio crosses a shallow lagoon to join Yumiko on the jetty. She tells him she can see the fire so clearly. This climactic encounter is shown in a long take lasting just over three minutes. As so often before, the camera maintains a studious distance, using a series of extreme long shots to follow the drama unfolding. Yumiko turns her back on the fire to face Tamio. As she approaches, he turns and walks away screen right. She follows. The camera moves accordingly, as if to reassure us that Tamio's appearance has broken the near-fatal spell of the phantom light. The camera shifts to center them as they stop and face one another.

Another director might have moved in close, inviting close-up scrutiny of gestures and facial expressions. Koreeda, true to his theme of anguished perplexity, lets dialogue speak for a situation still problematic. Finally, Yumiko breaks her silence. Why, she wails, did Ikuo want to die? Tamio answers her question with an anecdote about his father. The old man left the seafaring life because he was haunted by that same phantom light—the *maboroshi no hikari*. It beckoned so insistently he had no other choice. Tamio takes it for granted that anyone can be subject to death-wish temptations. And since he was born and bred here in sight of it, he adds, "The sea has the power." We realize that he is referring to the ancient understanding of sea as image of escape and oblivion, the *fons et origo* of life from which a human is born and to which he returns in the end.

Here again, we might note the difference between a long take by Koreeda and one by Mizoguchi. As we have seen, Mizoguchi's famous one-scene, one-shot method could focus on virtuoso performances by actors equipped to convey the full range of subtle emotions. Koreeda's young performers could not be expected to meet that high standard. One might say that this director works to a different standard. Certainly Koreeda's forte lies in the cinematic mode of representation we see here, as elsewhere, in his film. The pathos of Yumiko's struggle is rendered in this painterly mode. The camera poses these two tiny human figures against a vastness of sea and sky stretching out away from shore. We get the message: there is nothing more to say. The roar of the breakers grows louder. Tamio walks on ahead. After a pause alone on the jetty, Yumiko follows. This long take ends with a pause to consider the uninhabited vastness of the sea, as if inviting us to reflect on this woman's life and likely outcome now.

The Final Sequence

The closing sequence suggests that the cure for Yumiko's alienation is as near at hand as togetherness. The dreaded bicycle motif itself returns, redeemed by that notion. We see Yūichi, not Ikuo, riding now, taught by his new father as his new sister looks on. A cut to the house shows Yumiko and her father-in-law, Yoshiharu, seated on the balcony, gazing seaward. We see them first facing the camera, then in profile. Now we know them both as survivors of the phantom light. We notice Yumiko's white blouse, surely a hopeful shift away from her usual mournful black.

This scene inevitably invites comparison with Ozu's famous ending of *Tokyo Story* (1953). Certainly it looks like a young director's homage to the old master. The talk of weather is there. Yoshihiro says it is going to be a fine day. Yumiko agrees. What lover of Japanese cinema could overlook the likeness to Ozu's widower Shūkichi agreeing with the old woman next door when she says it's going to be a hot day?

Still, important differences exist in their approach to reliance on simple everyday detail. Everyone agrees that when it comes to simplicity, Ozu is a master nonpareil. He redeems banal detail routinely, using it to elicit complex responses in his audience. He does so at the end of *Tokyo Story*. He does it by making that brief last scene an echo of the one that opens the film. There we saw the same old woman saying the very same thing as Shukichi and his wife prepared to leave for Tokyo. The difference lies in the story

Ozu has told meantime. This parting parallel speaks for our awareness of Shūkichi's lonely resignation to his new life as a widower.

The affecting simplicity of this moment owes much to casting, too. Chishū Ryū (1904–1994) played in many Ozu films. Like his director, he had a gift for the ineffable, for understated eloquence, for the telling monosyllabic utterance. We hear that in Shūkichi's parting assent. We see it in the final profile view, in the way he moves his fan, in his lonely resigned expression gazing out to sea. There the director takes leave of the scene with a point-of-view shot of the river—another classic example of Ozu simplicity, his subtly eloquent use of uninhabited landscape.

Yumiko's father-in-law is played by Akira Emoto, another actor famous for his economy of speech. He earned rave reviews in films such as Shōhei Imamura's *Mr. Akagi* (Akagi Sensei, 1998) and Masayuki Suo's *Shall We Dance?* (1996). Talented as he is, he cannot match Ryū's hinting eloquence.

Koreeda gets that deft final touch from the camera. His gift for simplicity lies with visual images and diegetic sounds used as signifiers, inviting us to puzzle them out. One might say that Ozu makes us feel intuitively, while Koreeda makes us think. Here we are given father-in-law and daughter-in-law in profile, gazing out to sea. Not a word is spoken. Next we are given a point-of-view, high-angle, fixed shot of ocean down below and houses lining the shore. As usual, Koreeda juxtaposes both diegetic and nondiegetic sounds. A dog barks. A bicycle bell tinkles.

We know by now that the Sea of Japan is famous for rough weather. We have seen its troubled, overcast skies play their part in this story. But now the sky is clear. The sea is deep, rich blue. The light of common day fairly radiates all round. Every ominous hint of phantom light has vanished. We hear Yūichi's childish exclamations of delight as he teeters along on his bike. We don't see Yumiko; we only hear Yūichi call out happily "Mommy!"

A cut to his parents' bedroom speaks the final twenty-second piece. The room is empty. A small desk occupies the foreground. The window in the background is open. Thanks to Koreeda's deft use of deep space, we glimpse the distant sea. Windows heretofore have mirrored ominous hints of phantom light. They flashed the speeding lights of city commuter trains. They sped past urban blight and country landscapes seen by Yumiko in painful states of doubt. They played tricks with outdoor light, as in that troubling scene in this same room, drawing a gleam into a dagger shape. The police car window glittered with drops of nighttime rain as Yumiko sat tearless, stunned by her loss.

Since our view of the desk is a medium shot, we cannot be sure of another object, but we do see a watch. This shot bears an unmistakable resemblance to an earlier studious gaze at an alarm clock and electric bulb left lying on the table. The bulb had no power to shine (though it rocked gently back and forth, as if touched, ever so slightly). The watch in this final scene lends a definite touch of Ozu. As such, it would speak for the passing of things Yumiko must accept in order to live.

Koreeda leaves us to wonder there. Will she adjust or won't she? Surely she will. All the signifiers point to that happy outcome: to escape from the past and its perilous phantoms of sorrow.

–14–
Stressed-Out Nineties Youth in Laid-Back Sixties Dress
Takeshi Kitano's *Kids Return* (1995)

TAKESHI KITANO (b. 1947) took the long way around to the director's chair. He started out as a strip joint comic then enjoyed some success in the "Two Beats" comedy twosome that inspired his stage name, "Beat Takeshi." He became a regular on a number of TV shows and wrote sixty-odd books. He was cast as the lead in *Violent Cop* (Sono otoko kyōbō ni tsuki, 1989) but found himself doubling as director when the legendary Kinji Fukasaku (1930–2003) fell ill.

Fukasaku was the grand old man of *ninkyō eiga,* films about the Yakuza gangsters of Japan. His definitive contribution to this Tōei Studio specialty was the five-part *Battles without Honor* (Jinginaki tatakai, 1973–1975). Fukasaku reinvigorated the genre by giving it relevance to contemporary life.[1] He updated the look and setting, yet the conventions of the genre remained the same: a single Yakuza wins out against overwhelming odds in a struggle with a rival gang. Fukasaku's gangsters wear suits, not kimonos, yet Kitano found much that was "unrealistic" in his predecessor's formula.[2]

In *Violent Cop* Kitano developed a refreshingly innovative approach to the plot. His central figure is a policeman pitted against gangsters and dirty cops. The level of violence escalates accordingly, becoming a hallmark of Kitano's style. He directed and starred in two more such films, *Boiling Point* (San tai yon ekkusu jū-gatsu, 1990) and *Sonatine* (Sonachine, 1993). In between those two, he tried his hand at a characteristically offbeat beach genre film, *A Scene at the Sea* (Ano natsu, ichiban shizukana umi, 1991). Entirely free of violence or suspense, this film moves through the silent world shared by a deaf boy and girl.[3] The camera follows their move away from city confinement to a rather uneventful life in sight of the boundless sea the boy yearns to know as a surfer.

Kitano's big moment came in 1998 when *Fireworks* (Hanabi, 1997) won the grand prize at the Venice International Film Festival. The film explores the themes of friendship, guilt, and revenge as two policemen come into conflict with Yakuza gangsters. Kitano has risen to prominence at home and abroad.

His last four films attest to his versatility and wide-ranging interest. For example, *Kikujiro* (Kikujirō no natsu, 1998) is a drama of family life given the benefit of comic relief. Kitano has said that parent/child stories work best for him, and he may be right.[4] *Kikujiro* shares a boy's journey in search of his mother. This classical plot is greatly enhanced by the rather comical shifting relationship between the boy and his middle-aged companion (played by Kitano). *Zatoichi* (2003) is Kitano's contribution to a series immensely popular in the 1960s and 1970s. Here too he is cast as the hero, a swordsman and masseur who happens to be blind. Kitano's version is an interesting companion to the 1989 *Zatoichi* directed by actor Shintarō Katsu, who also played the lead.

The eleven films Kitano has directed to date include one of the best yet made in the so-called youth genre, *Kids Return* (Kizzu retān, 1995). His innovative approach to the plight of discontented youth is an achievement that gains in interest, seen in the context of postwar youth-culture film.

The hard-working "miracle" of postwar recovery in Japan spawned its share of youthful malcontents, as in America. The cultural contexts were as different as East and West, but the paradox was the same: the first generation raised on the higher standard of living their parents' hard work made possible was the first to question the personal and social value of study and work whose aim was security and material success. The plight of that and succeeding generations of discontented, rebellious youth has been a mainstay theme of Japanese cinema ever since.

The so-called *Taiyōzoku* (Sun-Tribe) films on this theme get their name from Takumi Furusawa's definitive, seminal adaptation of the young Shintarō Ishihara's 1956 novella *Season of the Sun* (Taiyō no kisetsu, 1957). Its story follows a group of youngsters whose ill-fated response to a materialistic society (defined in terms of fast cars and motorboats) defines itself in terms of sex and violence. Two other films mark 1956 as the starting point for a downright fad along these lines. The title of Kō Nakahira's *Kurutta kajitsu* translates as "crazed fruit," as if to suggest that some cultural quintessences are simply not for export. *Backlight* (Gyaku-kōsen) looks at the Japanese counterculture through the experience of a "Sun-Tribe" girl who has an affair with a middle-aged married man.

Dennis Washburn makes the insightful point that this genre sheds light on a growing rift in 1950s Japan as a conspicuous minority prospered while the vast majority of Japanese did not:

The problem of youth culture, and the dislocations suffered by the younger generation around the world in the postwar era was a popular subject of novels and films; and the students' willingness to exploit that problem as a subject for mass entertainment is an indication of the influences on the industry that arose from the effects of the so-called economic miracle.[5]

The genre would in fact go on to outlive the postwar boom as each generation of Japanese youth found reason to feel threatened by changing social and economic arrangements. Directors responded to the need accordingly, with results sometimes entirely predictable, sometimes boldly experimental. A few offer refreshingly thought-provoking approaches to youthful struggle with senses of loss and fear, confusion and alienation. Nagisa Ōshima and other so-called New Wave directors of the early 1960s brought their trademark versatile camera movement to bear on this brave new world of fast-paced sex and violence. David Desser sees the image of youth in most of these films as "hopelessly rebellious and powerlessly goal-less."[6]

By 1983 the genre was ready for the more focused form of rebellion offered by Shun'ichi Nagasaki (b. 1956) in *Rockin' Softly* (Rokku yo shizuka ni nagarero, 1988). Nagasaki (a man in his thirties at the time) gave his youth an on-screen chance to resist an aspect of the prevailing social order bound to be unpopular with the young: the nose-to-the-grindstone system of education in Japan. These high-school age rebels, however, are neither hopeless nor goal-less, since they plan to make it as a rock band. This is no gang of slouching in-fighting misfits but a band of brothers who cherish their bond and value camaraderie. Their rock band gives form and meaning, real and symbolic, to youthful yearning for freedom from the hidebound orthodoxy of exam-driven education. Even so, another obvious symbol of youth and freedom brings students and teachers closer together when one of the band has a fatal motorcycle accident.

Takeshi Kitano's *Kids Return* is an outstanding example of the genre itself and of this multifaceted director's contribution to films about youth counterculture in general. Kitano wrote the story and screenplay and edited the film himself. Its subject is the bond between two dropouts from an elite high school. The narrative gains momentum and strength from Kitano's inclusion of two episodic plot lines related to their classmates. Interestingly enough, he leaves out the aspect of sexual challenge his predecessors took full advantage of. Kitano prefers to work with another dynamic: the careful control of color imagery that adds an innovative touch to his film's stylistics.

Opening Sequence: Time and Place

The opening sequence of thirteen shots suggests a haphazard collage of disjointed images. But of course the attentive viewer soon catches their drift. The opening shot of a gift just unwrapped is forthrightly lyrical: a small paper doll and its blue box. This nostalgic touch hints of childhood's privileged access to parental affection. A cut to a theater introduces a long take lasting some forty-five seconds. This interval is rich in details we will later recognize as amply informative of major events yet to unfold. Just now we see a comedy duo waiting in the wings along with their manager. All three are young men. The manager's long hair, dyed blonde, is clearly meant to single him out. The comics are gaudily dressed in shiny suits, one burgundy, one off-white. We see them step out to face the audience. Their manager lurking behind the curtain occupies the foreground screen.

That long take yields to a long shot of a young man riding a bike. He is headed to our left, though the camera holds him framed in the center of the screen. Sudden lively music plays a synthesized accompaniment to solo guitar. It merges with an undertone of diegetic sound we recognize as bicycle pedals spinning round and round. Later we will know this youth as Shinji, one of the two protagonists. He is dressed for jogging in a quiet shade of blue. The camera takes note of a day-old beard. The next shot pulls back to offer a distant, fairly detailed view of the business at hand. Shinji stops at a gate, parks his bike, and enters, carrying a bag of rice. The camera loiters in the empty street. A woman's voice says thanks for the rice. Viewers familiar with Japanese culture will recognize this now-outdated mode of rice delivery.

The next few shots serve a reunion motif. Shinji's face in medium close-up shows surprise and joy. Another young man is seen approaching from his line of sight. He wears a gray leather jacket. We are surprised to see someone so young walking with a slight but noticeable stoop. A few lines of dialogue fill us in. These two used to be close friends. They have not met for quite a while. Shinji has given up boxing. Masaru is looking for a job. Shinji offers his old friend a ride. As they head off a sudden transition takes us into the past. The bicycle remains the same. The change in context is obvious. A younger, livelier Masaru is wearing a flashy red jumper. Shinji, still pedaling, is dressed much more conservatively in a black school uniform—no sign of whiskers here. This is a schoolboy. The music returns, alerting us to this shift back in time. The boys come to an overpass with concrete barriers on both sides. The camera pans down to give one barrier foreground magnitude, filling the screen with its nondescript gray. The title *Kids Return* (in English) appears.

The density of this brief sequence foreshadows the tightly structured narrative that follows. What appear to be fragments have a motif in common—youthful bonding put to the test by character and circumstance as the story unfolds. By the end each piece has found its place. Just as important is the way the opening sequence sets the pattern for the telling color scheme Kitano is famous for. His carefully controlled use of red and blue and gray throughout forms a symbolic core of visible cues to the courses of action taken by Shinji and Masaru.

Masaru (l., Ken Kaneko) and Shinji (r., Masanobu Andō) in
Kids Return (1995). © Bandai Visuals and Office Kitano.

The alert viewer may in fact be puzzled by anachronistic touches here and there. Events characteristic of the late 1960s or early 1970s appear to be credited to the early 1990s. The director is clearly counting on his Japanese audience to accept a notably free approach to late twentieth-century history. In some instances, Kitano is dipping into his own past life. The comic duo's *manzai* (cross-talk) act recalls his early struggle to make his mark as a dimwit straight man.[7] Bicycle deliveries of rice were already a thing of the past in 1995, though still in living memory—thanks in part, one might say, to the rerun afterlife that movies and television now give to ongoing cultural history.

Like Madison Avenue, Kitano picks and chooses historical/cultural facts and artifacts to send a message energized by imagery meant to be understood as a creative construct. If it suits his purpose to refer to a boxing and porno film fad more relevant to 1960s and 1970s Japan, so what? What does it matter that the company he chooses to exemplify a lifetime guarantee of mind-numbing security had folded some years before? We see quite clearly what this film thinks it means: that a high-school graduate should desire no better lot in life. Some misfit details of hair and clothes are wickedly easy to criticize, as one writer has done, referring to *Kids Return* as peopled with "1960s throwbacks in 1990s dress."[8]

Central Problem and Issues

The main text problem is timeless and general in one sense and in another sense highly specific in its cultural context. Two young men must find themselves through life experience. The story examines the choices they are offered and the ones they make, with all that means to their present and future well-being. We see how choices of life experience—theirs and some others as well—shape individuals and their relationships to themselves and others and to society as well. All this questing is rooted in classroom experience. Here the film is culturally highly specific. Though some secondary characters are satisfied to play along, Shinji and Masaru make a case for youthful dissatisfaction with the cramming grind that passed for education in 1990s Japan. Time and again the camera returns to the classroom with its rows of neat, obedient student elite being told by a teacher what will serve to pass an exam.

Masaru and Shinji are misfits from the start. Masaru is the rebel leader, the restive individualist. He wears the only red jacket in the school. Shinji is the follower, a cautious conformist at least to the extent of wearing the school's black uniform. Still, he values camaraderie more than academic success. Our first view of their youthful conspiracy takes us to the schoolhouse roof. They lower a doll on a string to dangle outside their classroom window. The doll sports studious nerd glasses. It is also obscenely male. What better taunt for a cut-and-dried math teacher whose approach to teaching makes ciphers of his students—mere do-as-you're-told passers of college entrance exams? The next several episodes show youthful frustration outgrowing boyish pranks. Masaru starts taking money from students open to bullying. Shinji mostly just plays along, as an accessory after the fact. Their pleasures are aimless and largely harmless: drinking coffee, slurping noodles, sneaking into a porn theater.

Their naughty-boy idyll ends suddenly. Masaru accosts a student whose companion turns out to be a professional boxer. Badly beaten, he drops out of sight. Has he dropped out of school? Kitano withholds that information. We see Shinji staring at Masaru's empty seat in class. We see how monotonous and empty the school routine is. Shinji does keep stopping by Masaru's house, ringing the bicycle bell that offers his friend a ride. Masaru never appears. Several times the camera returns to the school rooftop to show us Shinji there alone.

Suddenly they meet again, not far from school. Masaru asks Shinji to jog with him. Like Shinji, we do not know where they are headed, though we learn that Masaru now has a goal in life. He declares his intention to get even with the boxer who beat him up. But how? They come to a gym, where his plan is revealed. Masaru has been training to become a professional, a boxer whose goal is revenge. He will pack his punch as the Dynamite Kid. They are back to being friends. Shinji is back to playing along, kid brother to the Dynamite Kid. Ironically, his loyalty this time destroys their friendship quite by accident. Masaru, pushy as always, arranges a bout for his neophyte friend. Shinji wins impressively; the manager of the gym sees him as a natural. That is more than Masaru can take. Again, he vanishes from Shinji's life.

From this point on the plot moves back and forth between their separate lives. Causal lines diverge yet move in parallel in some respects. Each, for example, has his goal. Shinji has chosen boxing; Masaru, gangster careerism. Both turn out to be achievers. Shinji appears to thrive on a boxer's steady, rigorous training. Masaru's taste for violence moves him quickly up through the ranks from hard-knuckled goon to streetwise henchman close to the Yakuza boss. Then each is brought low by a crisis of choice.

Masaru's immediate superior is killed in a gangland feud. He is torn between conflicting loyalties. He wants revenge that the man at the top has nixed. Masaru cannot contain himself. In front of the others, he accuses the boss of backing down. He is a big boy now, and is punished accordingly: his fellow Yakuza beat him black and blue. Shinji is undone by his need for leadership. He finds it in Hayashi, a Mephistophelean archetype. This boxer in decline is a rich source of all the wrong advice. He even teaches his protégé how to cheat in the ring. Shinji is warned by the manager of the gym but proves too weak to shake off Hayashi's bad influence. Sure enough, his career is suddenly over. A medium shot of him alone in the locker room catches his sense of total defeat. It comes as a poignant echo of a series of rhythmically accelerated shots that mark his progress in the ring—match after winning match complete with photograph of the upstart young champ.

The two causal lines do intersect at one point. The camera returns us to the coffee shop where they hung out as boys. Shinji's face in close-up registers surprise. The camera shifts to his line-of-sight view of Masaru in his henchman role. Masaru is tending to business, not yet high ranking enough to sit and have coffee with the boss. He and Shinji do not really get a chance to talk. Masaru's parting comment is enough: "We'll see each other when

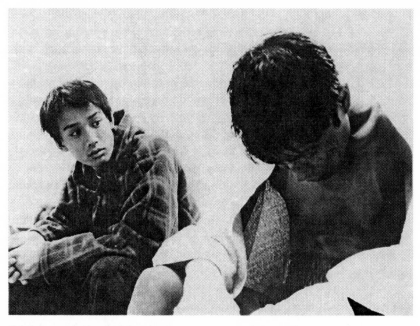

Shinji (l., Masanobu Andō) and Masaru (r., Ken Kaneko) in *Kids Return* (1995). © Bandai Visual and Office Kitano.

I'm a lieutenant and you a champ." Will their dreams be fulfilled? We are alerted to that possibility. Their next meeting seems promising. Masaru, as promised, drops by the gym. He has not yet made rank but is clearly getting there: silk shirt, tattoos, hard-faced entourage—the works. He has nice things to say about his old friend's triumphs in the ring. Yet the merging of causal lines abruptly ends there. Masaru invites Shinji to a classy restaurant but stands him up; some bit of gangster business kept him away.

Kitano enriches the plot with three parallel subplots. All concern classmates bullied and outdone by Masaru and Shinji. As might be expected, their contact with the two is anywhere but the classroom—school staircase, coffee shop, and gym. The academic hopes of these youngsters are dashed, not by careless rebellion but by failing to make the grade. They will not be going on to college.

Hiroshi is the quiet type, the only child of a single parent. His notion of happiness in life is entirely conventional. Devotion and dedication appear to pay off accordingly. He courts a coffee shop waitress. They marry. He lands a modest, dull job. He seems happy enough, yet his is the tragic case. Pressures at work and money woes at home have him driving a cab after hours. The last we see of him is not him at all. The camera searches the wreckage. It closes in on something dangling from the dashboard mirror—a tiny doll, possibly a good luck charm.

The *manzai* comic duo has a more ambitious goal. No corporate slavery for these two. They want to make it big onstage. Ironically, Masaru is their first reviewer, a classmate mocking their improvised performance in a corner of the school. He tells them to run away to the Kansai area, the better to learn their trade. We see them next in front of an Osaka theater known as the mecca for *manzai*. This plot line is in stark contrast to the others. These boys achieve their dream, as the opening sequence shows. Their trade itself implies a measure of harmony and friendship. Even so, we glimpse their struggle in two brief shots: one of them performing for an audience of just two; another of the same theater dotted with spectators here and there.

A narrative ellipsis obscures the causal line that links Masaru and Shinji. How has each fared since his hopes were dashed? Kitano tells us nothing about their lives at home. What do their parents do? Are there siblings? Only once do we see Shinji talking to a member of Masaru's family—is it his mother? Did family life have anything to do with these young strays? Kitano leaves us guessing. The ending of the film brings the story full circle, as we shall see.

Stylistic Devices: Color Cues and Sentimental Moments

Kitano's cinematic thought process is guided by color images more than by story, as he himself admits: "To make a unique film, I think images are more important than drama; what kind of color and what kind of images. Therefore, when I saw Fellini's *The Clowns,* I thought that was great. So many colors rush [pour] out of the screen."[9] He has this to say about his use of a color base admiring critics have dubbed "Kitano blue": "When you have a dark blue next to a light blue, it does not stand out in any way. To make a color conspicuous you have to bring a completely opposite color next to it. That's why I wanted the base color to be blue and then use other colors to punctuate the look of the film—give the film an edge."[10]

Like his other films, *Kids Return* makes magnificent use of Kitano's gift for color imagery. Blue is basic here too, with gray its effective complement. As may be expected, red is used as their counterpoint throughout. Daisuke Miyao has done excellent work on Kitano's color schemes in this and other films.[11] Here it will suffice to expand on and modify his observations.

Kids Return begins with a shot of a painting in pastels. The subject is a girl next to a gift box. Its blue and red offer a completely harmonious image of childhood innocence and joy. Who would guess from this glimpse that blue and red will come to clash as opposites? Yet the story of this film turns on that very possibility as Shinji and Masaru grow into opposites.

The opening sequence shows Kitano's deft use of shifting texture. Shinji and Masaru are introduced almost immediately. We do not know it yet, but this is the end of the story. They have met by chance, young men we will get to know as boys. Their colors here are suitably subdued. Masaru wears a grayish leather jacket with pants of a similar color. Shinji's jacket is blue. Sky and nearby buildings are light gray. These young men, like their surroundings, are suitably nondescript. Just what the educators ordered, one might say. What are these but decent, law-abiding citizens of Japan?

Shinji offers Masaru a ride. We do not know yet that this simple act harkens back to their time as boyhood friends. As they set off a sudden change of texture signals a return to the past. Even as they ride, the flashback sequence clothes them accordingly. Masaru's shirt is a daring red. Shinji's school uniform is obedient black, though the camera takes note of a blue shirt peeking out.

Red here is clearly symbolic of a young man's desire to resist authority. Miyao adds correctly that it is also clearly symptomatic of danger, violence, and even defeat.[12] Certainly it works out that way. Masaru's bully career at school ends with a bloody nose. We see him training for vengeance in red boxing gloves. Unbeknownst to us, he is probably wearing boxer shorts decorated with a bold red. Red is the color of his punishment; that gangland scene ends with him in a pool of his own blood.

The naked violence of that scene is in sharp contrast to Kitano's color orchestration of Hiroshi's fatal crash. The twisted wreckage of his cab is lit by the hectic red flashing of emergency response, yet the synthetic musical accompaniment is oddly engaging, almost lyrical, certainly sympathetic to the sadness we feel at this pitiful outcome.

Beginning with the opening sequence, Shinji's color cue is blue, as befits his more ordinary good intentions gone astray. His basic good-boy flaw is submissiveness. Masaru is a bad companion, a mentor he should not have tried to emulate. Miyao points to our first glimpse of his conversion encoded in the color scheme of a scene depicting Masaru's bully-boy behavior; the one in which he shows off his boxing skills to intimidated classmates while Shinji stands on the sidelines watching in a blue and white striped shirt.[13] After Shinji joins the boxing club, his dedication is shown in blue-dominant scenes. The camera keeps pace with his training runs on bluish roads. His outfit is blue. His trainer rides a bicycle under clear blue skies.

Kitano uses red to alert us to Shinji's vulnerability, sometimes obliquely and sometimes not. When Masaru quits boxing, he gives Shinji his pair of red gloves. Shinji in blue decks an opponent in red. He trains in a ring whose posts are red. When Hayashi replaces Masaru as another bad mentor, Shinji shows up at a Chinese eatery in a red training outfit. A red chopstick holder catches our attention, as Miyao sensitively observes.[14] Shinji's final match makes the most of red/blue tension. He, in red shorts, sprawls defeated on a blue mat. A freeze frame ends the scene, catching a white towel thrown by his angry trainer.

Kids Return is well endowed with memorable single shots. The most impressive one offers a distant view of Shinji alone on the roof of the school. Masaru is conspicuously missing. Gray sky and gray concrete dominate the screen. Shinji's tiny figure is the vanishing point in this uninviting look at a lonely boy's universe.

The Final Sequence

Kids Return ends as it began, with scattershot scraps of narrative used to introduce a steadier gaze at past and present outcomes. Here, of course, we know that various youthful dreams have come to commonplace grown-up ends. Shinji and Masaru have suffered but survived, while poor Hiroshi has not. Their fates are separate, yet this cinematic farewell links them in a series of intersecting shots.

First we see Shinji losing in the ring to the sound of a rueful guitar. A cut to a single glancing blow of a shot shows a taxi in a crash. A quick cut back to the ring shows Shinji down, the white towel flying up. A freeze-frame gives foreground magnitude to the towel. That yields to a cut back to the taxi's dangling doll. Hiroshi courted his waitress with a gift of a tiny figurine. The film's opening image was the little girl's doll. A shot looks at a patrol leaving the scene of the accident, their dome light flashing red. A final cut to the gym finds Shinji alone in the locker room.

The coda's narrative ellipsis takes us three or four years into the future. Here too, Kitano offers narrative legibility by way of circularity and repetition. We see the *manzai* duo playing to a packed house roaring with laughter. What better measure of success in life for two comedians? A cut to the manager in the wings confirms it with an obvious reprise of our first-ever view of these three.

A cut to a coffee shop shows Hiroshi's widow, Sachiko, saying no to a date, a gentle reminder of her loss. A cut to the gym samples change of a more aggressive variety. Two weaklings Masaru bullied at school once upon a time have joined the boxing club. One has made the cut. Spiked hair signals his 1990s bravado. He dances across the ring, throwing fierce practice punches, true to his moniker, "Tomahawk." Two admirers watch ringside. One is his buddy who had not made the grade but is suited up to act as his manager. The other is Tomahawk's girlfriend, sleek and spiky as befits. The camera sneaks a sly look at a picture on the wall: Shinji as a brand-new champ, one picture of many such now. What goes around comes around. If only Tomahawk could know.

The film picks up where it left off in the opening sequence. Shinji and Masaru ride the bike into the schoolyard. A long shot shows them circling round and round. It turns out to be a point-of-view shot from inside the classroom. The onlooker is a student in process of being scolded by a teacher out of the frame. He is charged with being unfocused. A cut to the man identifies him as the dreaded math teacher of days gone by. Time has taken its toll on him as well. His hair is streaked with gray. Only his dreary notion of education remains impervious to change. And so the rows of desks are filled with yet another generation of victims of the system's perfectly respectable hopes for them.

A cut to the schoolyard shows Shinji and Masaru still circling. Their talking and laughing echo on the soundtrack after the screen goes blank.

"Masaru, do you think we're finished already?" "Hell no! We haven't got started yet." Is there any hope for such as these? Will a return to friendship be a source of moral strength this time round? Will Masaru find work? Will either or both of them commit to a better kind of life?

Kitano's view of youths like these has its sentimental side, but *Kids Return* is too complex a film to let them—or us—off easy. That may be its strength: that it leaves us to work out the uncomfortable ambiguities.

–15–
Bittersweet Childhood
Yōichi Higashi's *Village of Dreams* (1996)

YŌICHI HIGASHI (b. 1934) needs some introducing, since his career got off to a rather slow start at home and a very slow start abroad. His 1978 film *The Third,* aka *Third Base* and *A Boy Called Third Base* (Sādo), won a number of prestigious Japanese awards but viewers elsewhere remained largely unaware of him until 1996, when *Village of Dreams* (E no naka no boku no mura) won the Silver Bear Award at the Berlin Film Festival. His first film, *Faisu* (A face), came out in 1963. It was a short documentary on billboard advertising in the metropolis. The face of his title is that, literally—outsized. Higashi shows what happens at the end of a billboard's public life—how the face gets scrapped.

This is one director whose production schedule appears to have been anything but hectic. In the next fifteen years he made only four feature-length films, yet two of them got attention. *Okinawa Archipelago* (Okinawa Rettō, 1969) was a documentary on the status of the island during the U.S. military occupation. *A Gentle Japanese* (Yasashii nipponjin, 1971) returns to Okinawa. It tells the story of a youth who survived a mass suicide on one of the islands in the wake of Japan's defeat in 1945. This film earned Higashi the New Director Award of the Association of Japanese Directors.

His real breakthrough came in 1978 with *The Third*. It was voted year's best picture by *Kinema jumpō*. The playwright Shūji Terayama wrote the script himself. The film is set in a juvenile house of corrections. Its protagonist had played third base in high school, hence the title *The Third*. Japan in the 1960s, like the United States in that decade, had reason to be worried about rising rates of juvenile delinquency. A number of directors made films that explored this phenomenon. Most, such as Susumu Hani's *Bad Boys* (Furyō shōnen 1960), studied the boys from the outside, as evidence of a social problem. Higashi did the opposite in *The Third,* looking at the world from the point of view of the juvenile offender himself. His youth sees himself as a reject—excluded by school and society at large.[1]

Higashi has made a dozen films since *The Third*. Two stand out as exceptional. *A River with No Bridge* (Hashi no nai kawa) appeared in 1992. It is Higashi's adaptation of Sue Sumii's novel on a subject not well known in the West: the class of outcasts that used to exist in Japan, the Burakumin. Yoichi Higashi came to Sumii's work through his interest in women as victims in Japanese society. Two of his films in that vein are *The Rape* (Za reipu, 1982) and *Metamorphosis* (Kashin, 1986). In *A River with No Bridge* he expands his interest in victimization to include both women and men—the suffering Burakumin. The film, like Sumii's novel in six parts, covers the years from 1909 to 1922. (Sumii published a seventh part after the film was released. It carries the story on past 1922.) Novelist and director are concerned with showing how the history of suffering among the Burakumin includes the anguish of their awakening to the possibility of social equality and their struggle to achieve it.[2]

Compared to that terrible story, *The Village of Dreams* is bathed in sweetness and light—though it too has a bitter taste. Ironically, that touch of sadness also refers to the Burakumin, as we shall see. Japanese audiences greeted it with great affection. *Kinema jumpō* ranked it fifth on its list of ten best pictures of 1996. (Best Picture that year went to Masayuki Suō's *Shall We Dance?*—a hit overseas as well.)

Geographic and Historical Settings and the Central Problem

The Japanese title of the film translates literally as "my village in the picture." It is based on the autobiographical children's picture book of that title by Seizō Tajima. As the opening sequence shows, he has an elder twin named Yukihiko. Except for the opening and closing sequences, the film is set in Shikoku—an isolated village near Kōchi City in Kōchi Prefecture. The brothers did in fact live there for four years, from the ages of seven to eleven.

As the film begins, the narrator's voice-over reminisces about that happy time. The speaker is middle-aged now. He visits his brother, who is now living in a suburb of Kyoto. They agree that the years in Shikoku were the most unforgettable of their lives. Since the brothers are both book illustrators, a montage of their pictures is used to transport us back in time to a place—and to a large extent a society, even an entire world—that has vanished like their youth. We see straightaway that this is a film about the changing times these men live in—and which, in fact, we live in, too.

The story itself is intimately connected to Japan's sudden transformation in the immediate postwar period. Even a village this far removed from the mainstream cannot escape the pressures of change. At one point we hear the grumpy old landlord complain about land reforms carried out under the auspices of General MacArthur. Land has been given to tenants who actually tilled its soil during the war.[3]

We also learn that this landlord has, in effect, adopted the family of these two boys. That too, as we shall see, is part of the story. Right from the outset the story casts an idyllic spell. It is, after all, the story of a world seen through the eyes of little boys fresh to everything in the world, and to their own sense of mischief and adventure. No wonder the critic Masayuki Nomura describes this film as a "subjective documentary seen from the two boys' point of view."[4]

The boys are played by real-life elementary school children from the place itself: Keigo Matsushima and Shōgo Matsushima. Higashi found them through a well-publicized audition search for twins in Kōchi Prefecture. The convincing naïveté of the twins is balanced with its equivalent in mature performance by actors Kyōzo Nagatsuka and Kumiko Akiyoshi, cast as their parents.

At a *bon* celebration (a major communal gathering), the village headman gives the twins' mother, Mrs. Tajima, a teacher, a piece of advice: she needs to work harder at fitting in. Her outsider status is complicated by the fact that her boys are in her class at school. Worse yet, Mrs. Tajima has a mind of her own. She ignores the principal's warning and enters her sons' paint-

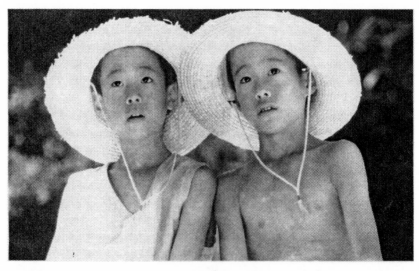

Seizō Tajima (l., Keigo Matsuyama) and Yukihiko Tajima (r., Shōgo Matsuyama) in *Village of Dreams* (1996). © Sigro, Co. Ltd.

ings in the prefectural art exhibit. She claims to be quite capable of distinguishing between her roles as mother and teacher. The principal thinks otherwise, as used as he is to dealing with village proprieties. He punishes Mrs. Tajima by transferring her to a hamlet even farther out in the sticks.

All these incidents of in/out opposition relate to the central problem of the film: how do the twins come to terms with their lives in this rural community? Will they become model pupils and sons acceptable to the villagers? Or will they refuse to conform, following their personal inclinations? The plot unfolds as the values of constraint are pitted against the values of freedom. Both Seizō and Yukihiko opt for the latter, counting on their bond as a source of strength. It is so strong that they feel no need to cultivate ties with fellow pupils or unfriendly neighbors. It follows that boys so inclined will take center stage as mischievous adventurers motivated by curiosity, not malice. They are curious at every level of life, exploring the unknown in areas as close to home as details of the female body and as far-flung and mysterious as the countryside they roam.

The film itself explores the process of growing up, not in the way traditionally emphasized—learning to fit the given social mold—but in terms of boys-will-be-boys adventures expanding their knowledge and creativity

Seizō (l., Keigo Matsuyama) and Yukihiko (r., Shōgo Matsuyama) in *Village of Dreams* (1996). © Sigro, Co. Ltd.

in often surprising ways. They even learn a lesson lost on most students of social conformity: namely, that outcasts such as their Burakumin friend Senji are deserving of respect and inclusion, too.

Higashi takes full advantage of the fact that the twins are exiled to unspoiled countryside. Their growing up is all of a piece with their increasing harmony with nature—a privilege of education denied most children in contemporary Japan. That same privilege extends to their artistic development as well.

The drama of their growth unfolds with the seasons, beginning with early summer. A series of episodes glimpses the carefree spirit of boys bursting with energy redoubled in some peculiar way by their mutual resemblance. Something fey and mischievous in their look suggests an attitude of Us against Them right from the start. The opening sequence of a fishing trip yields a note of conflict. The fusspot landlord complains about the smell of a catfish the boys have left in a bucket by the well. Later on, he orders the twins to cut grass for his goat. They take impish advantage, turning this chore into a slashing invasion of an old woman's garden next door. Their mother does her best to make peace, but the old lady is implacable. She insults Mrs. Tajima, calling her an "outsider" and accusing her of playing favorites in the classroom. The episode ends with a suggestion that the twins get their spirited independence from their mother. Even as she scolds them, she admits to not liking their neighbors much herself. She even says, with a disarming smile, that she wishes she had slashed a few of those plants herself.

Scene after scene adds to our sense of a special bond being strengthened by this time of outdoor adventuring. Then the plot takes a dramatic detour. Yukihiko very nearly drowns in a scene depicted with harrowing clarity. The ensuing hospital stay gives Seizō a taste of facing the world on his own. He finds a conch shell in the woods and takes it into an abandoned house, wanting to practice blowing it. He has stumbled on the shabby outcast Senji's hideout. Senji shows him the knack of getting the shell to sound. By the time his brother rejoins him, Seizō has learned how—and also what it means to have a friend other than his twin.

The narrative develops our sense of the parents, too. Their affection is sometimes obvious, sometimes revealed in subtle ways. At first the twins are left in their mother's care. She is kind and supportive, indulging their taste for adventure along with their creative bent. By encouraging their artistic gifts, she gives their energies scope and purpose. The prize-winning pictures are a direct reflection of their outdoor derring-do. One depicts the landlord's goat. Seeing it, we understand the opening scene of the film where the grown-up artist twins leaf through their colorful illustrations of child-hood scenes they remember with such affection—vivid portrayals of country pleasures such as fishing and chasing butterflies.

The father, rejoining his family, sounds a chilling note at first. He tells his boys to forget about making a living as artists. Later, however, the camera takes a noncommittal stance, catching him in the act of studying work they have left around. The mother says nothing, yet we know from her smile that the art has spoken for itself. In a sense, *Village of Dreams* is also a film about family solidarity surviving the stresses and strains of rapid post-war change by creating its own safe haven at one remove from the harsh realities of the outside world.

Narrative Devices: Imaginary Hags and Withheld Information

Since we, as viewers, are allowed to see worlds of both reality and imagi-nation through the eyes of these children, we find ourselves looking at some rather surprising "facts" of hyperactive young imagination. Among them are six convincingly real apparitions of village crones cast in fairytale roles, though the grown-up reflex insists on noting that old ladies do not really perch in trees. On two occasions (one in the final scene), we hear only their

Seizō (l., Keigo Matsuyama) and Yukihiko (r., Shōgo Matsuyama) in *Village of Dreams* (1996). © Sigro, Co. Ltd.

voice-over narration. Needless to say, the twins' artistic talent is part of the plot, yet what are these old women to them?

Their functions do vary. Out first glimpse occurs when the camera pans up a huge, ancient tree to the beating of a drum. Three old gossips are perched with unrealistic ease in the branches. Here they pass on a tidbit about Senji: he is an adopted waif, a former juvenile delinquent. Next time we see them, they exchange knowing glances, village busybodies shaking heavy heads over youthful pranks. A flashback reminds us that Senji had swiped some eels. The three hags go on to catch us up on the latest: Mr. Tajima has just rejoined his family. Bad news for naughty boys and a good thing, too.

Higashi makes good use of this narrative device. Like the all-knowing chorus in Noh and classic Greek drama, these crones help move the plot along, keeping us informed, smoothing transitions from scene to scene.[5] They also speak to more far-reaching concerns, such as the postwar changes affecting all of Japan, even this tiny rural community. One crone mentions in passing that the father of the twins is home for the summer from his job with the board of education in Kōchi City. Higashi is counting on his 1990s audience to put that fact in its 1950s context. Viewers familiar with Japanese history will recognize that the father's work entails the wholesale reorganization of Japanese schooling in accord with the process of democratization supervised by the American Occupation. In other words, the twins are growing up in a world of momentous change.

The third time the crones appear they are sitting under a tree in the foreground, commenting on the landlord's funeral taking place behind them. They relish talk of a rift between the old man's heirs. Surely his widow will contest any bequest to these outsiders he has, in effect, adopted. Their malicious aforethought misfires, however; a later episode shows the widow in a compliant mood.

A viewer alert to inference may wonder why these crones are found sitting not around the gossip's hearth, but outside in the bosom of nature. Those familiar with Japanese culture will connect them with Shintō notions of natural divinity serving, here, in a role roughly equivalent to the tutelary deities of classical myth in the West. They are guides to good conduct as well as clucking gossips.

The crones appear a fourth time to Seizō alone. His twin has been hospitalized. An extreme long shot shows them walking away from the camera along a deserted country path. Seizō enters the frame. The crones say nothing. He simply follows. They lead the way to the abandoned house where Senji shows him how to blow the conch shell.

Their sixth appearance casts the old ladies in a wind god role. Seizō is found seated near a temple. He has run away from the school, upset at seeing the innocent Senji punished for a prank he and his classmates played. He runs pursued by a cloud of vengeful dust aiming for his eyes, fit punishment for a bad-boy painter. The crones fend off that dire outcome with a helpful gust resulting in a coughing fit that leads to the quintessential real world childhood ailment: tonsillitis.

Seizō's redeeming compassion grows out of a harrowing scene Higashi uses to give the theme of prejudice a telling ironic twist. A group of mischiefs in Seizō's class slick the floor with wax, sending the principal sprawling. The principal demands that the perpetrators step forward. When no one does, he accuses the innocent Senji and knocks him to the floor. A close-up reads pain, outrage, and courageous defiance in the boy's expression. The principal responds with a series of harder blows. The camera looks away. Its gaze comes to rest on samples of student calligraphy pinned to the wall. Each sheet elaborates the Chinese character for "equality." The point is not lost on Japanese viewers aware that their country's new postwar constitution guarantees the rights of all citizens, even Senji's traditionally outcast minority group, the Burakumin. The principal's behavior speaks for the slow pace of change in this respect. He expels the victim of his brutal attack, declaring that no pupil rates a place in his school who cannot afford textbooks.

Thoughts on Mode of Representation

It is safe to say that *Village of Dreams* is one of the most visually pleasurable films made in recent years. Its emotional and aesthetic appeal undoubtedly owes much to close collaboration between the director and the cameraman Yoshio Shimizu. It is important to notice that Higashi aims to get beyond Shimizu's documentary style. He does this by blending two levels of reality: the actual factual world anyone can see and the world of childish fantasy. His deft use of color—green especially—makes a major contribution to the meeting of worlds in young imaginations. Our first such glimpse comes as the boys go fishing with their bare hands. Seizō wades into a stream whose lush green bank is the picture of everything wonderful about summer's rioting growth and this privilege of youth to play for entire carefree days on intimate terms with it. The camera dives into the clean, clear water, close behind Seizō's searching hands. The perky little goby easily escapes. Snatches of voice-over and subtitle dialogue let us in on a lively conversation between boy and fish.

The same boyish tendency to hyperactive imagination takes a rather more complex turn when the boys return home. They find the landlord's freshly washed loincloth lying in the courtyard. The object itself is common enough in the world of these boys, but since they are boys, its relation to the old man's body transfers it to another realm. Their response could be as simple as sniggering amusement or as complex as the one their imaginations seize upon. The transition from real-life gruff old authority figure to purely fantastic menace is entirely natural. The loincloth springs to life, catching them in its folds as orchestral instruments play an eldritch tune. Just as quickly this nightmare blinks off as the landlord's wife comes out to take the cloth inside.

Higashi makes good use of long shots throughout, a convenient means of giving legibility to the sense of harmony between these children and their natural setting. Coupled with a carefully controlled long take, this device achieves stylistic magnitude. Together they powerfully express a sense of bond.

An example of this comes in the scene where Seizō is making an eel trap. A close-up in the freeze-frame shows his forefinger pierced by a gimlet. A cut to a long, slightly higher-angle shot of Seizō on the veranda introduces a long take that lasts several minutes. The camera's distant gaze shows a little boy shocked into immobility. The father wheels his bicycle into the garden. Seeing what has happened, he goes to his son (still in the same shot) and removes the gimlet. Only then does Seizō start to whimper. His father scolds him, saying he should cry out loud or hush. Film time and real time agree as the father goes inside and comes back out with a bottle of hydrogen peroxide and a strip of cloth to serve as a bandage. Several shots of Seizō finishing the trap end with the father saying, "Get a big eel." The mother's affectionate way with her boys is familiar by now; this episode offers a glimpse of the genuine fatherly affection hidden beneath Mr. Tajima's stern and distant manner.

An equally moving two-minute long take reveals a growing intimacy between Seizō and the underclass girl Hatsumi. Thanks to Senji, he has gotten the knack of blowing the conch. We see him from a distance, walking across a bridge. The sparkling water casts bright shadows up onto the lush, green bank. A group of laborers enters screen right, each carrying a load of mulberry leaves. Hatsumi is one of them. The camera follows as they overtake Seizō. The camera stops with Hatsumi. Her family passes on, ignoring Seizō completely.

Seizō, proud of his new skill, blows the conch for Hatsumi. Her father's voice off screen calls her away. She hurries on. This fleeting encounter shows us that these children have moved beyond the barrier of class prejudice Hatsumi's family suffers from so obviously. Only she has the innocent courage to stop and speak to Seizō. The long take itself is reminiscent of earlier encounters. In one, Hatsumi is seen admiring the paintings done by the twins—Seizō's especially. In another, she passes by the river where the boys are swimming. Seizō joins the others in hiding his nakedness from this girl, though we sense a difference in his response.

The Final Sequence

The main body of the narrative ends with a graduation picture. Senji is missing. We were prepared for this sad outcome by one of the most moving moments in the film. The twins are heading home along a country path. They have been trapping eels, enough for a family feast. This recurring image may be simple, but it works like a charm, referring us time and again to the increasing confidence that comes with skill and practice, especially with kids as daring as these two. We glimpse them at the outset snaring a sizeable catfish. It is a trophy that outmatches their inexperience, escaping from a bucket overnight even as the boys wet their beds. We next see their frustrated efforts to fish with bamboo poles, the poles soon put to use as weapons in a duel. Next thing we know, they have taken to splashing in the creek, fishing with bare hands. Between them, they manage to catch a sassy little goby, though not before the camera gives the chase its underwater due.

The attempt to make an eel trap (a feat requiring skill) ends in injury. Seizō watches with particular care as their father makes the trap they use in their last adventure. This sign of his youthful yen for empowerment is neatly symbolic, too, of the stern educator's affection for his sons. The audience cannot miss the reference to coming of age implicit in the progress from fishing pole to eel trap. The alert Western viewer will have taken note of the difference in an earlier scene where grown-ups are shown working eel traps in broad midriver, itself a symbolic step up from the babbling brooks the twins explore.

This vein of symbolic persuasiveness returns as the twins snare two eels themselves. They basket their trophies, clearly triumphant, approach the camera, pause in the foreground, then turn to look back. No viewer East or West could fail to catch Higashi's drift. A line-of-sight shot shows a boy entering the background frame. We see that it is Senji, somewhat taller now, though still in ragged clothes. The twins call out his name. The shot continues as Senji waves and goes on his way, vanishing from view. The camera's distant gaze confirms our sense of the grave injustice done to Senji and others like him, those whose inferior social status condemns them to a life not just poor but tragically demeaning, too. And so he passes on, a figure sadly remote from daily life in this idyllic country setting. A voice-over we recognize as the middle-aged Seizō confirms our sense of this shot: "That was the last time we saw Senji."

This scene also serves as a moment of recapitulation. The country path by this time is what might be called referentially enriched, a device of narrative connecting commonplace facts and events with complex meanings and outcomes. Our first view comes at the outset when the twins head home from fishing in the pouring rain. They have caught a catfish. One steps in cowflop. Such simple archetypes of outdoor adventure serve our growing sense of the boys' life learning. Another fishing trip sequence on this path shows them meeting Senji; they compare catches. The twins are impressed but decline Senji's offer to share his, which have come from traps not his. As they go their separate ways, we are aware of the complex understanding growing between these boys despite what turns out to be an unbridgeable gap in their circumstances. In the meantime, this scene reminds us of Senji's earlier rescue of the twins when they were attacked by bullies along this path.

Higashi has used repetition so artfully that we are struck by an acute sense of change in the final scene. It speaks well for time elapsed and such a variety of associations with the joys and sorrows of these four years of youth. The final scene returns us to the opening. The twins stand outside Seizō's house in the suburbs of Kyoto. The camera pans up to the sky. The voices of the village crones are passing overhead, having their last say. Where are they headed? All they say is that there is no more room for them in the lives of the twins. The music that accompanied them before plays on as an overhead pan surveys the local scene. Mountains loom in sight of rice paddies here too, but this place is far removed from the village and countryside so dear to these men in their youth.

We register a sense of loss: the disappearance of myth and imagination faced by adults living in the modern world. The twins' village is gone, and so the divinity associated with it. And yet it *is* a village of dreams in a bittersweet sense. This film struck a chord in Japanese audiences still well populated with those who remember whole countrysides swept away in so few years after World War II. Taking the point of view of this film, we might well feel entitled to mixed emotions—sweet nostalgia for the past and bitter judgment too, seeing as how prosperity gives so much and takes away so much, also. Or, retreating to the view of the little boys themselves, fey and naughty as they are, we might sing a childish song titled simply "Furu-sato" (Home).

> There's the mountain where I chased a rabbit.
> There's the river where I caught catfish.
> Even today my thoughts return
> To that unforgettable home.

A Woman Director's Approach to the Country Family
Naomi Kawase's *Suzaku* (1997)

IN THE LAST FIFTEEN YEARS the list of notable Japanese women directors has grown steadily longer. After a slow and faltering start, it seems obvious that Japanese female filmmakers are coming into their own. Naomi Kawase (b. 1969) is an outstanding example of this trend. Her early 1990s apprenticeship in 8 mm documentaries apparently served her well. Her first full-length 35 mm feature, *Suzaku* (Moe no Suzaku), won her the Caméra d'Or for best new director at Cannes in 1997. She was twenty-eight. Cinema lovers East and West sat up and took notice, not just of her but of other women, too. Some had been making films in Japan long before Kawase's sudden rise to prominence; others, like her, are talents on the rise.

Any woman director's success in Japan will inevitably invite comparison with that of the incomparable Kinuyo Tanaka, whose distinguished acting career culminated in masterpieces such as *The Life of Oharu* (Saikaku ichidai onna, 1952) and *Ugetsu* (1953). Her drive and ambition were legendary early on, so it seems in retrospect only natural that mature assurance should take her behind the camera. Equally unsurprising was the amount of resistance she had to overcome just to get there. Against all such odds she made six films between 1953 and 1962. Her first, *Love Letters* (Koibumi, 1953), made her the first woman director in postwar Japanese cinema history. Sad to say, that small number also makes her the most prolific in mainstream features to date.[1]

Another outstanding woman made her mark in documentary films. Sumiko Haneda (b. 1926) got her start in 1958 with *Village School for Women* (Mura no fujingakkō). At age seventy-nine she is still at work, adding to an impressive array of over thirty films. Her recent masterpice is *The Life of Raichō Hiratsuka* (Hiratsuka Raichō no shogai, 2003), a two-hundred-minute biography of the octogenarian writer and activist for women's rights and world peace. Tomoko Fujiwara (b. 1932) is another documentary talent to mention in the same breath with Sumiko Haneda.

Sachi Hamano (b. 1948) is yet another. After many years in the so-called pink, or soft porn, industry, she has done herself proud in two main-stream features. *In Search of Midori Osaki* (Osaki Midori o sagahite) got rave reviews at the 1996 Tokyo International Film Festival. *Lily Festival* (Yurisai, 2001) deals with the sexuality of older Japanese women.

Hisako Matsui (b. 1946) has made two feature-length films on fairly large budgets: *Yukie* (1998) and *Oriume* (2001). Both explore the effects of Alzheimer's disease on care-giving family members.[2] Another emerging talent is the wunderkind Shiori Kazama (b. 1966), who made her first film in high school. She has nine to her credit now, among them the widely acclaimed 35 mm *How Old Is the River* (Fuyu no Kappa, 1994), *The Mars Canon* (Kasei no kyanon, 2001), and *The World's End* (Sekai no owari, 2004). All three document everyday love affairs of different kinds.

Of all these women, Kawase seems most likely to break Tanaka's record set so long ago. *The Weald* (Sonoudo monogatari, 1999), *Fireflies* (Hotaru, 2000), and *Sara Sōju* (2003) all explore the theme she seems most comfort-able with: issues of family life in and around her hometown Nara, the ancient capital of Japan. Elements of autobiography find their way in, too. Kawase has personal experience of family breakup and clearly values the support that children of broken homes receive from the elderly—grand-mothers especially. She herself was adopted by an old couple after her par-ents separated.

Her mostly highly praised film thus far is *Suzaku*. It foreshadows what has proved to be a consistent thematic concern more often the property of those some decades older. As it is, Kawase exhibits a precocious gift for harkening back to personal experience of a world reduced to a vanishing point by a century ending on a note of rapid change.

Yet Kawase brings a confident, personal touch to issues of family life deeply rooted in Japanese society. The story she tells is quietly sad, though filled with thought-provoking questions about the nature and structure of human relations in modern-day Japan. She depicts a rural middle-class fam-ily destroyed by the fluid, inconstant nature of the new economic order the Japanese have made their own with such conspicuous success.

She herself had this to say about her relation to the stories she tells: "I make films based on what I've actually seen and felt in my life—the sadness and the happiness and all the rest—in my own way. I haven't followed any filmmaking trend. Instead, my films have been formed by the environment in which I grew up."[3] Needless to say, the awards committee at Cannes was looking beyond her grasp of the subject at hand. One might say that in this case the Caméra d'Or recognizes a powerful synergy of stylistic and narrative means, as we shall see.

Kawase's first efforts in film show how *Suzaku* grew out of personal experience with the "incomplete" or dysfunctional family. In 1993 she made an 8 mm documentary, *Embracing* (Ni tsutsumarete), recording her long search for the father who deserted his family when she was a child. Another 8 mm documentary in 1995, *Katatsumori,* explores her relationship with the grandmother (by adoption) who raised her.[4] *Suzaku* continues this autobiographical and documentary approach. Its story is set in Nishiyoshino-mura, an isolated village in the south of Nara Prefecture. Kawase grew up in the area, as mentioned above, and spent some time in the village before shooting began. Her cast were amateurs, with one exception: the father, Kōzō (played by Jun Kunimura). Even village life appears "in character." A handheld camera was often used to shoot local events. In fact, the roving documentary camera itself plays a moving part in the film, as we shall see.

One noticeable omission is that mainstay of documentary filmmakers, the harsh indictment of the sociopolitical system responsible for the human tragedy at hand.[5] Kawase explained her position in an interview:

> My documentary *Tsutsumarete* was shown at the 1992 Image Forum Festival. At that time I noticed that a lot of filmmakers, especially women, were making documentaries about their own lives. Until then the image of the documentary had been films about social issues made by groups of people with a common agenda. But recently, filmmakers have been making more documentaries about themselves and their immediate environment, not the social conditions around them. I'm one of them.[6]

Suzaku invites reflection on fundamental issues of family, not challenge or confrontation. Kawase's expressive devices all accommodate that approach. Her camera eye studies nature up close and far away with obvious lyrical intent. Sometimes she rests our gaze on scenes for the better part of a minute, which, in cinema, has such power to bring thought and feeling together.

Some critics consider beginning-to-end analysis of a film the most horrific bore. I beg to differ, especially in the case of a film whose insights and surprises follow the natural order of events that destroy this family over time.

The Central Problem and Issues:
The Opening Sequence and the First Part

Suzaku was shot in just forty-five days. The director's reliance on the documentarian's economy of means is apparent from the outset. An opening shot of immense cedar trees on a windy day takes us into the heart of village life. The audience can be counted on to know that these trees are the basis of the rural economy in this backward region. These fine old trees will serve as a constant point of reference in the film, and so will the lyrical piano blending with the sound of wind stirring in the branches. Together they evoke the sweetly rueful sense of the film as it unfolds its tale of something precious lost.

This opening point of view connects with film's full title, *Moe no Suzaku*. Kawase herself explained this rather sophisticated reference:

> The word *moe* originally meant new green growth and by extension all of nature. I wanted to portray nature as a major character, along with the people in my film. *Suzaku* is one of the Chinese guardian deities of the four directions. *Suzaku* watches over the south. The title suggests that nature is under his protection.[7]

Such a title might refer to a family saga of struggle and ultimate survival in this idyllic setting on the ancient Yamato Plateau, watched over by its ancient deity. Here, however, the title serves a tragic irony, since we see the Tahara family falter and scatter in a matter of thirty years.

The story is in two parts. The first is set in 1971, when the last generation of the Tahara family is still in elementary school. The second takes place in the time leading up to 1986, the year now known to have been the high point of Japan's postwar economic "miracle." Woven into this narrative tapestry is the central problem: how does the rural family come to terms with Japan's modernization process? The first part shows the extended family leading a normal life, unaffected by modernization. Solidarity is what holds the entire family together. The second part works on the theme of dissolution. The Tahara family, as we shall see, were among the victims of that economic miracle. Kawase is in no hurry to be the bearer of bad news.

After the opening shot of cedars stirring in the wind, we come in on a scene of everyday family life in the country, anno 1971. This sequence is reminiscent of Ozu's classic depictions of middle-class family life. The camera takes note of the familiar old-fashioned country kitchen with its earthen floor and cauldron steaming over the fire—no electric rice cooker here. This dark room clearly belongs to people who have enough to eat, but no privileged possessions or status. An old woman and a young one are busily preparing breakfast. A young boy passes in and out, wearing wooden clogs. This shot lasts seventy-odd seconds. What we see is what we know. It looks like a mother-in-law and daughter-in-law working together, getting along. A boy has just gotten out of bed. A wind chime sounds in the second shot. It hangs in the living room, in sight of a mountain range stretching off and beyond. The camera backtracks to a young couple looking out at the mountains, seated in this living room. We have seen her; he must be her husband. This brief, purely visual introduction tells us that this family lives a fairly rudimentary country life, close to nature. A cut returns us to the kitchen, where the old woman is giving *miso* soup to the boy and a little girl. The suggestion here is that this family, composed of three generations, is rich in affection, if noticeably poor in material goods.

The pace of the film is rather slow, thanks in part to a good number of long takes. Even so, we are aware of a certain rhetorical tension building as the camera documents the life of this family in increasing detail.

The next two sequences speak for the isolated character of this little community. We see how the Tahara house stands by itself on the crest of a hill. The children walk to school along a path that leads through the woods. A series of long shots reminds us that these villagers are beholden to nature's bounty, not the cash-and-carry economy of urban life. When the children come home from school they find their grandmother tending a vegetable garden on a steep hillside. The camera studies this self-sufficient little garden for forty seconds. The aspect of hard necessity is spoken for by the very steepness of the hillside. The little girl is too weary to climb all the way to the top. The boy has to carry her. The camera cuts to another familiar village scene. Housewives gather around a peddler—a vital link with the outside world. The camera documents some vigorous haggling. Another cut shows children playing without the benefit of toys. They climb trees and splash one another with water. The father returns from work with a gift— not a toy, but a big beetle. But why are we here? What is the point of all this idyllic detail? Just when we might begin to wonder, a family picnic brings the note of sadness in.

Two long shots show the Tahara family walking through the woods together, five happy country people communing with nature. A third long take shows the children off and gone, the three adults sitting on the grass. Grandmother Sachiko, her son Kōzō, and his wife, Yasuyo, exchange fragments of conversation. A shift of mood is signaled by a temple gong. It echoes through the peaceful woods. In this shot, lasting one minute and twenty-four seconds, we learn a surprising amount of family history. We now know why these three people look so anxious, so sadly resigned. The boy, Eisuke, and the girl, Michiru, are not brother and sister. He is Kōzō's sister's child. She left the village a long time ago; we do not know why. The father of her child is not mentioned.

As we shall see, families in this little remote village need all the marrying-in reinforcement they can get. This early in the film we see the beginnings of rift in the Tahara family. Kōzō speaks bitterly of his sister's selfishness. The camera serves the director's documentary purposes, shifting to scrutinize Sachiko's face in close-up. She appears content, despite the loss of her only daughter. She says as much: "We've had a hard time. But now my life is easier and I'm happy."

This first part of the narrative climaxes in a scene conveyed in just six shots. Brief as it is, this episode plays an important double role in the film's overall design. A long shot shows Kōzō and the children at the mouth of a tunnel. In the next shot Kōzō asks Eisuke if he is afraid to walk into the darkness ahead. The camera pans to the open sky above, making the obvious comparison. A cut back to Eisuke alone shows him walking by himself. His face is taut with fear. The next shot shows Kōzō walking the children on through the tunnel, the three of them holding hands. Kōzō speaks to the boy as a father might to his son. He tells him to persevere, no matter how hard life may seem with his parents gone. The boy's expression in close-up speaks for his determination to try. This simple scene ends with another long shot of the three leaving the tunnel together. At this point it seems inconsequential, but the tunnel will return to greater effect in the second part of the narrative.

Narrative Ellipsis and the Second Part

Halfway through the film there is a narrative ellipsis. An abrupt time shift puts us in 1986. This year marks the high point of Japan's postwar prosperity. What does that mean to the Tahara family and to their remote little village? After a subtitle announcement "Fifteen years later" Kawase offers another leisurely, documentary approach to the matter at hand. She uses the same characteristic devices of the long take, lyrical piano accompaniment, and a fluid mix of realistic detail and idyllic inferences.

After the subtitle a following shot repeats the film's opening scenario. Sachiko and Yasuyo are making *miso* soup in a kitchen still centered around the old-fashioned cauldron. The electric pan is new, but nothing else seems changed. Who would guess from this scene that Japan's postwar constitution made women the equals of men? Eisuke comes in. How he has grown! He is a young man now, a wage earner. As he hands his monthly salary to Yasuyo, we realize that the family depends on him. Yasuyo reminds him to inquire about a new position opening up at his work place.

The next scene confirms our sense that the nation's prosperity has not extended to this remote area, that the Taharas are not the only hard-pressed family in the village. The village menfolk are meeting, seated around a table in a traditional Japanese room. The camera records the proceedings in a noncommittal documentary style. The village headman begins by announcing that the projected rail link has been canceled. The camera moves from speaker to speaker and group to group as all in the room express shock and dismay. Without this link to the outside world, to the new and different national economy, the village is doomed. Young people will move to find jobs far away. Young men who stay will never find brides willing to live in such a dead-end place.[8]

The scene ends with a shot of Kōzō seated in the foreground. The camera studies his troubled look, leaving the others out of focus in the background. He seems alienated, singled out, alone. That impression is reinforced by a conversation between Sachiko and Yasuyo. We learn that back in 1971 the village had been designated a "region too sparsely populated." The tunnel we saw Kōzō walking the children through had been part of a plan to revitalize the area. Yet trouble arose when the villagers split into factions for and against bringing the railroad in. Kōzō had been an active proponent of the railroad. His future depended on it, of that he was sure. Now, after all these years of waiting and hoping and projecting—nothing. We see him become a shadow of his former self. One afternoon he comes home early and sits in his room, listening to a record on the phonograph. The camera watches his motionless despair in a shot that lasts more than two minutes. The music is the same as before, something for piano, wistful and lyrical. This repeated view of Kōzō works in a subtle way to alert us to something different. We sense a mixture of urgency and ennui in his change of mood—even as he sits motionless.

Finally, a series of shots records his course of action. He picks up a camera and heads out of the house, followed by echoes of the music on the soundtrack. A cut shows his mother, Sachiko, in the living room. She is listening to the wind chime. Its note blends with the piano. We follow Kōzō at a distance as he walks a mountain path. He meets a neighbor on a bridge.

Another cut shows Sachiko resting contentedly. The silence is broken only by cicadas trilling in the light of afternoon.

These shots might be taken as a series of documentary notes on a sad but ordinary day in the life of the Tahara family. But the sequence closes on a view somehow disturbing, even alarming. Another long shot shows Kōzō wading through tall pampas grass, making his way toward the tunnel. Piano and wind chime cease. All we hear is the vacant, dry sound of tall grass brushed by the wind. Kōzō finds the tunnel closed with a bamboo barricade. We see at once what Kōzō sees and feels. This tunnel used at the outset of the film as a moral emblem fit to inspire a little boy with courage is here transformed into a very real artifact of hope turned to despair. The bamboo barricade has spoken.

Even before she uses this shocking image to bring Kōzō face to face with personal despair, Kawase has documented important evidence of increasing hardship in the village. One example connects this remote locale with a problem facing the Japanese wherever they live: the ever-increasing ratio of old to young in the population.[9] Here, in plainly documentary fashion, the director shows how a family sends grandfather and grandmother to a nursing home. A truck carrying an entire extended family stops at the Tahara house. Kōzō, Yasuyo, and Sachiko leave their gardening to greet the passengers who get out to stretch their legs. The head of the family says simply that he is "taking them." That is all he needs to say. Everyone knows what it means. Kōzō gives two children fresh tomatoes to eat. Even in these dire times, the villagers have their bonds. The travelers climb back into the truck and prepare to leave. The camera cuts to the departing grandparents and back to the Tahara family. Each party bows deeply, a gesture plain but eloquent. Nothing is said. Nothing needs to be said. The message of mutual respect and affection has been expressed the old-fashioned way.

So what will become of Kōzō now that he finds the tunnel blocked? Kawase leaves us wondering for several sequences more. One night the telephone rings. Here the one-scene, one-shot method is used to detail the reaction of the family. The shot lasts one minute and forty-five seconds. Michiru and Yasuyo run in. The camera pans right to include everyone as Eisuke answers the phone. He looks very much the man of the family. Sachiko stands next to him. The police have found a man in possession of Kōzō's camera. Eisuke moves out of frame, leaving the three women in the room. A scene in the police station merely confirms the fact of Kōzō's disappearance. Has he run away? Has he killed himself somewhere? Where? We never do learn. His fate lies outside Kawase's documentary scheme.

The tunnel image returns, this time to suggest an element of fatalistic circularity. Eisuke removes the barricade and goes in to investigate. A medium shot in profile shows him looking around, his eyes shining in the darkness. He is no longer afraid. A flashback speaks for his memory of that childhood visit. Now, robbed of the father/mentor showing him the way to courage, he bolts. An extreme long shot shows him running for the exit.

Eisuke has other tests before him. Michiru has fallen in love with her cousin. Her feelings are hinted at many times in this second part of the film. In one scene her shy, maiden manner of accepting a ride on Eisuke's motorcycle connects with a similar instance. In it, however, the rider is Yasuyo. The camera takes note of the young man's awareness of her hands tightly gripping him as they ride. His expression suggests a subtle affection. Is it merely filial? Could it be otherwise? We are given no clue to Yasuyo's feelings. Her face in close-up appears entirely noncommittal.

The possibility of a love triangle adds considerable tension to the narrative, though Kawase plays hide-and-seek with the basic facts of the matter. We see this in a scene depicting a sudden summer shower one afternoon shortly after Kōzō's disappearance. An extreme long shot shows Yasuyo walking away from the camera along a country path. Deep space is used to show her encountering Eisuke. Another extreme long shot shows them continuing on together, away from the camera.

A reverse set-up follows. For the first time we hear a voice. It is Eisuke calling out "Sis!" (a boy in his situation in Japan will call the aunt who mothers him "auntie," not the more affectionate "sis"). Yasuyo does not respond. She continues walking toward the camera, finally stopping in the middle of the path. Eisuke catches up to her. This shot lasts a good long minute. Then rain begins to fall. The couple take shelter under a roof and Yasuyo runs back out into the rain and away, followed by Eisuke.

A cut to the Tahara house shows Michiru seated alone in her room looking out at thunder and rain. Her puzzled, pained expression reminds us of her look in a previous scene. There she looked out the window of a bus at Eisuke giving Yasuyo a lift on his motorbike. Now she wears that same look of wondering jealousy. She seems to be wondering where is he—and where is she, the other woman? The next shot clears away the storm but not the poor girl's doubts. Storm clouds give way to clear sky and mountain vista. The guardian deity Suzaku is watching over all. Mulberry trees in the foreground look washed and refreshed, as if they welcomed the attentions of the storm. But has Suzaku swept away the turmoil of human emotions? A cut shows that Eisuke and Yasuyo have taken shelter in a dilapidated building. We hear no words exchanged, only silence broken by the chirping of a bird, now that the storm has passed on. Has anything . . . happened? We do not have a clue.

Another cut to a long shot shows Eisuke and Yasuyo approaching the Tahara house. The grandmother asks where they have been. Neither answers. They enter the house in silence, crossing the screen. Both are sopping wet. They look as if all their sorrow and anxiety over Kōzō's disappearance have been cleansed by Suzaku's sudden downpour. Has Michiru seen Eisuke and her mother entering the house together? Again we are given no clue. A concluding shot simply shows the grandmother in the living room. Michiru joins her, then Eisuke comes in.

A dedicated psychoanalytical critic might feel inclined to see a touch of Oedipal conflict here. I think it more likely that Eisuke's feelings for Yasuyo are as simply factual as his grief for the loss of his father figure, Kōzō. He is a motherless child raised by his aunt. It seems only natural that his yearning for mother love should tend her way, especially now with Kōzō gone. What takes center stage in the causal line of the Michiru-Eisuke liaison is her changing affection, which is perhaps more surprising. As children, they were raised as brother and sister. Now she must school him—and herself—to see one another in a different light.

The next scene after the storm takes place on the night of a festival. The air outdoors at dusk is filled with the sounds of summer. Frogs croak and crickets chirp as Eisuke and Michiru stroll in a long take lasting over two minutes. Again, Michiru wears the lover's expression of anguished doubt we saw that afternoon of the storm. Now, obviously, she has decided to make her inclinations known. She clings to Eisuke, weeping. He suggests that they go home. The camera follows them, taking note of the electric lantern lighting their footsteps home. Kawase uses this simple detail to link this growing-up moment to earlier scenes from childhood when these two walked a country path to school and back. Now we see them holding hands in such a different sense. A series of shots taken by a handheld camera shows them moving with the crowd past the busy, colorful stalls of festival vendors. The film's romantic piano plays a gradual crescendo, as if to celebrate their love. Kawase uses this ordinary documentary highpoint to appeal to our sense of passing time and the timeless rhythm of growing up and falling in love and growing old to die. What remains to be seen is how forces near at hand and far away precipitate the crisis that will scatter the Tahara family once and for all.

The film has done its documentary work, showing how the village is doomed to decline. Yasuyo's health was already fragile before Kōzō disappeared. She had been forced to find work at a country inn and had collapsed there once. Now suddenly failing health makes her an invalid.

Sachiko is not the tyrant mother-in-law of stereotype. Her concern for Yasuyo is genuine when she suggests that the poor woman return to her family. Michiru, of course, will go with her. This is a terrible moment for Sachiko, too. Old as she is, she must start anew with Eisuke, moving with him to live and work at a country inn.

Yasuyo and Michiru react differently to this crisis. Again Kawase uses a long take—nearly two minutes—to introduce their tête-à-tête for the first time. Silence and dialogue alternate in a rhythmical manner as if to belie the tension between them. Michiru is insisting that they stay.

Next we see a notably restrained scene between Eisuke and Michiru. She opens his door. The camera rests an unhurried gaze on the young lovers standing in the doorway. They find little to say, though everything about them speaks for affection. Michiru is the one who tries putting it into words. She says she is fond of him. Her expression is serious, as befits, since she adds, rather abruptly, that she will be leaving with her mother. We get a sense that Michiru has just this moment made up her mind to follow obligation, not personal inclination. They look at one other in silence. Then Eisuke says only "good night." As she turns to leave he calls her back.

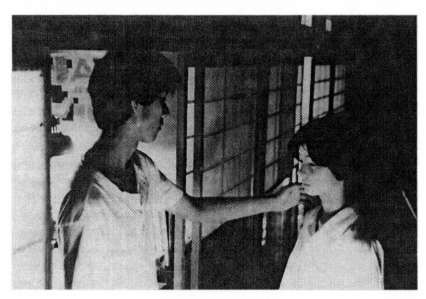

Eisuke (l., Kōtarō Shibata) and Michiru (Michiko Ono) in *Suzaku* (1997). © Bittre's End.

A cut shows them alone together one last time on the rooftop, despairing young lovers seeking out a starry sky. Kawase invests this moment with quiet romance. They sit close together admiring the vastness of the universe, their tiny village spread out down below. The lyrical piano theme plays out, leaving behind only the odd intermittent single note.

The Final Sequence

The film ends with a coda, which, in effect, documents the documentary. Again we see breakfast being made in a country kitchen. Now three generations of women—Sachiko, Yasuyo, and Michiru—perform the morning ritual. The kitchen is the same behind-the-times place. These women seem doomed to be behind the times as well. The village itself, we are forced to think, will be lost in time, its women doing woman's work forever and a day. Again, a full, significant cinema minute is given to this seemingly inconsequential scene. Breakfast reminds us that the head of the house has vanished, and with him so many related hopes. Here, Kawase does something surprising. She revives the past by showing documentary footage taken by Kōzō with his 8 mm camera. It had been found in the tunnel. We see the things he saw that day he disappeared.

Oshima did something similar in *The Man Who Left His Will on Film* (Tōkyō sensō sengo hiwa, 1968). Here Kōzō's legacy records his feelings of closeness to nature and community. He dwells in loving, almost obsessive, detail on flowers, trees, and grass, all vibrant with life. These views alternate with pictures of villagers young and old. The amateur shutterbug catches folks in center-front shots, smiling obligingly at the camera. Who would guess that they are leading lives increasingly desperate in this forgotten place? Accustomed as we are to Kawase's leisurely long takes, here we are surprised by the jaunty pace of these hand-held camera glimpses. The effect is that of a montage.

That previous rhythm suddenly returns as we witness the final separation in a long take of just under four minutes. The four remaining Tahara family members come out of the house. Our need for closure is served by a number of details. Sachiko speaks of the innkeeper's kindness, letting her and Eisuke live at the workplace. We hear the sound of water falling into the well. That calls to mind the times we have seen the family pause there to wash and the children's mischievous splashing long ago.

This scene documents, in real time, the long, awkward minutes of saying good-bye in real life. Here, as there, good manners are used to shoo away the pain. Even here, where the pain of separation is so real, we see bows and handshakes—though Michiru does sob. The young lovers get no final embrace, only a bow each to each as the grandmother dabs silent tears. The camera speeds up slightly, panning left and right to record the motions of departure. Finally, Eisuke and Sachiko bow as the van moves away. Two brief glimpses say all there is to say on behalf of the two young lovers. A medium shot shows Michiru in tears. A point-of-view shot records her farewell gaze at the roof of the house.

A cut omits some small interval of time, taking us to Eisuke burning old letters and boxes. He is no doubt merely preparing to move to smaller quarters. Even so, we are curious about his mood but cannot read it, given his lowered posture shown in medium shot. It looks as if we are being warned against drifting into merely sentimental interest in the outcome here.

The camera pans laterally toward the house to end the film with its longest shot—four minutes and forty seconds. Sachiko sits quietly, then begins to sing a children's song. It tells of a game of hide-and-seek. Two children hiding in a tree hold hands and look at the sky. The camera comes to rest on Sachiko's face as she sings, then closes her eyes. She seems to have fallen asleep. The camera closes in slowly as if to make sure that she is all right. This gesture creates an ambiguous impression. Are we to assume that this good old soul has passed on peacefully in her sleep? Or is she only old

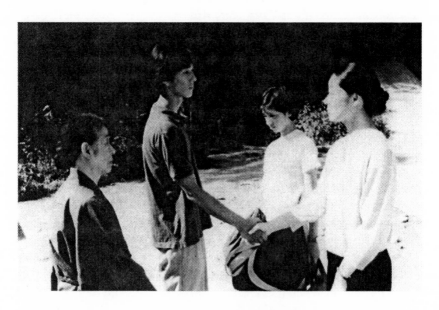

Sachiko (l., Sachiko Izumi), Eisuke (c.l., Kōtarō Shibata), Michiru (c.r., Michiko Ono), and Yasuyo (r., Yasuyo Hamamura) in *Suzaku* (1997). © Bittre's End.

and tired and apt to doze? (I am inclined to think the latter, though Kawase's scenario says that she has passed into her final sleep.)

The camera's attention wanders, as if to suggest that Sachiko and Eisuke are where they are and remain in tune with nature, like the children in the song. An upward pan looks to the wind chime. A diagonal pan reaches back down to Sachiko still leaning against a pillar of the house. The wind chime tinkles a lullaby sound. The camera moves diagonally to include Eisuke, now standing in the yard. Then it pans up for a rhythmical glide along the rooftop. Blue sky fills the screen. Children's voices sing Sachiko's song.

I am inclined to praise the restraint and economy of this ending. It seems to gain a lot by omitting much that might be expected. In place of surging emotions and plot all tidily knotted up, we have recurring, everyday images the film itself has enriched with meaning. One might say that Kawase, like Ozu, is offering us matter for reflection. We see it in our final view of Sachiko. Her sleeping face seems well nigh expressionless, transcendent, resigned to fate. But of course Kawase and Ozu do very different camera work. Ozu is a perfectionist intent on eliminating any hint of asymmetry. Kawase values spontaneity more. Yet her parting look at the grandmother Sachiko invites comparison with Ozu's old father in *Tokyo Story* (1953). He typifies eloquent economy at the ending of the film, looking out at the sea, fanning himself. Despite her documentary, ostensibly casual approach, Kawase achieves a similar effect here. She shows us a passing generation resigned and younger generations pressing on—to what end, she is wisely unwilling to say.

Some viewers have been surprised to find that a film so strong on documentation has left some obvious questions unanswered. Where do Yasuyo's parents live? What can she and Michiru expect to happen to them there? And for that matter, is there no hope that the two young lovers will meet again?

Asked to explain this lack of narrative legibility, Kawase answered: "I don't attempt to solve this problem of family breakdown. I wouldn't dare."[10] My own thought is that we should accept *Suzaku* for the rarity it is, a semi-documentary that invites reflection on important, unanswerable questions about life. Those who insist on looking for hints of problem solving might do well to consider what Kawase has to say about the importance of our human bond with nature. Certainly by the end of the film we see why her title honors the spirit of Shintoism associated with nature worship in a world continually ravaged by its "civilizations."

Notes

Introduction

More references on the films briefly mentioned in introduction will be provided in the individual chapters to follow.

1. Donald Richie, *Japanese Cinema: Film Style and National Character* (Garden City, NY: Anchor Books, 1971), ix.

2. Mitsuhiro Yoshimoto, *Kurosawa: Film Studies and Japanese Cinema* (Durham, NC: Duke University Press, 2000), 10.

3. These important characteristics are well documented in a number of books. For concise information, see Donald Richie, *Japanese Cinema: An Introduction* (Hong Kong: Oxford University Press, 1990). Noël Burch also offers though-provoking, if often dogmatic, observations on these early practices. See *To the Distant Observer: Form and Meaning in the Japanese Cinema* (Berkeley: University of California Press, 1979).

4. Joseph Anderson, "Japanese Film" in *Encyclopaedia of Japan* (Tokyo: Kodansha International, 1984), 269. Also see Joseph Anderson, "Spoken Silents in the Japanese Cinema," *Journal of Film and Video* 30, no. 1 (1988): 23–26; and Don Kirihara, "A Reconsideration of the Institution of the Benshi," *Film Reader* 6 (1985): 41–53.

5. *Kōdan* is a popular story type that tells the adventures of heroic samurai, most having to do with family feuds and vendetta. *Rakugo* originated as comic tales accentuated with equally funny gestures and vocalizations in the late sixteenth century. This genre made great progress toward the end of the seventeenth century, gradually shifting audiences from feudal lords to the man in the street.

6. For a comprehensive study of the Japanese Pure Film movement, see Joanne Bernardi, *Writing in Light: The Silent Scenario and the Japanese Pure Film Movement* (Detroit: Wayne University Press, 2001).

7. *Shingeki*, which literally means "new theater," occurred as part of the Meiji enlightenment. A leader of this New Theater movement was Shōyō Tsubouchi (1859–1935), an advocate of realism in fiction and drama. His follower Hōgetsu Shimamura (1873–1918) upheld a theory of European naturalism as a basis for the modern theater. Together, they were instrumental in introducing many European plays, especially those of Ibsen. Hōgetsu's production of Ibsen's *A Doll's House* with the actress Sumiko Matsui made an important contribution to the development of *shingeki*. Kenji Mizoguchi's *The Love of Sumako the Actress* (Joyū Sumako no koi,

1947) and Teinosuke Kinugasa's *Actress* (Joyū, 1947) portrayed the couple's involvement in the *shingeki* movement. The culmination of the *shingeki* drive came in 1908 with the organization of Jiyūgekijō (the Liberty Theater) by Kaoru Osanai and Sadanji Ichikawa II (1880–1940). Together, they introduced modern plays by Ibsen, Chekhov, and Hauptmann. For further information on *shingeki,* see Thomas Rimer, *Towards a Modern Theater: Kishida Kunio* (Princeton, NJ: Princeton University Press, 1974).

8. For a complete study of Gosho's major films, see Arthur Nolletti Jr., *The Cinema of Gosho Heinosuke: Laughter through Tears* (Bloomington: Indiana University Press, forthcoming).

9. For more detailed information, see Keiko McDonald, *From Book to Screen: Modern Japanese Literature in Film* (Armonk, NY: M. E. Sharpe, 2000), 17–43.

10. For a comprehensive history of Japanese cinema from its beginning through the war period, see Peter High, *Teikoku no ginmaku* (The imperial screen: A cultural history) (Nagoya: Nagoya Daigaku Shuppankai, 1995).

11. Donald Richie, *A Hundred Years of Japanese Cinema* (New York: Kodansha International, 2001), 216.

12. For more information, see Kyōko Hirano, *Mr. Smith Goes to Tokyo: Japanese Cinema under the American Occupation: 1945–1952* (Washington, DC: Smithsonian Institution, 1992), 47–103.

13. For a detailed analysis of *Twenty-four Eyes,* see David Desser, "*Twenty-four Eyes* (Nijūshi no hitomi)," in *Teaching Guide for Childhood and Education in Japan,* ed. Merry White and David Desser (New York: Japan Society of New York, 1990), 30–34; and Keiko McDonald, *Cinema East: A Critical Study of Major Japanese Films* (London: Fairleigh Dickinson University Press, 1983), 231–254.

14. The major references on *Rashomon* include Donald Richie, ed., *Rashomon* (New Brunswick, NJ: Rutgers University Press, 1990). See also Donald Richie, *The Films of Akira Kurosawa,* expanded ed. (Berkeley: University of California Press, 1996), 70–80; Stephen Prince, *The Warrior's Camera: The Cinema of Akira Kurosawa,* rev. and expanded ed. (Princeton, NJ: Princeton University Press, 1999), 127–136; and David Desser, *The Samurai Films of Akira Kurosawa* (Ann Arbor, MI: UMI Research Press, 1983), 65–71.

15. For a more comprehensive study of Sun-Tribe films, see Michael Raine, "Ishihara Yujiro: Youth, Celebrity, and the Male Body in Late 1950s Japan," in *Word and Image in Japanese Cinema,* ed. Dennis Washburn and Carole Cavanaugh (New York: Cambridge University Press, 2001), 204–209.

16. For a detailed study of Japan's New Wave cinema, see David Desser, *Eros Plus Massacre: An Introduction to the Japanese New Wave Cinema* (Bloomington: Indiana University Press, 1988).

17. For a study of Fukasaku's Yakuza films, see Keiko McDonald, "Kinji Fukasaku: An Introduction," *Film Criticism* 8, no. 1 (1983): 20–32; and "The Yakuza Film: An Introduction," in *Reframing Japanese Cinema: Authorship, Genre and History,*

ed. David Desser and Arthur Nolletti Jr. (Bloomington: Indiana University Press, 1988), 165–192.

18. For a study of *Japan Sinks,* see Susan Napier, "Pacific Sites: the Japanese Imagination of Disaster from Godzilla to Akira," in *Contemporary Japanese Culture,* ed. John Treat (Honolulu, University of Hawai'i Press, 1996), 225–239.

19. Richie, *One Hundred Years of Japanese Cinema,* 218.

20. Ibid.

21. Ibid., 219.

22. Mark Schilling, *Contemporary Japanese Film* (New York: Weatherhill, 1999), 70.

23. For example, see David Bordwell, *Ozu and the Poetics of Cinema,* 224–249, 256–259. He offers detailed analyses of *I Was Born, But . . .* and *Story of Floating Weeds.* Joan Bernardi's study of *A Page of Madness* not only places the film in the context of avant-garde art in late 1920s Japan, but examines critics' responses to the 1971 rerelease with more complete footage. See her "Silent Cinema as Experimentation, Improvisation, and Cineáste Sensation: Kinugasa Teinosuke's *A Page of Madness* (1926)" in *Japanese Film: Texts and Context,* ed. Alastair Phillips and Julian Stringer (London: Routledge, forthcoming). See also Richard Cohen, *"A Page of Madness,"* Film Quarterly 29, no. 4 (1976): 47–51.

24. *Muddy River* was available on video with English subtitles in the mid 1980s in the United States. However, it soon went out of circulation.

Chapter 1. Kenji Mizoguchi's *Sisters of the Gion*

1. For a more comprehensive study of Mizoguchi's work, see Keiko McDonald, *Mizoguchi* (Boston: Twayne, 1983). The following are also helpful: Dudley Andrew and Paul Andrew, *Kenji Mizoguchi: A Guide to References and Resources* (Boston: G. K. Hall, 1981, 1984); Dudley Andrew and Carole Cavanaugh, *Sanshō Dayū* (London: BFI, 2002); Keiko McDonald, ed., *Ugetsu* (New Bruswick, NJ: Rutgers University Press, 1993); and Donald Kirihara, *Patterns of Time: Mizoguchi and the 1930s* (Madison: University of Wisconsin Press, 1992). Also see Dudley Andrew, "The Passion of Identification in the Late Films of Kenji Mizoguchi," in *Films in the Aura of Art* (Princeton, NJ: Princeton University Press, 1984), 172–201. This chapter examines the dichotomous nature of Mizoguchi's women and his ambivalent attitudes toward their plight as found in his late works such as *The Life of Oharu* and *Miss Oyu* (Oyū-sama, 1951).

2. Andrew and Andrew, *Kenji Mizoguchi,* 26.

3. For an informative discussion of Mizoguchi's camera work in his representative films such as *The Story of the Last Chrysanthemum* (Zangiku monogatari, 1939), see Tadao Satō, *Currents in Japanese Cinema,* trans. Gregory Barrett (Tokyo: Kodansha, 1982), 178–185.

4. The Chinese characters for the original title were misread as "Gion no shi-

mai." They should have been read as "Gion no kyōdai." I am grateful to Dr. Kyōko Hirano, a former director of the Film Center, Japan Society of New York, for pointing this out.

5. See Donald Richie, *Japanese Cinema: Film Style and National Character* (Garden City, N.Y.: Anchor Books, 1971), 118–119. Noël Burch, *To the Distant Observer: Form and Meaning in the Japanese Cinema* (Berkeley: University of California Press, 1979), 217–246. For a more recent study, see Kirihara, *Patterns of Time*. Critic Tadao Satō's pinpointed discussion of Mizoguchi's artistry in his representative films is also available in English. See Tadao Satō, *Currents in Japanese Cinema*.

6. In recent years a few cultural videos on the life of a geisha have become available. *The Secret Life of Geisha* (1999), distributed by A&E Television Networks, incorporates many interviews with *maiko* (apprentice geisha) and geisha in the Gion as well as their clients.

7. Yoshikata Yoda, *Mizoguchi Kenji: Hito to Geijutsu* (Kenji Mizoguchi: His life and art) (Tokyo: Tabata Shoten, 1970), 62–63.

8. Ibid, 62.

9. Kenji Mizoguchi, "Tsuchi no nioi" (The smell of the earth), *Kinema jumpō* 21 (July 1936): 60.

10. Noël Burch, *To the Distant Observer: The Form and the Meaning of the Japanese Cinema* (Berkeley: University of California Press, 1979), 226.

11. Ibid., 227.

12. Ibid.

13. For a shot-by-shot analysis of the final scene, see Keiko McDonald, *Mizoguchi*, 43–45.

14. For a thorough discussion on this subject, see Takeo Doi, *The Anatomy of Dependence*, trans. John Bester (Tokyo: Kodansha, 1981).

15. The original script included a telling scene on the subject of male ego. On a train bound for his hometown, Furusawa celebrates his future with Sadakichi, his former employee. Asked by Sadakichi what he is going to do with Umekichi, he cheerfully replies that he will send her some money for heart balm. He adds that when all is said and done, a geisha like her is only in it for the money.

16. Andrew and Andrew, *Kenji Mizoguchi*, 29.

Chapter 2. Akira Kurosawa's *Drunken Angel*

This is a revision of my article on *Drunken Angel* that originally appeared in Post Script 20, no. 1 (2000), the special issue on Akira Kurosawa.

1. In addition to Donald Richie's *The Films of Akira Kurosawa*, Prince's *The Warrior's Camera*, and Desser's *The Samurai Films of Akira Kurosawa* mentioned earlier, the major publications on Kurosawa in English include Patricia Ellen, *Akira Kurosawa: A Guide to References and Resources* (Boston: G. K. Hall, 1979); and James Godwin, ed., *Akira Kurosawa and Intertextual Cinema* (Baltimore: John Hopkins University Press, 1994).

2. Quoted by Richie, *The Films of Akira Kurosawa*, 243.

3. For detailed analyses of *Rashomon*, see Donald Richie, ed., *Rashomon* (New Brunswick, NJ: Rutgers University Press, 1990). See also Desser, *The Samurai Films of Akira Kurosawa*, 65–71; and Keiko McDonald, "The Dialectic of Light and Darkness in Kurosawa's *Rashomon*" in *Cinema East: A Critical Study of Major Japanese Films* (East Brunswick, NJ: Fairleigh Dickinson University Press, 1983), 23–35.

4. Quoted by Richie, *The Films of Akira Kurosawa*, 47.

5. Ibid.

6. Kurosawa discovered Mifune while the actor was working on Senkichi Taniguchi's *To the End of the Silver Mountain* (Ginrei no hate, 1947). Critic Tadao Satō wrote this about Mifune's performance: "Film-goers were used to actors whose faces reflected a certain complacent satisfaction with being a star. Yet here was a completely different look. This actor's face expressed resentment against everything around him. . . . It was the face that many in the audience yearned to show the world but didn't dare. They became instant fans of Mifune, doting on his disdainful expression as much as on the rebellious roles he played." See Tadao Satō, *Kurosawa Akira no sekai* (The world of Akira Kurosawa) (Tokyo: San'ichi Shobō, 1976), p. 121.

7. Stephen Prince, *The Warrior's Camera: The Cinema of Akira Kurosawa*, rev. and exp. ed. (Princeton, NJ: Princeton University Press, 1999), 81. For a more extensive analysis of the cesspool symbolism, see 79–85.

8. Nagisa Ōshima, "*Yoidore tenshi* kara manabu mono" (What I learn from *The Drunken Angel*), quoted by Satō in *Kurosawa Akira no sekai*, 126.

9. Nobuhiko Kobayashi, "Daisukurīn de minaoshite hoshii eigateki miryoku" (Charming moments on the big screen I'd like you to revisit), *Kinema junpō* 1268 (October 1988), 88. According to Kobayashi, Mifune's gangster glamour in this film had an immediate effect on the Yakuza around Shibuya in Tokyo. Matsunaga's suit and white muffler redefined the tough-guy look.

10. Tadao Satō, *Kurosawa Akira zensakuhin-shu* (Akira Kurosawa: A complete collection of his works) (Tokyo: Tōhō, 1980), 53. A number of critics claim that as an avid lover of music, especially classics, Kurosawa knew very well how vital a role music played in the film. For example, see Shiki Ichirō, *Kurosawa Akira to Ozu Yasujirō* (Akira Kurosawa and Yasujirō Ozu) (Tokyo: Hōbunkan, 2000), 194.

11. David Bordwell, *Ozu and the Poetics of Cinema* (Princeton, NJ: Princeton University Press, 1988), 68–69. Also see Donald Richie, *Ozu* (Berkeley: University of California Press, 1971), 183–184.

12. See Richie, *The Films of Akira Kurosawa*, 53.

13. Tadao Satō, *Kurosawa Akira kaidai* (Akira Kurosawa: Interpretation) (Tokyo: Iwanami, 1990), 90–91. I am very grateful to Vladimir Padunov, a colleague of mine in film studies at the University of Pittsburgh, for providing me with the following information. Timoshenko was more famous for the production of formulaic comedies in the second half of his career, especially around 1935. *Sniper*, aka *The Art of Killing*, was the only film he made in 1931.

14. Richie, *The Films of Akira Kurosawa,* 52.

15. Satō, *Kurosawa Akira zensakuhin-shū,* 53.

Chapter 3. Shirō Toyoda's *The Mistress*

1. For a comprehensive study of the Japanese cinema industry's involvement in so-called *bungei-eiga* (adaptations of literary works) from 1935 to 1941, see Keiko McDonald, *From Book to Screen: Modern Japanese Literature in Films* (Armonk, NY: M. E. Sharpe, 2000), 17–45.

2. Ōgai's many works are now available through English translations. For example, see Tomas Rimer, ed. *Youth and Other Stories* (Honolulu: University of Hawai'i Press, 1994). For a most recent English translation of *Gan,* see Burton Watson, trans. *The Wild Goose* (Ann Arbor: University of Michigan Center for Japanese Studies, 1995). Thomas Rimer's seminal study, *Mori Ōgai* (Boston: Twayne, 1970), offers a thought-provoking overview of the novelist's work.

3. The author's analysis of the heroine in *Snow Country* appears in Thomas Rimer and Keiko McDonald, *Japanese Literature on Screen* (New York: Japan Society, 1989), 50–58.

4. George Bluestone, *Novel into Film* (Berkeley: University of California Press, 1957), 21.

5. Ōgai Mori, *The Wild Geese,* trans. Kingo Ochiai and Sanford Goldstein (Tokyo: Tuttle, 1959), 33.

6. For a socialist feminist approach to patriarchy revealed in both the novel and the film, see Tamae Prindle, "Money, Sex, and Power: A Socialist Feminist Analysis of Mori Ōgai's *The Wild Geese* and Toyoda Shirō's *The Mistress,*" a paper presented at the 1997 AAS Conference in Chicago, 1997.

7. Ōgai, *The Wild Geese,* 46–47.

8. Ibid., 57.

9. Ibid., 76.

10. For example, the critic Shunji Chiba explores a "mythological" dimension of the snake incident mentioned by the narrator. Chiba points out the universal theme of the heroic exploit shared by myths East and West. For example, according to Chiba, both a story in *Kojiki* (The record of ancient matters) and the Perseus-Andromeda myth concern a hero who fights a destructive python to save the life of a maiden. See Shunji Chiba, "'Mado no onna' kō: *Gan* o megutte " (Rethinking of the heroine "Woman in the Window": On *The Wild Goose*), in *Mori Ōgai kenkyū* (Study of Ōgai Mori) 2 (Tokyo: Izumi Shoin, 1988), 40–41.

11. Critic Masao Miyoshi considers shipping Okada out off to Germany as the only solution, not just "another plot detail." He claims that Okada's further stay in Japan would lead to his inevitable "involvement with Otama." See Masao Miyoshi, *Accomplices of Silence: The Modern Japanese Novel* (Berkeley: University of California Press, 1974), 46–47.

12. For a more detailed analysis of Ōgai's use of the first-person narrator, see Miyoshi, *Accomplices of Silence*, 46–54.

13. Ōgai, *The Wild Geese*, 119.

14. For an insightful study of themes of exploitation and male anxiety and impotence shared by Ōgai's *The Mistress* and the Hollywood melodrama *Blonde Venus* by Josef von Sternberg, see David Desser, "*The Mistress:* The Economy of Sexuality," *Post Script* 11, no. 1 (1991), 20–27.

Chapter 4. Hiroshi Inagaki's *Samurai* Trilogy

1. Takahiro Shimaji et al., eds. *Nihon eiga kantoku zenshu* (Encyclopedia of Japanese film directors) (Tokyo: Kinema Jumpō, 1976), 47.

2. For a comprehensive analysis of Inagaki's *Chūshingura* available on video with English subtitles, see Keiko McDonald, *Japanese Classical Theater in Films* (Rutherford, NJ: Associated University Presses, 1995), 247–256.

3. Tadao Satō, "Musashi no Shōwa jidai: Kindaiteki jiga ni mezameta kengō" (Musashi films in the Showa period: The master swordsman who was awakened to a modern type of ego), *Hitotoki* 3, no. 6 (2003): 24.

4. An English translation of this novel is available. See Eiji Yoshikawa, *Musashi,* trans. Charles S. Terry (New York: Harper and Row, 1981).

5. For an analysis of Kohata's version, see Alain Silver, *The Samurai Film* (New York: A. S. Barnes, 1977), 94–103.

6. For a study of the myth of Musashi, see Gregory Barrett, *Archetypes in Japanese Film* (London: Associated University Presses, 1989), 44–56. Barrett shows how filmmakers adopted traditional storytellers' invented episodes related to Musashi's training. He also covers various *Musashi* film versions, such as Uchida's five-part series (1961–1965) and the NHK drama serialized between April 1984 and March 1985. The most recent NHK Musashi drama, featuring the famous Kabuki actor Shin'nosuke Ichikawa, began to be serialized in 2003.

7. *The Book of Five Rings* focuses on the strategy of warfare and single combat. Musashi analyses many aspects of swordsmanship as they relate to any situation requiring tactical assessment and operation. Musashi's work has been used as a handbook by many Japanese businessmen. A number of English translations have appeared over the years. Among them is *A Book of Five Rings,* trans. Victor Harris (New York: Overland Press, 1972).

8. Will Wright, *Six Guns and Society: A Structural Study of the Western* (Berkeley: University of California Press, 1975).

9. For an English translation of this work, see Donald Keene, ed. *The Anthology of Japanese Literature: From the Earliest Era to the Mid-Nineteenth Century* (New York: Grove Press, 1955), 197–207.

10. Eiji Yoshikawa, *Musashi,* 317.

11. Ibid., 456.

12. Ibid., 970.

Chapter 5. Yasujirō Ozu's *Floating Weeds*

1. Daisuke Miyao, "Translator's Introduction," in Kijū Yoshida, *Ozu's Anti-Cinema*, trans. Daisuke Miyao and Kyōko Hirano (Ann Arbor: Center for Japanese Studies, University of Michigan, 2003), xiii. The Kanji characters for Yoshida's first name can be read as "Kijū" or "Yoshishige." Though his first name was originally "Yoshishige," he recently changed it into "Kijū" for the sake of readability for Western audiences when his most recent film, *Women in the Mirror* (Kagami no onnata-chi, 2003), was released in France.

2. For a comprehensive study of Ozu's *Tokyo Story*, see David Desser, ed., *Tokyo Story* (Cambridge: Cambridge University Press, 1997); and Yoshida, *Ozu's Anti-Cinema*, pp. 87–120. See also Keiko McDonald, "A Basic Narrative Mode in Yasujiro Ozu's *Tokyo Story*," in *Cinema East: A Critical Study of Major Japanese Films* (Rutherford, NJ: Fairleigh Dickinson University Press, 1983), 201–227.

3. For a detailed analysis of *Ohayo*, see David Desser, "Ohayo," in *Teaching Guide for Childhod and Education in Japan* (New York: Japan Society of New York, 1989), pp. 25–29. Also see David Bordwell, *Ozu and the Poetics of Cinema* (Princeton, NJ: Princeton University Press, 1988), 348–354.

4. Donald Richie, *Ozu: His Life and Film* (Berkeley: University of California Press, 1974), 8–9.

5. Miyagawa reminisces about the difficulty he had accommodating Ozu's preference for a low-angled camera position and his own choice of a crane shot over it in a number of scenes. Linda Ehrlich and Akiko Shibagaki, "Miyagawa Kazuo: My Life as a Cameraman," *Post Script* 11, no. 1 (1991): 5–19.

6. Certainly there are a few notable exceptions. The final scene of *Early Summer* (1951) shows a tracking shot. See Bordwell, *Ozu and the Poetics of Cinema* (Princeton, NJ: Princeton University Press, 1988), 321.

7. See Richie, *Ozu*, and Bordwell, *Ozu and the Poetics of Cinema*.

8. See Tadao Satō, *Ozu no geijutsu* (The Art of Ozu, 1971), and Yoshida, *Ozu's Anti-Cinema*.

9. Donald Keene, ed. *The Anthology of Japanese Literature: From the Earliest Era to the Mid-Nineteenth Century* (New York: Grove Press, 1958), 79.

10. Ibid., 362.

11. Richie, *Ozu*, 61.

12. Hasumi Shigehiko, *Kantoku: Ozu Yasujirō* (Director Yasujirō Ozu) (Tokyo: Tsukuma Shobō, 1983), p. 240.

13. Yoshida, *Ozu's Anti-Cinema*, 48.

14. Richie, *Ozu*, 173.

15. Ibid., 57

16. Compiled in *The Literature of America* 2, ed. Irving Howe et al. (New York: McGraw-Hill, 1971), 424.

17. Richie, *Ozu*, 173.

Chapter 6. Kaneto Shindō's *Onibaba*

1. For detailed information on the Lucky Dragon incident, see Shinjirō Tanaka, "Death Ash: Experience of Twenty-three Japanese Fishermen," *Japan Quarterly* 2, no. 1 (1955): 36–42.

2. For a summary of various critics' responses to this film, see Joan Mellen, *Voices from the Japanese Cinema* (New York: Liveright, 1976), 74–76.

3. Quoted in Masaji Saitō, "Sakuhin Kenkyū: *Kanawa*" (A Study of *Kanawa*), *Eiga hyōron* 276 (1974): 5–6. The translation is mine.

4. *"Onibaba,"* in *Nihon eiga sakuhin zenshū* (A complete collection of Japanese films) (Tokyo: Kinema Jumpō, 1980), p. 61.

5. In his book, *Theory of Film Practice,* Noël Burch uses the term "parameters" to describe cinematic techniques. David Bordwell's choice of diction "parametric narration" takes its cue from Burch's term. Bordwell argues that the "parametric" is synonymous with "style centered," "dialectical," or "permutational." According to Bordwell, in a "parametric narration" film, the deployment of stylistic features weighs more heavily than "syuzhet-defined functions." See David Bordwell, *Narration in the Fiction Film* (Madison: University of Wisconsin Press, 1985), 274–334.

6. Quoted by Joan Mellen in *Voices from the Japanese Cinema,* 80.

7. Ibid., 85.

8. For a discussion of the *han'nya* mask, see Iwao Kongō, *Nō to Nōmen* (Noh and Noh Masks) (Osaka: Sōgensha, 1983), 83–87.

9. For a discussion of those three basic movements of the Noh mask, see Donald Keene, *Nō: The Classical Theater of Japan,* rev. ed. (Tokyo: Kodansha, 1961), 62. Also see *Nō e no sasoi: Jo-ha-kyū to ma no saiensu* (Invitation to Noh: Science in Jo-Ha-Kyū and Space), 215.

10. Pointing out the contemporary relevance of both the samurai and the old woman's disfigured faces, Adam Lowenstein argues the film's allegorical engagement with Hiroshima. See "Allegorizing Hiroshima: Shindo Kaneto's *Onibaba* as Trauma Text," in *Trauma and Cinema: Cross-Cultural Explorations,* ed. Ann Kaplan and Bang Wang (Hong Kong: Hong Kong University Press, 2004), 145–162. For a comprehensive study of the Hiroshima-Nagasaki experience as shown in films, see Mick Broderick ed., *Hibakusha Cinema: Hiroshima, Nagasaki and the Nuclear Image in Japanese Film* (New York: Kegan Paul, 1996).

11. Ibid.

12. Joan Mellen, *Waves in Geiji's Door: Japan through Its Cinema* (New York: Rheinholt, 1976), 111–112.

13. Robin Wood, "An Introduction to the American Horror Film," in *American Nightmare: Essays on the Horror Film,* ed. Robin Wood and Richard Lippe (Toronto: Festival of Festivals, 1979), p. 10.

14. Mellen, *Voices from the Japanese Cinema,* 86–87.

15. Ibid., 87.

Chapter 7. Kōhei Oguri's *Muddy River*

1. Donald Richie, *A Hundred Years of Japanese Film* (Tokyo: Kodansha International, 2001), 235.

2. David Owen, *"Muddy River,"* a program note for the Japanese Film Series at the Japan Society of New York (n.d.). Scott Nygren also sees the film as a reaction against "the stylistic innovations and self-reflexivity" of the Japanese "New Wave" films made in the 1960s in that it shows a return to "'humanist' films in the 1950s." See Scott Nygren, "New Narrative Film in Japan: Stress Fractures in Cross-Cultural Postmodernism," *Post Script* 11, no. 1 (1991): 48–56.

3. Miyamoto's novel of the same title won the thirteenth Osamu Dasai Prize for Literature in 1977.

4. For an insightful study of the first three films by Oguri, see Linda Ehrlich "Water Flowing Underground: The Films of Oguri Kohei," *Japan Forum* 4, no. 2 (1992): 145–161.

5. Mark Schilling, *Contemporary Japanese Film* (New York: Weatherhill, 1997), 274. For a more detailed analysis of this film, see Linda Ehrlich "Stillness in Motion: *The Sleeping Man* (Nemuru oroko) of Oguri Kohei," *Journal of Film and Religion* 3, no. 1 (1999).

6. For Shimizu's major films about children, see Keiko McDonald, "Saving the Children: Films by the Most 'Casual' of Directors, Hiroshi Shimizu," in *Word and Image in Japanese Cinema,* ed. Dennis Washburn and Carole Cavanaugh (Cambridge: Cambridge University Press, 2000), 174–201.

7. For more information on the Jinmu boom, see William W. Kelley, "Metropolitan Japan," in *Postwar Japan as History,* ed. Andrew Gordon (Berkeley: University of California Press, 1993), 204. Kelley claims that in 1955 Japan's economic achievement reached prewar levels because improved mechanization shifted the labor force from agricultural to industrial production.

8. Quoted by Donald Richie in *"Muddy River—*A Japanese Movie That Defied the Odds," *New York Times,* January 23, 1983, page unknown.

9. Ibid.

10. Ibid.

11. Owen, *"Muddy River."*

12. Linda Ehrlich, "The Films of Oguri Kōhei: Sleeping Men and Awakening Children," a public lecture given at the University of Pittsburgh on November 4, 2002. Ehrlich argues that the major characters in Oguri's films are mostly marginal people, such as the underclass Nobuo and Kiichi's family in *Muddy River* and the Korean protagonist in *For Kayako*. Also see Tadao Satō, *Nihon eigashi* (History of Japanese cinema), vol. 3 (Tokyo: Iwanami, 1995), p. 271. Sato observes that *Muddy River* superbly realizes the theme of search for "the poverty of the past."

Chapter 8. Yoshimitsu Morita's *The Family Game*

This article is an extensive revision of my article "Family, Education and Postmodern Society: Yoshimitsu Morita's *The Family Game*," which appeared in *East-West Film Journal* 4, no. 1 (December 1989).

1. Hideo Hesebe, et al. *Omoide no Morita Yoshimitsu Morita* (Remembering Morita Yoshimitsu) (Tokyo: Kinema Jumpō, 1985), 119.

2. For an intensive analysis of this film, see "Yoshimitsu Morita's *Something Like Yoshiwara*: The Cultural Perspective," *East-West Film Journal* 2, no. 2 (June 1988): 13–22.

3. For a comparative analysis of Sōseki's novel and its film version, see Keiko McDonald, *From Book to Screen: Modern Japanese Literature on Screen* (Armonk, NY: M. E. Sharpe, 2000), 256–268.

4. Scott L. Malcomson, "Mitsuo Yanagimachi," *Film Criticism* 7, no. 1 (Fall 1983): 15.

5. Ted Bestor, "The Japanese Family: An Overview" in *Teaching Guide on the Japanese Family*, ed. Ted Bestor (New York: Japan Society, 1988), 16.

6. Ibid., 16–17.

7. Quoted by Hideo Nagabe in "Mittsu no Morita Yoshimitsu-ron" (Three essays on Morita Yoshimitsu), in *Omoide no Morita Yoshimitsu* (Remembering Yoshimitsu Morita), 23.

8. Donald Richie, *"The Family Game,"* in *Teaching Guide on the Japanese Family,* 26.

9. Will Wright, *Six Guns and Society* (Berkeley: University of California Press, 1976), 40.

10. Adam Knee correctly points out that this behavior does not imply that Yoshimoto has "a homosexual interest" in Shigeyuki but that this "suggestion of sexual threat" is a one of the methods Morita uses to curb the viewer's natural tendency to view the tutor as merely a benevolent surrogate father. See Adam Knee, *"The Family Game* Is Up: Morita Revises Ozu," *Post Script* 11, no. 1 (Fall 1991): 46.

11. Richie, *"The Family Game,"* 29.

12. William Cadbury, "Character and the Mock Heroic in Barchester Towers," *Texas Studies in Literature and Language* 5 (1963): 569.

13. Saburō Kawabe, "*Kazoku Gēmu*: Taidan Morita Yoshimitsu vs. Kawamoto Shirō" (*The Family Game*: Dialogue between Yoshimitsu Morita and Shirō Kawamoto) *Kinema jumpō* 813 (March 1985): 56.

Chapter 9. Masahiro Shinoda's *MacArthur's Children*

1. For a comprehensive study of Japan's New Wave cinema, see David Desser, *Eros Plus Massacre: An Introduction to the Japanese New Wave Cinema* (Bloomington: Indiana University Press, 1988).

2. For comparative analyses of these Chikamatsu plays and Shinoda's film adaptations, see Keiko McDonald, *The Japanese Classical Theater in Films* (Cranbury, NJ: Associated University Presses, 1994), 208–223.

3. For a comparative study of Ōgai's story and Shinoda's film adaptation, see Keiko McDonald, *From Book to Screen: Modern Japanese Literature in Films* (Armonk, NY: M. E. Sharpe, 2000), 237–268.

4. Quoted in Midori Yajima, *"Yari no Gonza"* (On *Gonza: The Spearman*), *Kinema junpō* 927 (January 1986): 52.

5. For a comprehensive history of Japan's defeat and the ensuing era of the Occupation, see John W. Dower, *Embracing Defeat: Japan in the Wake of World War II* (Boston: Harvard University Press, 2000).

6. Linda Ehrlich, "Erasing and Refocusing: Two Films of the Occupation," in *The Confusion Era: Art and Culture of Japan during the Allied Occupation, 1945–1952,* ed. Mark Sandler (Washington, DC: Smithsonian Institution Press, 1997), 40.

7. Ibid., 41.

8. Ibid., 42.

9. William R. May, "Sports," in *Handbook of Japanese Popular Culture,* ed. Richard Gid Powers and Hidetoshi Kato (Westport, CT: Greenwood Press, 1989), 172.

10. Kyōko Hirano, "An Interview with Masahiro Shinoda," *Cineaste* 14, no. 3 (1986): 51.

11. Rob Silverman, *"MacArthur's Children"* in *Cineaste* 14, no. 3 (1986): 52.

Chapter 10. Jūzō Itami's *A Taxing Woman*

1. Itami's acting career began in 1960. Although he appeared in Nicholas Ray's *Fifty Days in Peking* (1961) and Richard Brooks's *Lord Jim* (1965), his career appeared to be going nowhere. That changed in 1983 when he was cast as the father in Morita's *The Family Game*. He also appeared as a naval admiral in Shinoda's *MacArthur's Children* (Setouchi shōnen yakyūdan, 1984).

2. For a study of his major works, see Mark Schilling, "Juzo Itami," in *Contemporary Japanese Film* (New York: Weatherhill, 1999), pp. 74–83.

3. Donald Richie, *A Hundred Years of Japanese Film* (Tokyo: Kodansha International, 2001), 218.

4. For a detailed study of *Tampopo*, see "In the Show House of Modernity, Exhaustive Listing in Itami Jūzō's Tampopo," in *Word and Image in Japanese Cinema,* ed. Dennis Washburn and Carole Cavanaugh (Cambridge: Cambridge University Press, 2000), 126–48; and Tamae Prindle, "Globally Yours: Jūzō Itami's *Tampopo*," *Japanese Studies* 1 (1996): 61–71.

5. Schilling, *Contemporary Japanese Film,* 253.

6. Ibid., 77.

7. See Jūzō Itami, *Marusa no onna: Nikki* (*A Taxing Woman:* Diary) (Tokyo: Bungeishunjū, 1987).

8. Yoshio Sugimoto. *An Introduction to Japanese Society* (Cambridge: Cambridge University Press, 1997), 140.

9. During the era of the Occupation, Mizoguchi made three "feminist" films in response to the changing sociopolitical climate. *Victory of Women* (Josei no shōri, 1946), *The Love of Actress Sumako* (Joyū Sumako no koi, 1947), and *My Love Burns* (Waga koi wa moenu, 1949) all show women protagonists struggling for independence in postwar Japan. For a detailed analysis of these films, see Keiko McDonald, "Whatever Happened to Passive Suffering? Women on Screen," in *The Confusion Era: Art and Culture of Japan during the Allied Occupation, 1945–1952*, ed. Mark Sandler (Washington, DC: Smithsonian Institution Press, 1997), 53–71.

Chapter 11. Hayao Miyazaki's *My Neighbor Totoro*

1. For a detailed discussion of *Ghost in the Shell* (1995), see Susan J. Napier, *Anime from Akira to Princess Mononoke* (New York: Palgrave, 2001), 103–116.

2. For a concise history of Japanese animated films, see Daisuke Miyao, "Anime: The History of Japanese Animated Films," *The Japan Society Newsletter* (December 1998): 1, 3. Also see Donald Richie, *A Hundred Years of Japanese Film* (London: Kodansha International, 2001), 246–253.

3. Tadao Sato, *Nihon eiga-shi* (The history of Japanese cinema), vol. 2 (Tokyo: Iwanami, 1995), 102–103.

4. Miyao, "Anime," 3.

5. Sato, *Nihon-eiga-shi*, 2: 103–105.

6. For example, see Napier, *Anime from Akira to Princess Mononoke*, 121–38.

7. Ted Bestor, "The Japanese Family: An Overview" in *Teaching Guide on the Japanese Family*, ed. Ted Bestor (New York: Japan Society, 1988), 16.

8. David Bordwell, *Planet Hong Kong: Popular Cinema and the Art of Entertainment* (Cambridge, MA: Harvard University Press, 2000), 178.

9. Chieko Tanaka, "*Tonari no Totoro*: Nihon to shizen o egaku: Miyazaki Hayao kantoku intabyū) (*My Neighbor Totoro*: Portraying Japan and its natural wonders: Interview with director Hayao Miyazaki) *Kinema jumpo* 983 (1989): 78–79.

10. Jūzō Isaka, *Miyazaki hayao no susume: Hayao Miyazaki Fantasy World* (Hayao Miyazaki: A reader) (Tokyo: 21st Century Box, 2001), 20–21.

11. Tanaka, "*Tonari no Totoro*," 80.

12. Bordwell, *Planet Hong Kong*, 178.

13. Quoted by Katsumi Hirano in "*Tonari no Totoro*: Arakajime tsuihō sareta kodomotachi no supiritto" (*My Neighbor Totoro*: The spirits of the children already dispelled), in *Filmmakers 6: Miyazaki Hayao*, ed. Takeshi Yōrō (Tokyo: Kinema Jumpō, n.d.), 130.

14. Napier, *Anime from Akira to Princess Mononoke*, 120.

15. Ibid., 119.

16. Ibid., 127.

17. Translation by Earl Miner in *An Introduction to Japanese Court Poetry* (Stanford, CA: Stanford University Press, 1968), 68.

18. Napier, *Anime from Akira to Princess Mononoke,* 138.

19. Fuyuhiko Kamijima, "Rimeiku de wa naku riteiku e no michibiki: Miyazaki eiga ni okeru samazama na diteiru" (Invitation to re-taking, not re-making: Various details in Miyazaki films), in *Filmmakers 6: Miyazaki Hayao,* 36.

20. Yoichi Shibuya, *Kurosawa Akira, Miyazaki Hayao, Kitano Takeshi: Nihon no sannin no enshutsuka* (Akira Kurosawa, Hayao Miyazaki, and Takeshi Kitano: Three Japanese filmmakers) (Tokyo: Rokkingu On, 1993). The book is a collection of five long interviews Shibuya had with the three directors.

Chapter 12. Akira Kurosawa's *Madadayo*

1. For example, see Jonathan Rosenbaum, "*Madadayo:* Kurosawa, Japan, 1993," *Film Comment* 36, no. 4 (2000): 73–74.

2. See Donald Richie, *The Films of Akira Kurosawa,* exp. ed. (Berkeley: University of California Press, 1996), 227–228. Also see Stephen Prince, *The Warrior's Camera: The Cinema of Akira Kurosawa,* revised and expanded edition (Princeton, NJ: Princeton University Press, 1999), 329–339; and Mitsuhiro Yoshimoto, *Kurosawa: Film Studies and Japanese Cinema* (Durham, NC: Duke University Press, 2000), 372–374. Prince's expanded edition contains two additional chapters devoted to detailed analyses of Kurosawa's last three films—*Dreams* (Yume, 1990), *Rhapsody in August* (Hachigatsu no Kyōshikyoku, 1991), and *Madadayo*—and the author's assessment of the director's achievements.

3. Saisei Murō, one of Japan's leading writers, praises Uchida's stylistic finesse, claiming that no modern essayist can surpass him. See "Kaisetsu" (Commentary), in *Uchida Hyakken-shū* (Collection of Uchida's works), ed. Saburō Hirayama (Tokyo: Yaoi Shobō, 1981), 193.

4. Several essays on Nora are compiled in Hyakken Uchida, *Shinkan Uchida Hyakken zenshū* (Tokyo: Fukutake Shoten, 1988).

5. Mitsuhiro Yoshimoto, *Kurosawa: Film Studies and Japanese Cinema,* 373.

6. The so-called Hōsei incident (Hōsei sōdō) of 1934 was one of the most disturbing examples of campus unrest in Japanese university history. The "liberated" atmosphere of the newly accredited Hōsei University attracted many literary talents, among them Sōseki's disciples. In 1934, however, students and liberal faculty joined forces to clash with professors they considered opposed to academic freedom. As a result, forty-five such professors were forced to resign. Among them were a noted Noh scholar, Toyoichirō Nogami, the writer Haruo Satō, and Hyakken Uchida himself.

7. Earl Miner, *An Introduction to Japanese Court Poetry* (Stanford, CA: Stanford University Press, 1968), 87–88.

8. Ibid.

9. Donald Keene, ed., *Anthology of Japanese Literature from the Earliest Era to the Mid-Nineteenth Century* (New York: Grove Press, 1955), 197.

10. Ibid., 204.

11. Nagaharu Yodogawa, "Ima kawaita tsuchi ni, karekaketa ki ni, kireina mizu o sosoide kureta meisaku" (The masterpiece like clean water that gave life to dry soil and withering trees), in *Kurosawa Sakuhin: Mādadayo* (Kurosawa's work: *Madadayo*), pamphlet (Tokyo: Tōhō, 1993), 7.

Chapter 13. Hirokazu Koreeda's *Maboroshi*

This is a revision of my article that originally appeared in *Asian Cinema* 13 (Spring/Summer 2002). I am grateful to Dr. John Lent, the journal's editor-in-chief, for permitting me to reprint it.

1. For example, see Mark Schilling, "Wonderful Life," in *Contemporary Japanese Film* (New York: Weatherhill, 1999), 375–376. For a study of *Distance,* see *Cinema Rise,* no. 107 (2001); the entire volume is devoted to discussion of this film and also contains the screenplay.

2. For a brief introduction to Koreeda's work, see Donald Richie, *A Hundred Years of Japanese Film* (Tokyo: Kodansha International, 2001), 241–243.

3. Quoted by Mark Schilling in "Hirokazu Koreeda," in *Contemporary Japanese Film,* 117.

4. For example, see March Schilling, "Maboroshi no hikari," in *Contemporary Japanese Film,* 249.

5. For example, Donald Richie mentions that the distant view of the funeral procession in a long take is reminiscent of Mizoguchi's method in films such as *The Water Magician* (Taki no shiraito, 1933), *The Life of Oharu,* and *Ugetsu.* Koreeda claims, however, that though he admires Mizoguchi, he was never conscious of the master's style while shooting this sequence. From the outset, he intended to take it by combining a long take and a long shot. See "Taidan: Donald Richie: Koreeda Hirokazu" (Dialogue between Donald Richie and Hirokazu Koreeda), *Kinema jumpō* 1180 (January 1996): 66.

6. The film is based on Teru Miyamoto's novella of the same title. See Teru Miyamoto, *Maboroshi no hikari* (Phantom light) (Tokyo: Shinchōsha, 1983).

7. For example, the critic Ken'ichi Ōkubo argues that this gesture creates the particular sentiment appropriate for this film. See "Shishashitsu: Koreda Hirokazu Kantoku sakuhin: *Maboroshi no hikari*" (Screening room: Hirokazu Koreeda: *Maboroshi*), *Kinema jumpō* 1175 (November 1995), 168.

8. Ibid.

9. Translated by Earl Miner in *Introduction to Japanese Court Poetry* (Princeton, NJ: Princeton University Press, 1979), 40.

10. I am grateful to David Desser for pointing out that the long take has become a staple cinematic device among a number of contemporary Japanese directors. For example, Makoto Shinosaki's *Okaeri* (1995), Shinji Aoyama's *Eureka* (Yūrika, 2000), and Naomi Kawase's *Suzaku* (Moe no Suzaku, 1997) effectively employ this method.

Chapter 14. Takeshi Kitano's *Kids Return*

1. For a development of the Yakuza genre in Japanese cinema, see Keiko McDonald, "The Yakuza Film: An Introduction" in *Reframing Japanese Cinema: Authorship, Genre and History,* ed. Arthur Nolletti Jr. and David Desser (Bloomington: Indiana University Press, 1988), 165–192.

2. For a concise introduction to Kitano's representative films, see Donald Richie, *A Hundred Years of Japanese Film* (New York: Kodansha International, 2001), 223–227.

3. For a brief analysis of this film, see Mark Schilling, "Ano Natsu, Ichiban Shizukana Umi," in *Contemporary Japanese Film* (Tokyo: Weatherhill, 1999), 140.

4. Mark Schilling, *Contemporary Japanese Film,* 94.

5. Dennis Washburn, "A Story of Cruel Youth: Kon Ichikawa's *Enjo* and the Art of Adapting in 1950s Japan," in *Kon Ichikawa,* ed. James Quandt (Toronto: Cinematheque, 2001), 156.

6. David Desser, *Eros Plus Massacre: An Introduction to the Japanese New Wave Cinema* (Bloomington: Indiana University Press, 1988), 43.

7. Kitano started out as an entertainer in a strip joint, then he went on to form a comedy duo known as Two Beats (hence his stage name, Beat Takeshi). See Mark Shillings, "Takeshi Kitano," in *Contemporary Japanese Film,* 91.

8. Mark Schillings, *"Kids Return"* in *Contemporary Japanese Film,* 228. Some critics point out that Kitano fails to define the temporal setting of the film clearly. See "Kitano Takeshi: *Kids Return:* Zadankai" (Takeshi Kitano's *Kids Return:* Roundtable discussion), *Kinema junpō,* 378 (Spring 1996): 6–16. One participant claims that the coffee shop and the movie theater in the film have the ambiance of the 1970s though the overall mood is associated with youth life and culture of the 1960s.

9. Quoted by Daisuke Miyao in "Blue vs. Red: Takeshi Kitano's Color Scheme," *Post Script* (special issue on contemporary Japanese Cinema, ed. Keiko McDonald) 18, no. 1 (Fall 1998): 114. Originally appeared in "Interview," *Studio Voice* 263 (November 1997): 43. For a study of various Japanese directors' use of color schemes, see David Desser, "Gate of Flesh (tones): Color in the Japanese Cinema," in *Cinematic Landscape: Observations on the Visual Arts and Cinema of China and Japan,* eds. Linda C. Ehrlich and David Desser (Austin: University of Texas Press, 1994), 299–321.

10. Quoted by Miyao in "Blue vs. Red: Takeshi Kitano's Color Scheme." Originally appeared in "Intabyū" (Interview), *Kinema junpō* 1198 (August 1996): 46.

11. See Miyao, "Blue vs. Red: Takeshi Kitano's Color Scheme."

12. Ibid., 123.

13. Ibid.

14. Ibid.

Chapter 15. Yōichi Higashi's *Village of Dreams*

1. Kazuo Kuroki et al., eds., *Nihon eiga terebi kantoku zenshū* (Japanese film and television directors) (Tokyo: Kinema Jumpō, 1988), 332.

2. For a comparative analysis of the film and the novel, see Keiko McDonald, *From Book to Screen: Modern Japanese Literature in Films* (Armonk, NY: M. E. Sharpe, 2000), 159–177.

3. Occupation legislation permitted the Japanese government to buy all land owned by absentee landlords. It also permitted the government to purchase most of the land from resident landlords, limiting their holdings to a maximum of 12 *cho* (19.6 acres). All the land thus acquired was sold to former tenants at preinflation prices. See Edwin O. Reischauer et al. *East Asia: The Modern Transformation* (Boston: Houghton Mifflin, 1965), 816. For a more comprehensive study of land reform in the era of Occupation, see Ronald Philip Dore, *Land Reform in Japan* (London: Oxford University Press, 1959).

4. Masayuki Noura, "Fikushon to dokyumento no sakai o koeru majutsuteki riarizumu" (Magical realism that transcends the boundary between fiction and the documentary), *Kinema jumpō* 1197 (July 1996): 77.

5. The script was cowritten by the director Higashi and Takehiro Nakajima. Higashi says that those elderly women first appeared as ordinary villagers in the second draft. In the third draft, they were treated as divine guardians of the village. See Yōichi Higashi, "*E no naka no boku no mura* no shinario ni tsuite" (On the scenario for *Village of Dreams*), *Shinario* 52, no. 8 (August 1996): 11.

Chapter 16. Naomi Kawase's *Suzaku*

This chapter is a revision of my article that originally appeared in *Post Script* 18, no. 1 (Fall 1998), a special issue on contemporary Japanese cinema, guest-edited by me.

1. For a more detailed discussion of Tanaka's accomplishments as a director, see Keiko McDonald, "Kinuyo Tanaka (1924–1976), the First Woman Director in Postwar Japan," in *Across Time and Genre Conference Proceedings,* ed. Janice Brown and Sonja Arntzen (Edmonton: University of Alberta Press, 2002), 107–110.

2. For a comprehensive study of Matsui's films, see Keiko McDonald, "A Woman Director's Rising Star: The First Two Films of Hisako Matsui (b. 1946)," *Asian Cinema* (Fall 2003): 55–74.

3. Mark Schilling, "Interview with Sento Naomi." Originally circulated among Kine Japan members through the Internet in 1997. A part of this interview was incorporated into his article "Naomi Sento: Documenting the Word," *Winds* (May 1998): 42–43.

4. *Embracing* won Kawase the Award for Excellence at the 1993 Image Forum Festival and also a FIPRESCI Prize Special Mention. *Katatsumori* was given the Award for Excellence at the prestigious Yamagata International Documentary Film

Festival. For a further study of these two films, see Aiko Nakanishi, "Hyō: *Ni tsu-tsumarete: Katatsumori*" (Review: *Embracing: Katatsumori*), *Kinema Jumpō* 1238 (November 1997): 90–91.

5. For a comprehensive study of Japanese documentary films up to the 1970s, see Yoshio Tanigawa, *Dokyumentarī-eiga no genten: sono shisō to hōhō* (Starting point of documentary film: Ideology and methodology) (Tokyo: Fūjusha, 1997). For a detailed study of prewar documentary films done in English, see Mark Abe Nornes, *Japanese Documentary Film: The Meiji Era through Hiroshima* (Minneapolis: University of Minnesota, 2003). For a critical analysis of the major documentary films made in the 1960s and the early 1970s, see David Desser, *Eros Plus Massacre: An Introduction to the Japanese New Wave Cinema* (Bloomington: Indiana University Press, 1988), 158–170. Desser claims that among various independent filmmakers of documentaries in this period, Shinsuke Ogawa and Noriaki Tsuchimoto were most strongly committed to student struggles and other social issues.

6. Schilling, "Interview with Sento Naomi," originally circulated among Kine Japan members through the Internet in 1997.

7. Yōichi Nakagawa, "Kawase Naomi Kantoku: *Moe no Suzaku* no Kannu jushō o kataru" (Director Naomi Kawase speaking of her Cannes award film, *Suzaku*), *Shine Furonto* (Cine front) 22, no. 6 (June 1997): 39.

8. One sociologist explains this phenomenon as follows:

Residents in depopulated areas are alienated both economically and cultur-ally. With youngsters leaving their villages for work in cities, older people find it difficult to sustain the agricultural, forestry, and fishery economies of those areas. With the liberalization of the agricultural market, the farming population has gradually lost government protection and competitive morale. Negative images of agricultural work make it difficult for young male farmers to attract spouses; an increasing number of them resort to arranged marriages with women from the Philippines, Sri Lanka, and other Asian countries.

See Yoshio Sugimoto, *An Introduction to Japanese Society* (Cambridge: Cambridge University Press, 1997), 61.

9. Sugimoto, *An Introduction to Japanese Society,* 75. He also observes as follows:

Japan has become an aging society with an increasing aged population and decreasing numbers in the active workforce. An official estimate made by the Ministry of Health in 1991 is that the number of senior citizens over sixty-four years of age will exceed that of children below fifteen before the end of the twentieth century. If one defines those between sixty-four and fifteen as the active population and those outside range as the inactive popu-lation, whereas five actives support two inactives in the early 1990s, by around 2020 two actives will have to sustain one inactive.

10. Nakagawa, "Kawase Naomi Kantoku," 30.

Selected Bibliography

Anderson, Joseph L. "Spoken Silents in the Japanese Cinema," *Journal of Film and Video* 40, no. 1 (Winter 1988): 13–33.

———, and Donald Richie. *The Japanese Film: Art and Industry*. Exp. ed. Princeton, NJ: Princeton University Press, 1982.

Andrew, Dudley. *Films in the Aura of Art*. Princeton, NJ: Princeton University Press, 1984.

———, and Paul Andrew. *Kenji Mizoguchi: A Guide to References and Resources*. Boston: G. K. Hall, 1981.

———, and Carole Cavanaugh. *Sanshō Dayū*. London: BFI, 2002.

Barrett, Gregory. *Archetypes in Japanese Film*. London: Associated University Presses, 1989.

Bernardi, Joanne. *Writing in Light: The Silent Scenario and the Japanese Pure Film Movement*. Detroit: Wayne University Press, 2001.

Bestor, Ted. "The Japanese Family: An Overview," in *Teaching Guide on the Japanese Family*. New York: Japan Society, 1988. 1–20.

Bluestone, George. *Novel into Film*. Berkeley: University of California Press, 1957.

Bock, Audie. *Japanese Film Directors*. Tokyo: Kodansha International, 1976.

———. *Naruse: A Master of the Japanese Cinema*. Chicago: Art Institute of Chicago, 1984.

Bordwell, David. *Making Meaning: Inference and Rhetoric in the Interpretation of Cinema*. Cambridge, MA: Harvard University Press, 1991.

———. *Narration in the Fiction Film*. Madison: University of Wisconsin Press, 1985.

———. *Ozu and the Poetics of Cinema*. Princeton, NJ: Princeton University Press, 1988.

———. *Planet Hong Kong: Popular Cinema and the Art of Entertainment*. Cambridge, MA: Harvard University Press, 2000.

Broderick, Mick, ed. *Hibakusha Cinema: Hiroshima, Nagasaki and the Nuclear Image in Japanese Film*. London: Kegan Paul International, 1966.

Burch, Noël. *To the Distant Observer: The Form and the Meaning of the Japanese Cinema*. Berkeley: University of California Press, 1979.

Cadbury, William, "Character and the Mock Heroic in *Barchester Towers*," *Texas Studies in Literature and Language* 5 (1963): 509–519.

Carroll, Noël. *Mystifying Movies: Fads and Fallacies in Contemporary Film Theory*. New York: Columbia University Press, 1988.

———. *Theorizing the Moving Image*. New York: Cambridge University Press, 2001.

Cazdyn, Eric. *The Flash of Capital: Film and Geopolitics in Japan*. Durham, NC: Duke University Press, 2002.

Chatman, Seymour. *Coming to Terms: The Rhetoric of Narrative in Fiction and Film*. Ithaca, NY: Cornell University Press, 1990.

————. *Story and Discourse: Narrative Structure in Fiction and Film*. Ithaca, NY: Cornell University Press, 1978.

Chiba, Nobuo. *Eiga to Tanizaki* (Film and Tanizaki). Tokyo: Seiabō, 1989.

————, et al. *Sekai no eiga sakka: Nihon eigashi* (Film directors of the world: The history of Japanese cinema), vol. 31. Tokyo: Kinema Jumpō, 1976.

Chiba, Shunji. "'Mado no onna' kō: *Gan* o megutte" (Rethinking of the heroine "Woman in the Window": *On The Wild Geese*), in *Mori Ōgai kenkyū* (Study of Ōgai Mori), 2 (Tokyo: Izumi shoin, 1988). 16–47.

David, Darrell William. *Picturing Japaneseness: Monumental Style, National Identity, Japanese Film*. New York: Columbia University Press, 1996.

Desser, David. *Eros Plus Massacre: An Introduction to the Japanese New Wave Cinema*. Bloomington: Indiana University Press, 1988.

————. *The Samurai Films of Akira Kurosawa*. Ann Arbor, MI: UMI Research Press, 1983.

————, ed. *Tokyo Story*. Cambridge: Cambridge University Press, 1997.

Dower, John W. *Embracing Defeat: Japan in the Wake of World War II*. Cambridge, MA: Harvard University Press, 2000.

Ehrlich, Linda. "Erasing and Refocusing: Two Films of Occupation," in *The Confusion Era: Art and Culture of Japan During the Allied Occupation, 1945–1952*, ed. Mark Sandler. Washington, DC: Smithsonian Institution Press, 1997. 39–51.

————. "Stillness in Motion: *The Sleeping Man* (Nemuru otoko) of Oguri Kōhei," *Journal of Film and Religion* 3, no. 1 (Spring 1999). Electronic journal.

————. "Water Flowing Underground: The Films of Oguri Kohei." *Japan Forum* 4, no. 2 (April 1992): 145–161.

————, and David Desser, eds. *Cinematic Landscape: Observations on the Visual Arts and Cinema of China and Japan*. Austin: University of Texas Press, 1994.

Ellen, Patricia. *Akira Kurosawa: A Guide to References and Resources* (Boston: G.K. Hall, 1979).

Godwin, James, ed. *Akira Kurosawa and Intertextual Cinema*. Baltimore: John Hopkins University Press, 1994.

Gordon, Andrew, ed. *Postwar Japan as History*. Berkeley: University of California Press, 1993.

Grant, Barry Keith, ed. *The Dread of Difference: Gender and the Horror Film*. Austin: University of Texas Press, 1996.

Hasumi, Shigehiko. *Kantoku: Ozu Yasujirō* (Director Yasujirō Ozu). Tokyo: Chikuma Shobō, 1983.

Higashi, Yōichi. "*E no naka no boku no mura* no shinario ni tsuite" (On the scenario for *Village of Dreams*). *Shinario* 52, no. 8 (August 1996): 10–11.

Hirano, Kyōko. "An Interview with Masahiro Shinoda" *Cineaste* 14, no. 3 (1986): 51.

———. *Mr. Smith Goes to Tokyo: Japanese Cinema under the American Occupation, 1945–1952.* Washington, DC: Smithsonian Institution Press, 1992.

Hirayama, Saburō, ed. *Uchida Hyakken-shū* (Collection of Hyakken Uchida's works). Tokyo: Yayoi Shobō, 1981.

Kawabe, Saburō. *"Kazoku Gēmu:* Taidan Morita Yoshimitsu vs. Kawamoto Shirō" (*The Family Game:* Dialogue between Yoshimitsu Morita and Shirō Kawamoto), *Kinema junpō* 813 (March 1985): 56–61.

Keene, Donald, ed. *The Anthology of Japanese Literature: From the Earliest Era to the Mid-Nineteenth Century.* New York: Grove Press, 1955.

Kirihara, Donald. *Patterns of Time: Mizoguchi and the 1930s.* Madison: University of Wisconsin Press, 1992.

Knee, Adam. *"The Family Game* Is Up: Morita Revises Ozu," *Post Script* 11, no. 1 (Fall 1991): 20–27.

Kobayashi, Nobuhiko. "Daisukurīn de minaoshite hoshii eigateki miryoku" (Charming moments on the big screen I'd like you to revisit), *Kinema junpō* 1268 (October 1988): 88–89.

Kongo, Iwao. *Nō to nomen* (Noh and Noh masks). Osaka: Sōgensha, 1983.

Lau, Jenny Kwok Wah, ed. *Multiple Modernities: Cinemas and Popular Media in Transcultural East Asia.* Philadelphia: Temple University Press, 1993.

Konparu, Kunio. *No e no sasoi: Jo-ha-kyū to ma no saiensu* (Invitation to Noh: Science in *jo-ha-kyū* and space). Tokyo: Tankosha, 1980.

Malcomson, Scott L. "Mitsuo Yanagimachi," *Film Criticism* 7, no. 1 (Fall 1983): 12–19.

McDonald, Keiko. *Cinema East: A Critical Study of Major Japanese Films.* East Brunswick, NJ: Fairleigh Dickinson University Press, 1983.

———. *From Book to Screen: Modern Japanese Literature in Films.* Armonk, NY: M. E. Sharpe, 2000.

———. *Japanese Classical Theater in Films.* Cranbury, NJ: Associated University Presses, 1994.

———. *Mizoguchi.* Boston: Twayne, 1984.

———, ed. *Ugetsu.* New Bruswick, NJ: Rutgers University Press, 1993.

———. "Whatever Happened to Passive Suffering: Women on Screen in Occupation-Era Japan," in *The Confusion Era: Art and Culture of Japan during the Allied Occupation, 1945–1952,* ed. Mark Sandler. Washington, DC: Smithsonian Institution, 1997. 53–71.

———. "A Woman Director's Rising Star: The First Two Films of Hisako Matsui (b. 1946)," *Asian Cinema* (Fall 2003): 55–74.

McDougal, Stuart Y. *Made into Movies: From Literature to Film.* New York: Holt, Rinehart, and Winston, 1985.

Miyao, Daisuke. "Anime: The History of Japanese Animated Films," *The Japan Society Newsletter* (December 1998), 1–3.

————. "Blue Vs. Red: Takeshi Kitano's Color Scheme," *Post Script* 18, no. 1 (1998): 112–127.

Miner, Earl. *An Introduction to Japanese Court Poetry*. Stanford, CA: Stanford University Press, 1968.

Miyamoto, Musashi. *A Book of Five Rings,* trans. Victor Harris. New York: Overland Press, 1972.

Mizoguchi, Kenji. "Tsuchi no nioi: *Gion no kyōdai* o tsukuru mae ni" (The smell of the earth: Before making *Sisters of the Gion*), *Kinema jumpō* 582 (July 1936): 60–61.

Mori, Ōgai. *The Wild Geese.* Trans. Kingo Ochiai and Sanford Goldstein. Tokyo: Tuttle, 1959.

Nagabe, Hideo, et al. *Omoide no Morita Yoshimitsu* (Remembering Yoshimitsu Morita). Tokyo: Kinema Jumpō, 1985.

Nakagawa, Yōichi. "Kawase Naomi Kantoku: *Moe no Suzaku* no Kannu jushō o kataru" (Director Naomi Kawase speaking of her Cannes award film, *Suzaku*), *Shine Furonto* 22, no. 6 (1997): 38–39.

Napier, Susan J. *Anime: From Akira to Princess Mononoke: Experiencing Contemporary Japanese Animation.* New York: Palgrave, 2000.

Nolletti, Arthur, Jr., and David Desser, eds. *Reframing Japanese Cinema: Authorship, Genre and History.* Bloomington: Indiana University Press, 1992.

Nornes, Mark Abe. *Japanese Documentary Film: The Meiji Era through Hiroshima.* Minneapolis: University of Minnesota, 2003.

Prince, Stephen. *The Warrior's Camera: The Cinema of Akira Kurosawa,* exp. ed. Princeton, NJ: Princeton University Press, 1999.

Prindle, Tamae. "Globally Yours: Jūzō Itami's *Tampopo,*" *Japanese Studies* 1 (1996): 61–71.

Richie, Donald. "The Family Game," in *Teaching Guide on the Japanese Family.* New York: Japan Society, 1988. 27–30.

————. *The Films of Akira Kurosawa,* exp. and updated ed. Berkeley: University of California Press, 1996.

————. *A Hundred Years of Japanese Film: A Concise History with a Selective Guide to Videos and DVDs.* Tokyo: Kodansha International, 2001.

————. *Japanese Cinema: Film Style and National Character.* New York: Doubleday, 1971.

————. *Japanese Cinema: An Introduction.* Hong Kong: Oxford University Press, 1990.

————. *Ozu: His Life and Films.* Berkeley: University of California Press, 1971.

————. "Yasujiro Ozu: The Syntax of His Films." *Film Quarterly* 17 (Winter 1963–1964): 11–16.

Rimer, Thomas, ed. *Ogai: Youth and Other Stories.* Honolulu: University of Hawai'i Press, 1994.

Rosenbaum, Jonathan. "*Madadayo:* Kurosawa, Japan, 1993," *Film Comment* 36, no. 4 (2000): 73–74.

Selected Bibliography

Sandler, Mark, ed. *The Confusion Era: Art and Culture of Japan during the Allied Occupation, 1945–1952*. Washington, DC: Smithsonian Institution Press, 1997.

Sarris, Andrew. "*Muddy River*," *Village Voice* (January 25, 1982): 47.

Satō, Tadao. *Currents in Japanese Cinema*, trans. Gregory Barrett. Tokyo: Kodansha, 1982.

———. *Kurosawa Akira kaidai* (Akira Kurosawa: Interpretation). Tokyo: Iwanami, 1990.

———. *Kurosawa Akira no sekai* (The world of Akira Kurosawa). Tokyo: San'ichi Shobō, 1976.

———. *Kurosawa Akira zenshū* (Akira Kurosawa: A complete collection of his works). Tokyo: Tōhō Co. Ltd., 1980.

———. *Mizoguchi Kenji no sekai* (The world of Kenji Mizoguchi). Tokyo: Tsukuma Shobō, 1982.

———. *Nihon eigashi* (The history of Japanese cinema), 4 vols. Tokyo: Iwanami, 1995.

———. *Ozu Yasujirō no geijutsu* (The art of Yasujirō Ozu). Tokyo: Ashahi Shibunsha, 1971.

Schilling, Mark. *Contemporary Japanese Film*. New York: Weatherhill, 1999.

———. "Naomi Sento: Documenting the Word," *Winds* (May 1998): 42–43.

Schrader, Paul. *Transcendental Style in Film: Ozu, Bresson, Dreyer*. Berkeley: University of California Press, 1972.

Shibuya, Yōichi. *Kurosawa Akira, Miyazaki Hayato, Kitano Takeshi: Nihon no sannin no Enshutsuka* (Akira Kurosawa, Hayao Miyazaki, and Takeshi Kitano: Three Japanese directors). Tokyo: Rokkingu On, 1993.

Silberman, Rob. "*MacArthur's Children*," *Cineaste* 14, no. 3 (1986): 50, 52.

Sugimoto, Yoshio. *An Introduction to Japanese Society*. Cambridge: Cambridge University Press, 1997.

Tanaka, Chieko. "*Tonari no Totoro*: Nihon to shizen o egaku: Miyazaki Hayao kantoku intabyū" (*My Neighbor Totoro*: Portraying Japan and its natural wonders: Interview with director Hayao Miyazaki), *Kinema jumpō* 983 (1989): 78–83.

Tanigawa, Yoshio. *Dokyumentarī eiga no genten: Sono shisō to hōhō* (Starting point of documentary film: Ideology and methodology). Tokyo: Fujūsha, 1997.

Treat, John Whittier, ed. *Contemporary Japanese Culture*. Honolulu: University of Hawai'i Press, 1996.

Turim, Maureen. *The Films of Oshima Nagisa*. Berkeley: University of California Press, 1988.

Washburn, Dennis. "A Story of Cruel Youth: Kon Ichikawa's *Enjo* and the Art of Adapting in 1950s Japan," in *Kon Ichikawa*, ed. James Quandt. Toronto: Cinematheque Ontario, 2001. 155–174.

———, and Carole Cavanaugh, eds. *Word and Image in Japanese Cinema*. Cambridge: Cambridge University Press, 2000.

Wright, Will. *Six Guns and Society: A Structural Study of the Western*. Berkeley: University of California Press, 1976.

Yoda, Yoshikata. *Mizoguchi Kenji: Hito to geijutsu* (Kenji Mizoguchi: His life and art). Tokyo: Tabata Shoten, 1970.

Yodogawa, Nagaharu. "Ima kawaita tsuchi ni, karekaketa ki ni, kireina mizu o soso-ide kureta meisaku" (The masterpiece like clean water that gave life to dry soil and withering trees), in *Kurosawa Sakuhin: Madadayo* (Kurosawa's work: *Madadayo*). Pamphlet. Tokyo: Tōhō, 1993. 7.

Yoshida, Kijū. *Ozu's Anti-Cinema*. Trans. Kyōko Hirano and Miyao Daisuke. Ann Arbor: University of Michigan Center for Japanese Studies, 2003.

Yoshikawa, Eiji. *Musashi*. Trans. Charles S. Terry. New York: Harper & Row, 1981.

Yoshimoto, Mitsuhiro. *Kurosawa: Film Studies and Japanese Cinema*. Durham, NC: Duke University Press, 2000.

Index

About the Author

DR. KEIKO MCDONALD is a professor of Japanese cinema and literature at the University of Pittsburgh. Her major books include *Cinema East: A Critical Study of Major Japanese Films* (1983), *Mizoguchi* (1984), *Japanese Classical Theater in Films* (1994), and *From Book to Screen: Modern Japanese Literature in Films* (2000). She has also coedited *Nara Encounters* (1997) with Dr. Thomas Rimer, and is currently completing a book on the filmmaker Hiroshi Shimizu and another on Japanese women directors.

Production Notes for McDonald / Reading a Japanese Film

Cover and interior designed by University of Hawai'i Press
Production Staff with text in Bembo and display in Post Antiqua

Composition by Josie Herr

Printing and binding by The Maple-Vail Book Manufacturing Group

Printed on 60# Text White Opaque, 426 ppi

Printed in the United Kingdom
by Lightning Source UK Ltd.
133080UK00001B/370-381/A